Fifty Cents An Hour

The Builders and Boomtowns
of the
Fort Peck Dam

Lois Lonnquist

D0671143

MtSky Press
Helena, Montana
2006

Fifty Cents an Hour:

The Builders and Boomtowns of the Fort Peck Dam
© 2006 MtSky Press

Front Cover design by author Lois (Smith) Lonnquist
Dredge cut northwest of the Fort Peck Dam, photo by the author.
Spillway worker Leonard Smith, photo by Jim Simpson, Fort Peck 1939.
Homes and vehicles, photo by Paul McFarland, project worker, 1936.

Back Cover
Gatehouses over the four Fort Peck Dam tunnels, photo by the author.

Maps drawn from Montana Highway Department road maps and
U.S. Army Corps of Engineers illustrations.

Second Edition 2007
Third Edition   2010
Printed in the USA

Library of Congress Cataloging-in-Publication Data
Lonnquist, Lois, 1935–
Fifty Cents An Hour: The Builders and Boomtowns of the Fort Peck Dam /
Lois Lonnquist
       p. cm.

Includes bibliographical references and index.

ISBN 13 978-0-9786963-0-6 (softcover)
ISBN 10 0-9786963-0-1   (softcover)

1. Montana — History — 1930-1940 — Fort Peck Dam.
2. Montana — Missouri River — Fort Peck Dam Boomtowns –
   Boomtown homes and family life — Social conditions.
3. Public Works Administration (PWA) Project No. 30, 1933-1940.

MtSky Press
P.O. Box 6444
Helena, MT 59604
www.FortPeckBoomtowns.com

Mom Stella (Fisher) Smith
Lois, Lucille, Stanley

To my brother Stan and sister Lucille
Boomtown Babies

In memory of our Mom and Dad
W. Leonard and Stella Smith
Like so many others of their generation,
they believed "charity will weaken you"

For The Fort Peck Project People
Write in the dust — it took us all

Thank You!

My book is possible because a great army of professional and amateur historians, librarians, and volunteers have diligently collected and preserved our nation's history in public and private libraries, museums, historical centers, newspaper files, government documents available on the Internet, and in family scrapbooks handed down through the generations.

Thank you Brian Shovers, Dave Walter, and the Montana Historical Society Library staff; Helena Lewis & Clark Library staff; Montana State Library staff; Carroll College Library staff; and MSU Bozeman librarians.

Thank you *Glasgow Courier* editor Samar Fay, and *Courier* staff past and present; the U.S. Army Corps of Engineers Fort Peck District staff, especially Michele Fromdahl, director of the Fort Peck Interpretive Center, and JoAnn Solem, John Daggett, Darin McMurry, Roy Snyder (ret.), and 1930s Corps photographer Robert Midthun; James Smith, Jr., editor of the *Rural Montana* magazine; and librarians in the Glasgow, Harlem, Circle, Miles City public libraries; Pioneer Museum, Glasgow, volunteers Bernard "Bunky" Sullivan, Kitty Lou Rusher, and Doris Franzen; and Sharon Emond and Jane Ereaux of the Phillips County Museum, Malta.

Thanks to everyone who shared stories and photographs including:

Earl Culver, Lois Damstrom, Larry DuBeau, John Egosque, Alvin Fisher, Bob Gilluly, Donna Goodwin, Doris Hanson, Dale Heidner, Nora Irwin, John Johnson, Janet Knox, Leona LaJoie, Sherman Martin, Iris Milne, Donald and Mary Mohn, James Peterson, Merle Plank, Marvin Presser, Robert and Dorothy Hurly, Art Hale, Donna Moore, Janet (Hagen) Murphy, Paul and Jill McFarland, Lynn Nyquist, Hal Ramsbacher and brothers John and Tom, Doris (Moon) Reichelt, Rafe Sigmunstad, Dorothy Skyberg, Ivy Stebbleton, Karen Sundhagen, Carl Tarum, LuAnn Tichman, Jean (Hurly) White, William "Bill" and Wanda Whisennand, Chuck and Rene Worley, and especially Polly Wischman. Thank you Jerry Smith for proofreading.

I thank my fantastic husband Del for his love, endless patience, computer expertise, photo support, motivational talks, singing my new songs with me, and so very, very much more. Thank you dear family for your assistance and encouragement: Allen, Pam, Linda, Diana, Ilidio, Janis, Mike, Joni, Gary, Roger, Janice, and all my "grands" and "greats."

After the first edition of my book was released, I received several letters and phone calls from former project workers and others who lived in the Fort Peck area. Thank you all for your many memories of the "dam days," and for your contributions to my ongoing research.
We thank God for hard times that make good times even better.
We are all rooted in the dust of the earth.

Lois Lonnquist

Contents

Preface

One of the most fascinating chapters in Montana history covers the construction of the Fort Peck Dam in the northeastern corner of the state, during the nation's 1930s Great Depression. It is the story of the wild Missouri river, and the thousands of drought-plagued, unemployed workers hired to tame it.

Fifty Cents an Hour is an account of the builders and the building of the largest hydraulically filled earth dam in the world. It shares the daily lives of the workers, their families, and the thousands of others who passed through the Fort Peck Project area. It is a history of the eighteen-plus boomtowns, the Hi-Line communities that supplied rock, the nearby incorporated towns of Glasgow and Nashua, and the government town of Fort Peck during the construction years.

This journal account of the overall construction provides the setting around which everything else revolved.

This book focuses on a period of time in Montana unequaled in its severity and suffering for so many honest, hard-working, independent men and women. I was inspired to write it by the stories I heard told by my northeastern Montana family and friends who worked at the dam and lived in Wheeler and the other boomtowns. I was motivated to write it by the observations of two perceptive newspaper men:

Wheeler will be gone in three more years. There may never be another one. Somebody had better record it for posterity, before it's too late. Reporter Ernie Pyle, Washington Daily News, 9/18/1936.

So far, no genius of literature has done a good job for the boom towns around Fort Peck. Their worst features, and we admit they have some, have been exploited to the skies.... But night life is only one part of the story in the project towns. Hundreds of self-respecting, law abiding people make their homes in them.... Someday, perhaps, the whole picture of this life will be drawn impartially and carefully by some understanding writer... he cannot do the job by spending a few days (or nights) in some of the better known spots.
Editor Sam Gilluly, Glasgow Courier, 2/9/1937.

I am not a "genius of literature" or a "he," but I have great respect for the people of the Fort Peck Project who pulled together and held on for a better tomorrow. I have tried to draw the impartial picture of them to which editor Gilluly refers, using the same heart and humor that made them tough people in tough times.

My research led me back through Montana's devastating drought years of the 1930s and into President Franklin Delano Roosevelt's numerous *New Deal* programs to salvage the nation.

I studied the weekly progress reports prepared by the Army Corps of Engineers to get a grasp on the tremendously complicated plans and coordination it took to build the dam and spillway. I read more than a thousand 1930s newspapers and articles, and listened to nearly two-hundred oral histories recorded by some former project people. I interviewed many of the remaining workers and boomtown residents. They added their personal experiences to my large volume of facts and figures. Those who have passed on, shared their stories in letters, journals, obituaries, and pictures left behind.

The diary of my Grandma Lucy Fisher, told me much about the hardships of the Depression and of my family working at the dam.

My father was one of the thousands of unemployed family men who desperately needed a job and paycheck early in 1936. He stood in a reemployment line until he found work on a gravel train, with a transfer to the spillway, at 50 cents an hour. I was a baby when we moved to Wheeler, our home through 1939. My brother and sister were born there. Our mother took in sewing and earned more than $400 at 25 cents to $5 per garment for mending old and making new shirts, pants, and dresses. She sewed many nights by lamplight on the treadle Singer sewing machine she bought with some of her earnings.

For my parents, and for most of the others at the project, the jobs provided stepping stones and they were thankful to have them. Mom and Dad made lifelong friends. Their years at the dam, a mixture of happy events and tragic times, were among their most memorable.

There was so much more I wanted to write about and so many more people whose stories personified the great spirit, perseverance, and laughter and tears of all. The Fort Peck story would fill volumes!

Many of the workers called themselves just "common guys." This history is to honor them and the other good and gentle, tough as nails, extraordinary "common" people. It cuts a little slack for the rest.

Through my many hours of research and my many trips to the Fort Peck area with my husband Del, I have, again, *lived at the dam* in the 1930s. I now know what has brought so many former project people back there in life – and in ashes.

Lois Lonnquist

The "project area" covers the dam, spillway, construction sites, town of Fort Peck, and the boomtowns. It includes Glasgow and Nashua. The "project people" are Corps personnel, government workers, and all who lived and worked in the project area.

Chronology

1930   State of Montana is 41 years old (Territory: 41st state 1889)
        Great Depression throughout the nation

1931   Valley County, eastern Montana suffering severe drought

1932   President-elect Franklin D. Roosevelt offers *New Deal*
        Army Corps of Engineers visit likely Fort Peck dam site

1933   Gov. John E. Erickson resigns (appointed to U.S. Senate)
        Lt. Gov. Frank H. Cooney becomes Montana Governor
        Public Works Administration (PWA) Project No. 30 plan
        Sen. Burton K. Wheeler pushes building a Fort Peck dam
        Reemployment Service hires first workers October 23
        Workers earn 50 cents to $1.20 an hour, 34-hour week

1934   Boomtowns springing up. Fort Peck town constructed

1935   Governor Frank H. Cooney dies of heart failure
        W. Elmer Holt President Pro-Tempore of Senate
            assumes office of Governor until 1937
        Works Progress Administration (WPA) jobs in Montana
        Montana Highway Patrol (MHP) created by the Legislature
        President Franklin D. Roosevelt signs Social Security Act
        President dedicates Boulder (Hoover) Dam on Colorado River
            Cost $48,890,995; 96 workers die during construction

1936   Farmers face most devastating grain shortage in state's history
        Roy E. Ayers elected Montana governor in November

1937   Missouri River diverted through four mile-long tunnels
        President dedicates the Bonneville Dam, Columbia River,
        five years to build, cost $88M

1938   Fort Peck dam earth movement "slide" kills eight workers

1939   Dam nearing completion, workers leaving project area

1940   Fort Peck Dam Project done. Plans to build a powerhouse
        Federal agency surveying for Fort Peck Wildlife Area

Fort Peck Dam largest hydraulic-fill dam in the world

Part 1

Taming the Wild Missouri River
"The Big Muddy," "Mighty Mo"

The Missouri springs from the merger of the Jefferson, Gallatin, and Madison rivers about three miles north of Three Forks, Montana. It winds north past Townsend, Helena, Great Falls, Fort Benton; east through the Fort Peck dam tunnels, and out of Montana at Bainville.

Across the North Dakota border it adds the Yellowstone River and runs through South Dakota. It touches the borders of Nebraska, Iowa, Kansas, and Missouri on its way to St. Louis to join the "Mighty Mississippi." Here the Missouri ends its 2,315 mile run and gives up its name as the rivers roll south to the Gulf of Mexico.

Before the Fort Peck dam was built in the 1930s, the Missouri ran wild and free. Sometime in December it froze over solid enough for travelers and animals to cross. In spring it broke into ice cakes that swirled around in the swiftly flowing, caramel colored runoff from flooding gumbo and sandstone coulees, creeks, and small rivers. As it swelled it became a moody monster picking up snags, debris, and dead trees to dump with its floodwaters on the sandbars and lowlands.

A second flood occurred in June when snow on the mountain tops melted and water rushed down the streams and over the river banks.

As the Missouri ran through the mountains it gathered sand, silt, and gravel, but instead of dumping them on the floodplain, it lined its channel bed with 100 or more feet of the accumulated alluvium.

The Missouri could be treacherous with its quicksand, sandbars, ice air-holes, and constantly changing channels.

During the Lewis and Clark expedition, Meriwether Lewis wrote in his journal on April 13, 1805: *We found a number of carcases of the Buffaloe lying long shore, which had been drowned by falling through the ice in winter and lodged on shore by the high water when the river broke up about the first of this month.*

The river had its nurturing side as well: Annual floods scattered cottonwood tree seeds and watered willows along its banks, animals drank from the river, and hundreds of species of fish thrived in its muddy water. People used the Missouri River for recreation and as a roadway, and found a multitude of uses for the water and ice.

Indian tribes and fur traders claimed the upper Missouri River before Lewis and Clark drew attention to it in 1805-1806. In 1838 the government spent $20,000 to send Capt. Robert E. Lee (General Lee of the Civil War Confederate Army) and a clearing crew with two snag boats, on a 300-mile journey up the river from St. Louis. They removed "2,245 snags and 1,700 overhanging trees."

Hundreds of steamboats full of passengers and freight traveled up the Missouri from St. Louis to Fort Benton after 1840. An estimated three-hundred of them, and hundreds of smaller boats, hit snags or had other accidents that sent them to the bottom of the river. The last recorded steamer trip was made September 12, 1888.

Montana Historical Society librarian David Hilger wrote to the Army Corps of Engineers in 1936 of three steamers under water in the Fort Peck area: The *Tacony* went down at Fort Peck sometime in 1870, "reason unknown." The *Red Cloud*, reason unknown, was sunk July 11, 1882, at the river's Eighth Point. The sternwheeler *Butte* caught fire and sank twelve miles north of Fort Peck on July 13, 1883.

In 1884 the U.S. Congress formed the Missouri River Commission (retired in 1902) to draft a river development plan that included flood control, navigation, and a dam. Survey maps were made in 1890.

The Army Corps of Engineers became involved in the early 1900s. The Fort Peck Dam was built in the 1930s when President Franklin D. Roosevelt's Great Depression *New Deal* combined the need for jobs for thousands of unemployed workers, with the need for a dam.

To make a bed for the dam and lake the government purchased farms and ranches along the river to add to land it already owned. Schoolhouses, homes, barns, and sheds were auctioned to the highest bidders. All structures had to be moved or burned.

In October 1933 government workers began clearing the land. Trees became lumber, poles, and firewood. Brush was burned. Men with hand tools, small machines, and teams of horses spent thousands of hours removing obstacles of all kinds. Crews went out to make sure nothing was left behind to become an underwater hazard.

A worker told how his crew cut barbed wire fences and blew up small bridges to block access to the river bank. He recalled burning the remaining buildings, especially one well built barn. "A lot of them were junk, but one of them in particular just hurt you right there...." He added that before the torching the men held a little ceremony.

The importance of clearing all the waterways was emphasized in September 1936 when the dredge Jefferson passed over the wreckage of the *Tacony,* and its pumps were clogged with bolts and boards.

Graves. *Permission is requested to remove the body described below, from its present burial place in the Fort Peck Reservoir to a spot above the water level of the said reservoir:*

Name of deceased: *C.H.M.*   Age*: About 30 years.*

Where buried: *Range 39 east, Montana Meridian.*

Date of death: *Probably in 1905.*   Cause: *Struck by lightning.*

Method of removal: *U.S. Government motor vehicle.*

Place of interment: *Near Willow Creek...Valley County, Montana.*

Applicant: *U.S. Engineer Office, Fort Peck, Montana.*

Authority to move the grave, *signed by James C. Crowder, a friend of the deceased, Glasgow, Montana.*

Signed R. Lee, Captain, Corps of Engineers executive assistant.

"Permission is hereby granted." *Signed by Valley County Health Officer Mark D. Hoyt, Nov. 27, 1937.*

Public records were searched and long time residents interviewed to locate graves in the area to be covered by Fort Peck Lake. Some graves dating back to the early 1800s were found in isolated areas, their markers missing or unreadable. Bones were moved to registered graveyards and markers placed with the available information.

Gravediggers located the grave of a cowboy drowned "long ago" in the river. His body was wrapped in a horse blanket and buried beneath a cottonwood. His tomato can marker was nailed to the tree.

Among the other graves were those of two children who died of diphtheria in the early 1900s and were buried next to their home.

Old Fort Peck. *Lewis and Clark passed by the site in May 1805.*

Fort Peck was established as a trading post in 1867 by the Durfee & Peck Company, on the Missouri River bank, about a mile west of the future dam. The fort was 300 square feet in size, protected by 12-feet high cottonwood log walls. Inside were quarters for the men, a stable, blacksmith's shop, storehouse, corral, and slaughterhouse.

Fur traders, and friendly Indians who set up teepees, stopped by. Military men negotiating with the Indians before the Custer Massacre stayed there. Fort Peck was the Milk River Indian Agency 1873-1879.

The fort was abandoned after the river bank washed away and the shale ledge it sat on thirty-five feet above the water was no longer safe. Erosion continued until the fort dropped down and sank in the main channel of the relentless river, around the turn of the century.

In the early 1900s old trenches, ovens, and barricades remained. For a time wooden burial boxes from the cemetery, originally a half-mile from the river, stuck out from the hillside on cutbank shelves before they too dropped into the water. Legend says that one of them may have held the remains of an Indian princess.

The Fort Peck Homestead "Fort Peck Point" was the first of the numbered points of land on the river west of the fort. A story in Valley County's *Footprints In The Valley* tells how in 1894 "a stretch of ground beyond the knoll in front of the cabin suddenly sank down several feet." The ground was littered with Indian relics, blue beads, white saucers, and "odd things" washed out of Indian graves. Skulls, stones with "queer figures," coins and agates were scattered around.

The river soon covered the homestead and land once dominated by wild animals and big cattle ranch herds that wintered on the shore.

The Hanging Tree stood at the mouth of Timber Creek. Legend says two to six men were hung from its branches for their dastardly deeds. No graves were found, but there was evidence of a dugout.

Dinosaur and buffalo bones rest in their water bed beneath the dam and lake, deep enough to be undisturbed by the construction.

The Missouri River does not graciously give up the treasures it has stored. One can only wonder what else lies buried at its bottom.

Farmers and Ranchers along the River

Consent to purchase or condemn all necessary lands is hereby given and concurrent jurisdiction is ceded to the United States over the Fort Peck Dam ... any lands now owned or that may be acquired by the United States and that touch the body of water, all such land and water being situated in the counties of Valley, Phillips, McCone, Garfield, Petroleum, and Fergus, state of Montana. Montana Codes Annotated, En. Sec. 1, Ch. 50, Ex. L. 1933.

News that the government was purchasing land along the Missouri River for the Fort Peck dam and reservoir was met with mixed emotions by the hundred or so farmers and ranchers who would have to give up their homes. Landowners who were deep in debt were happy to sell before they lost their land to the bank, or in a sheriff's sale for back taxes. Elderly homesteaders unable to work their farms and unable to sell them were thankful to get out with money in hand.

But some farmers and ranchers who had invested years in the land given them by the Homestead Act, did not want to sell. Many had large families to do the work, and alfalfa crops to carry them through the dry years. They wanted to stay in their riverside communities.

Army Corps of Engineers Appraisal report 1935

Aerial photos ... were used to appraise and acquire the land.... Section corners are located ..., and individual property lines are plotted.... About 275,000 acres of land are required for the dam site, the town of Fort Peck, and ... reservoir. About 150,000 acres are owned privately; 20,000 are owned by the state of Montana; the rest, 105,000, is public domain land. The Department of Agriculture examined and appraised all privately and state-owned land and submitted a report on each parcel.... The unit value of each physical parcel of land in the tract and all physical improvements such as buildings, fences, wells, etc. are appraised by a field appraisal party ... the total appraised value, together with a report, is submitted to the Land Acquisition Section to assist with the purchase.

Lt. E.G. Plank is in direct charge of land acquisition and H.A. Ward, the Department of Agriculture, is in charge of appraisals.

Field appraisal parties often traveled by boat due to a lack of roads along the river. Their visit met with offers of hot coffee or hot words.

By early 1934 several landowners had accepted their appraisals and checks. Farmers in the construction area were paid extra to move on short notice, others were allowed to stay up to two years.

Land acquisitions continued through 1935. During November the acting secretary of War announced approval for another 1,575 acres in the project area at $15,350.29, with landowners allowed to stay on the land until May 1, 1937, at no charge.

Disputes arose over some appraisals. Land owners wrote letters of protest to the government and to local newspapers. A few formed associations and demanded further negotiations, saying the hardship of people who came out to Montana with "practically nothing" to an "isolated and remote locality" deserved more. They stated their land and alfalfa crops were the most prosperous in Valley County and should be appraised at pre-drought valuations, not those of October 1933. Most disputes were settled in federal court in 1936 and 1937.

Legal issues arose in July 1937 when some farmers questioned the Land Department as to ownership of thousands of acres of former river bottom turned dry land after the river was diverted.

The controversy over whether or not the government paid a fair price for land, continued for years; even the landowners did not agree.

Leaving the land

Stories of anguish were told of residents leaving their homes. One family stayed until water rose in the lake. They were "forced to flee over the hills." An old man, whose wife had passed away, sold his stock and said goodbye to his neighbors. He drowned in the Big Dry. A woman refused to leave home until faced with forcible removal.

A little girl recalled her parent's separation before their farm was sold. As the broken family left with their belongings loaded in a pick-up, their buildings were set on fire, a sight she "never forgot."

An elderly bachelor accepted his check, saying when the water rose he would sit back and watch his land "get a good soaking."

Some farmers declared it a "bad day for river rats" then left for jobs on the dam and homes in the new boomtowns. When the project ended many bought farms and resettled in northeastern Montana. Several older couples retired to Glasgow and Nashua.

The community Thanksgiving dinner was a tradition for the settlers of the first ten points of land along the Missouri river. In their family history in *Footprints In The Valley* Arthur and Joyce Ferguson, who settled on Fifth Point in 1917, remembered the last celebration:

George and Mary Pointer of Fourth Point, hosts of the first dinner, hosted the last in 1933. Two-hundred neighbors came bringing chairs, and covered dishes of food to place on the plank and sawhorse tables. Mrs. Dave Francis, whose family farm was the first to go, invited the eight Corps majors and drivers she cooked for at her home. They brought "several five pound boxes of chocolates." After dinner local musicians tuned up fiddles and guitars and played for one last dance.

The people moved away as the project progressed. Soon the night lights along the river came from work sites instead of windows.

Dryland Farmers and Ranchers

News of project jobs brought hope to the drought-ridden dryland farmers, cattle ranchers, and sheep ranchers.

Dryland farming began in northeastern Montana in the early 1900s when thousands of young men and women, many with families, rode in on Jim Hill's Great Northern railroad to become homesteaders. Drawn by his ads for free land, people from all walks of life traveled to Montana from east and Midwest America between 1906-1920.

Hundreds of Europeans who bought in to Hill's offer of low-cost trans-Atlantic ship fare, railroad rides from St. Paul to Montana, and help locating land, joined the migration. Boxcars, averaging $20 each, hauled their farm equipment, seeds, livestock, and household goods. If so desired, the family could ride along in the boxcar.

Locators, for a varying fee, helped newcomers file their claims on land available through the Homestead Act, and prepare to "prove up."

Homesteaders built sod, log, and small frame homes or ordered house kits from Sears. Neighbors helped each other get settled and then developed active communities with schools and churches.

During America's involvement in World War I (1917-1919) the government pushed farmers to grow more food crops. Banks financed new equipment. More land was plowed. When the war ended, prices and sales dropped, leaving many over-extended farmers deep in debt.

The mid-1920s rain stopped falling. A severe drought hit in 1929. Creeks dried up, crops failed, and winds blew away the newly plowed topsoil. Hundreds of homesteaders were driven out by 1931. Others applied for seed loans and staked their hopes on "next year."

Swarms of grasshoppers destroyed the meager crops in 1935. Undeterred by tons of hopper poison on the ground and sprayed from bi-planes, they were back with a vengeance in 1936 through 1939.

Farmers tried conservation plans and bought poultry to eat insects. They planted sugar beets in the mid-1930s and fed 280,000 sheep and 15,000 cows on beet molasses, tops, and pulp in feed rations.

Most cattle ranchers arrived in Montana in the late 1800s, trailing herds of Texas longhorns north to the open range. In spite of harsh winters, cattle barons established large "spreads" and hired hundreds of cowboys. When homesteaders came with plows and fences, many of the large ranches became small ranches with wheat fields.

In the 1930s ranchers watched drought destroy their pastures and dry up their dams. Their cows ate thistles in 1934, but even thistles did not grow in 1935. A few ranchers could afford to buy feed but others drove their cattle to stockyards and shipped them to St. Paul.

Sheep ranchers were without pasture, and fighting wood ticks that paralyzed their sheep. They joined cattle ranchers to kill thousands of coyotes preying on their animals, and to control the huge numbers of rabbits, magpies, and rattlesnakes in places they had not been before.

As the drought dragged on, farmers and ranchers struggled with despair, fatigue, health problems, and delinquent taxes. Most hung on, but others, weary with old age, illness, and loss of loved ones lined up their unsold machinery, closed their doors, and left Montana forever.

Small businesses dependent on the rural trade were hurting. Relief agencies, churches, and organizations were short of funds. By 1931 the Valley County Red Cross had almost depleted its resources, and asked for help. In 1933 the St. Louis national office sent $56,000 and nearly 27 railroad cars of food, clothing, and other assistance.

Most Montanans desperately needed the Fort Peck project jobs.

Part 2

Fort Peck Dam - Project No. 30 - 1932-1940

1932

On October 23, 1932, Col. R.C. Moore, the U.S. Army Corps of Engineers division engineer, and Capt. Theodore Wyman, Jr., from the Kansas City headquarters, arrived in Glasgow to meet Mayor Leo B. Coleman. The men drove twenty-three miles southeast down a dirt road past dryland farms to the Missouri River Valley. They stopped at the Dave Francis farm northeast of Old Fort Peck and looked at a dam site considered during a Corps survey trip up the Missouri in 1928.

The *Glasgow Courier* reported the town "rife with speculation" about a dam project and "practically everyone was cheerful." Senator Burton K. Wheeler called a Fort Peck project "entirely feasible."

A few Corps engineers conducted preliminary tests at the dam site then returned to Kansas for the winter.

1933

Plans for the Fort Peck project were on the drawing board at the Missouri River Division office in Kansas City early in 1933. In June ten Corps surveyors arrived in Glasgow on the train. Their equipment missed the trip, so the Valley County surveyor loaned them a transit to get started. Within a week, twenty additional surveyors, engineers, and geologists arrived to start boring test holes and to study the river.

Some of the Corpsmen brought their families and rented homes in Glasgow. Others boarded with farmers at the dam site. Most bunked in granaries or tents while four work sites were set up at Fifth Point, Bear Creek, Big Dry Creek, and along the river in McCone County.

The first death of a project worker occurred on October 5, 1933. A scow load of machinery overturned in the Missouri River during core drilling. Three crewmen were injured; 35-year-old Victor Carlson, of Michigan, a ten-year employee of private contractor E. J. Longyear Explorations of Minneapolis, was drowned.

October 6, 1933, the *Glasgow Courier* headlines announced in big, bold type ***Army Head Recommends Fort Peck Dam.*** The initial allotment of Public Works Administration (PWA) funds was $15M, with $9,500,000 more approved three days later. Suddenly words like "millions," "tons," "gigantic," "huge scale" appeared in every story in the *Courier* and other newspapers around the state and nation.

Public Works Administration (PWA) Project No. 30 was approved October 13, 1933, by newly elected President Franklin D. Roosevelt. It was construction for employment, the melding of 40 years of Missouri River flood control planning and the need for jobs for thousands of unemployed workers during the Great Depression.

"The Dam"

With its 100M cubic yards of material, Fort Peck Dam will be by far the largest earth dam in the world and the largest hydraulic-fill dam, exceeding Gatun Dam in Panama (largest) by nearly five times. Major Thomas B. Larkin, Fort Peck district engineer.

No engineering job of this magnitude had ever been attempted with so short a time for planning. Major Clark Kittrell.

It would take an extraordinary plan to build the dam, one that allowed for unprecedented solutions to unique problems presented by a wild river running over unstable shale, silt, and sand. The site was in an isolated area, the weather was given to extremes, the work was to be done by a highly motivated but mostly untrained work force, and it would all begin in the dead of a Montana winter.

Permanent structures would include a 250 feet high by 9,000 feet long main dam (four miles overall); a mile-long spillway and 16 gates; four mile-long tunnels each with its own control shaft and gatehouse; a Corps Administration Building, and an Employees Hotel.

One major feature to be built, and never seen again, would be the two-mile long, steel sheeting cutoff wall; driven from 100 to 150 feet through river alluvium to bedrock under the dam, "high on the east abutment across the width of the valley to high on the west bank."

A priority on the construction list was the government town of Fort Peck for Corps personnel; and dorms and barracks for workers.

The Corps' To Do list was long, with many tasks to be carried out simultaneously: Test the river and the valley beds where years of flooding had covered Bearpaw shale with hundreds of feet of silt, gravel, and clay. Clear trees, brush, and buildings from the dam site and lake bed. Strip the dam and spillway grounds.

Build bridges, railroads and trestles. Assemble the four huge dredges and fleet of smaller boats, and dig a winter harbor for them. Build pipelines and boosters, and place hydraulic fill. Build up gravel toes on each end of the dam and borrow pits on each side. Deliver millions of tons of supplies, and huge boulders and gravel to the dam and spillway. The list went on.

Meanwhile, Corps officials, still short staffed from Depression era cutbacks, signed large and small construction company contracts. And, as ordered by President Roosevelt, hastened to line up as many jobs as possible for the thousands of unemployed workers to be hired.

Large construction company contracts signed by 1935.

Camp/Town Buildings: Madsen Construction Co., Mpls; Johnson, Drake & Piper, Inc., Mpls.; C.F. Haglin Co., Mpls.
Core Drilling: Longyear Exploration Co., Mpls.; S.J. Mathews, Tulsa; Mott Core Drilling Co., Huntington, W.V.; Diamond Drilling Co., Spokane;
Diversion Tunnels: Mason & Walsh Co., New York.
Electric Distribution System: P.O. Montgomery Co., Dallas.
Electric Feeders to Dredges/Tunnels: A.S. Schulman Co., Chicago.
Electric Transmission Line: Ziebarth & Walker, Los Angeles.
Gas-Distribution System: Municipal Service Co., Kansas City.
Gathering Field Boulders: Tobin Quarries, Inc., and R.W. Newton McDowell Inc., both of Kansas City.
Gravel/Aggregates: J.L. Shiely & Becker County Sand & Gravel, St. Paul.
Loading Out Field Boulders: Tomlinson-Arkwright Co., Great Falls.
Milk River Railroad Bridge: Minneapolis Bridge Co., Mpls.
Missouri River Bridge/Trestle: Massman Construction, Kansas City.
Sewage and Water System: C.F. Lytle, Sioux City, Iowa.
Spillway/Structures: Martin Wunderlich, Jefferson City, Mo.; Spillway Brothers, Inc., Kansas City; Addison Miller & Fielding & Shepley, St. Paul.
Steel Pile Cutoff Wall: Frazier-Davis Construction Co., St. Louis.
Streets & Roads (Fort Peck town): Morrison-Knudsen Co., Spokane.
Stripping Dam Site and Trestles work: Addison Miller, Inc., St Paul.
Substations & Buildings: Westinghouse Elec., Co., Pittsburgh; Allis Chalmers Mfg., Co., Milwaukee; W.C. Smith, Inc., Duluth.
Trestles: Morrison-Glasscock-Connor Co., Kansas City;
Tunnel emergency control gates: Bartlett Hayward Co., Baltimore.
Water-Filtration Plant: Gjellfald Construction Co., Forest City, Iowa.

Hundreds of contracts for services and supplies were signed during the dam and spillway construction. Montana contractors were employed whenever possible. Projects required everything from huge construction equipment to teams of well trained horses and their drivers.

Some adjustments were made along the way as the need arose for change. All told, the expertise of the Army Corps of Engineers and private contractors, combined with the skills, hard working hands and sweat of the brow of laborers made the project a reality.

The First Government Jobs

During the summer of 1933 the National Reemployment Service (NRS) opened offices to register unemployed workers living in their Montana county for six months or more. Thousands of men walked or traveled by truckloads to fill out applications. They were told, "Keep in touch. The office manager will call once, then call someone else."

Keeping in touch was a hardship as few men had telephones or the means to pay for meals and lodging while they waited.

By order of the NRS, unemployed veterans and married men with dependents, living in Valley County, would be hired first. Men from nearby counties would be next, then statewide. Single men were told there was little hope for jobs in the near future, but register and wait.

No out-of-state workers would be hired until all of the able-bodied Montanans had jobs. Large notices were posted in railroad stations and public places in other states to keep ineligible job seekers away.

The "rustling" of jobs by contacting contractors then registering, was forbidden. All acquisitions had to be processed through the NRS.

Civil Service rules for the Fort Peck District applied only to grades above common laborer, working directly for the government. Large contractors (most were from out of state) other than suppliers, could bring in their skilled workers and executive personnel, but laborers had to be hired under PWA rules and processed by the NRS.

Classified labor grade workers were hired from the Civil Service register by examination. In March 1934 CS examiners announced 91 different exams. There were 12,000 applications for 144 positions.

First government workers

October 23, 1933, the first 70 Valley County men went to work. They met at the Glasgow reemployment office where men with trucks

Courtesy of Marvin Presser

gave rides to men without. These World War I veterans, farmers, and ranchers in their patched overalls and worn out boots, bounced over 22 miles of country road to the dam site. They joked about their patches, so thankful to have jobs they little noticed the rain and sleet coming down.

At the river they formed two crews, each with a foreman, one to start cutting brush and the other to build a tool house.

For fifty cents an hour for a thirty-hour week, they took up axes and handsaws and went to work. While they stacked brush, rain turned the gumbo to mud that stuck on their boots, and clogged the truck wheels.

Hundreds of men were still waiting at the reemployment office for the government's order of a half-carload of tools from Minneapolis.

Daily the NRS called as many workers as possible. Stores ran out of axes, saws, mattocks, and other hand tools before the shipment from Minneapolis arrived. Workers were given acquisition books to buy tools. Some men brought their own and received tool rent.

There was no housing. The men lived in their vehicles, tents, and sheepherder style houses on trailers until they could bring in or build shacks. Winter was coming down. Oil barrel heaters began showing up at the worksites to warm cold hands and to brew hot coffee.

November 2, 1933, McCone County's reemployment office called 100 men to work on the east side of the river. They were told to bring their own bedding, cooking utensils, and lodging.

Four-hundred men from Valley and McCone counties now had jobs. There was jubilation when their paychecks came from Kansas!

In November 1933, Maj. T.B. Larkin, a West Point graduate with an impressive service record during World War I, and further training and experience with the Military Engineers, was appointed district engineer at Fort Peck. He set up temporary headquarters in the First National Bank in Glasgow while the Administration Building in Fort Peck was being built. He rented a home and sent for his family.

Major Larkin's first Corps assistants were: Maj. Clark Kittrell, operations; Capt. C.N. Iry, Capt. A.W. Pence, Capt. D.A.D. Ogden, Capt. R. Lee, Capt. C.H. Chorpening, Capt. J. B. Hughes, Capt. J.R. Harding, Lt. E.G. Plank. Principal civilian engineers: T.W. Ragsdale, C.S. Smith, and O.F. Brinton.

Roads and Rails

In 1933 there was one main dirt and gravel road between the dam site and Glasgow. The Corps needed a heavy-duty highway for the hundreds of trucks hauling supplies and lumber from US Highway 2 and the Great Northern railroad to the boatyard and dam.

Government crews graded and graveled the road but the going was still rough. Truck drivers who slid into the ditches on ice and snow often called on farmers and their teams of horses to pull them out.

Plans were approved for a Fort Peck-Glasgow highway to be built in the spring, but the existing road had to serve until then.

The Corps needed a twelve-mile railroad spur from the Great Northern main line at Wiota to the dam site. It would serve as a major link in moving massive amounts of construction materials and lumber to the boatyard and dam. It would later carry train loads of rock from the quarries along the Hi-Line to the dam.

Unable to find a contractor to build the railroad during the winter, engineers brought in machinery and hired laborers to do the job.

Great Northern crews built a switching track and water tank, and an office, cookshack, and other buildings to complete the Wiota Spur.

First winter 1933-34

Carpenters worked around the clock to build five barracks and a mess hall at the boatyard. Workers built shacks and pitched tents in the first boomtown, along the river between the boatyard and dam site.

Six-hundred government laborers, private contractor supervisors, and Corpsmen were on the job through the cold weather. They endured a shortage of facilities and supplies. That first winter was one of great hardship for all the men involved.

In spite of the cold weather, many projects got underway. Montana Power and Mountain State Telephone & Telegraph installed lines. Private contractors planned their work sites and prepared for spring.

1934

In January the Minneapolis Bridge Company went to work on the permanent 3-span plate-girder railroad bridge across the Milk River, two miles south of Wiota. It was finished in time for the first train to cross on April 16, sixty days ahead of schedule.

To create jobs, the Corps ordered stockpiling of rock for later use at the dam. Work began along the Hi-Line in February. The first five truck drivers from Chinook were hired. Five contractors in Valley County were awarded contracts. Work began on the first dredge hull. Preliminary construction of the Fort Peck-Glasgow highway began.

Employment February 15 was 1,017 workers on three shifts.

Emp. March 15 (1,521) included 1,290 Montanans and 241 non-resident district contractor administrators and supervisors.

In February the Corps announced that the Massman Construction Company would build the Missouri River bridge and nearly six miles of elevated steel and wood trestle encircling the damsite over the river and valley. The 200-foot bridge would span the river on the center line of the downstream gravel toe, 60 feet above the main channel. Work began on a $984,771 contract March 1, with 180 days to finish.

Spring snow, mud, and unseasonable cold raised havoc with trucks hauling steel, timbers, pilings, and machinery over narrow dirt roads from Glasgow and Nashua. Workers endured hardships and several were injured as they rushed to finish the bridge so trains and trucks could cross with millions of tons of materials needed at the tunnels and spillway. The first train of two engines and 16 cars, loaded with material for Mason & Walsh, crossed the bridge on October 1, 1934.

During April tunnel workers started work on the four mile-long tunnels. Boatyard carpenters were finishing the four dredges: the Jefferson, Madison, Gallatin, and Missouri. The high-tension power line "Blue Ox" between Great Falls and the dam was ready for use.

Emp. May 15 (2,999)

By June the twelve contractors building the town of Fort Peck were progressing in "orderly confusion." Several boomtowns had grown up around the construction sites. Work trucks began picking up workers in the towns to transport them to their jobs.

Most contractors had camps for supervisors and key employees at the tunnels, spillway, and larger work sites. Workers lived in tents or small barracks and ate in mess halls.

The Corps set up several camps in 1934. Some drilling inspectors moved into a deserted building. They covered the dirt floor with cottonwood, lined the walls with blueprint paper to keep out the wind, and furnished their "blue room" with a potbelly stove and cots.

Emp. July 1 (6,000)

All construction sites at the dam, tunnels, and boatyard were in full operation. Rock picking began in August with some 300 workers stockpiling rock in Phillips County.

Disputes arose over employment eligibility for some farmers. The labor board reviewed complaints by a few union reps who had moved into the project area to raise work and wage issues.

Thousands of Montanans were still searching for jobs. The state Relief Commission projected winter 1934-1935 rolls at 135,000.

A portion of the First Boomtown   Army Corps of Engineers - Fort Peck

Paul's truck   Courtesy of Paul McFarland

First Homes   Courtesy of Marvin Presser

23

Fort Peck Ferry   Courtesy of Paul McFarland

Tunnels   Army Corps of Engineers   Spillway   Photo by author

Tanker used in the tunnels   Courtesy of Paul McFarland

Boatyards

Dredge Missouri

Fort Peck Dam Casing
Photos Courtesy of Corps of Engineers-Fort Peck

Building the Wiota Spur to the dam during the winter of 1933-34

U.S. Army Corps of Engineers

Worksites of the dam, spillway, four tunnels, and bridges.

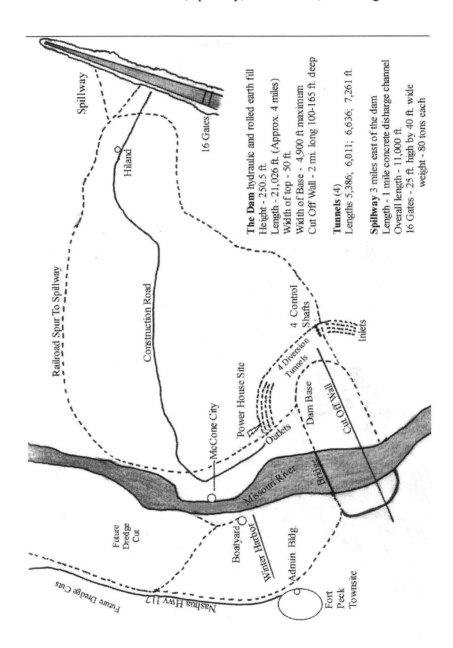

The Dam hydraulic and rolled earth fill
Height - 250.5 ft.
Length - 21,026 ft. (Approx. 4 miles)
Width of top - 50 ft.
Width of Base - 4,900 ft maximum
Cut Off Wall - 2 mi. long 100-165 ft. deep

Tunnels (4)
Lengths 5,386; 6,011; 6,636; 7,261 ft.

Spillway 3 miles east of the dam
Length - 1 mile concrete disharge channel
Overall length - 11,000 ft.
16 Gates - 25 ft. high by 40 ft. wide
weight - 80 tons each

FDR Visits The Project

This great Nation will endure ... the only thing we have to fear is fear itself. President Franklin D. Roosevelt, March 4, 1933.

August 6, 1934, President and Mrs. (Eleanor) Roosevelt and their entourage arrived in Glasgow on a special Great Northern train. A huge crowd of residents, visitors, and members of the Fort Peck Indian Reservation tribes dressed in their headdresses and traditional clothes, were at the railroad station to greet them.

After a warm welcome, the president's party transferred to eighteen cars to travel to the project on the newly built and oiled highway to Fort Peck. Glasgow's National Guard Company G stood at attention along the road. They were picked up later to hear Roosevelt's speech.

Thousands of boomtown residents and visitors lined the highway through Wheeler and along the motorcade route. President Roosevelt was immensely popular. The people listened to his weekly radio "Fireside Chats," and felt they knew and could trust him. Most of them had a picture of him on the wall of their home or business.

Eager to show their appreciation, they waved and cheered as the smiling president, Mrs. Roosevelt, Corps District Engineer Maj. T.B. Larkin, and Secretary of War George H. Dern drove by.

Workers were proud to have the president visit their worksites and everything was ready for his inspection. Even the "Cat House" sign had been removed from the caterpillar garage lest it be offensive. Grateful men waved, cheered, and thanked Roosevelt for their jobs.

While the president's party drove through the project and town of Fort Peck, his Great Northern train was moved to Nashua and down the Wiota spur to the engineer's warehouse where he delivered his twenty-minute speech from the caboose.

Surrounded by dignitaries, including Senator Burton K. Wheeler, Roosevelt congratulated workers on their progress. His rousing and inspirational speech was heard by thousands at the dam site, and by countless listeners to radio stations KFBB in Great Falls and KGCX in Wolf Point. Photos of the event and the text of the president's speech were printed in local and state newspapers the next day.

Among the gifts the president received from the project people was a diamond willow cane with a gold tip and special inscription.

Back to work. In September the Massman Construction camp near the railroad bridge was bought by Frazier-Davis Company for use while building the steel cutoff wall. Cranes, hydraulic hammers, and other equipment needed to place the wall were on their way.

Workers with twenty-five trucks and three huge power shovels began building the six-mile railroad extension from the dam to the spillway. The first men from Daniels County were hired. The Missouri River bridge and trestle were ready and the first engine and sixteen cars of gravel from Saco, crossed in October. The first dredge was launched. Crews began work on the spillway structure.

Phenomenal progress had been made before the project's first anniversary October 23, 1934: electrical energy was surging through the 288-mile line from the Rainbow substation at Great Falls, and, the new filtration plant had been completed.

Winter Layoffs 1934-35

Cold weather forced the Corps and several contractors to lay off some 1,029 workers during November and December. There were no other jobs, no unemployment checks, and very little government aid.

Workers with farms went home. Others moved in with relatives. But most had boomtown homes, children in school, and no place else to go. Layoffs were devastating for families already struggling to pay for food, fuel, and rent. Grocery stores, that could, allowed tabs. Employed friends and family brought food. Newly formed churches and organizations collected clothing and donated what money they had to help out until the men went back to work. Many families were too proud to ask for assistance. Their suffering was great.

1935

Emp. Jan. 1 (5,000)

Work at the spillway continued through most of January. Spillway Builders had 500 men operating caterpillars, shovels, and 63 White dump trucks, with 45 more trucks on order. Martin Wunderlich crews were grading the steep hillsides. Record distance drives were made in the tunnels. Borrow pits were cleared. Gen. Edward Markham asked for $20M more to finish the project.

Emp. Feb. 15 (5,322)

Steel plates, stretching out a mile, were sunk 150 feet for the cutoff wall. A record 64 feet were drilled in pilot Tunnel No. 3 in 24 hours. Concrete work began. Frigid temperatures froze ice 40 inches thick in parts of the river.

To take their minds off the sub-zero cold, workers guessed when the ice would break up, and when the first mile-long pilot tunnel would be "holed through." (March 28, with almost "perfect alignment.")

In March, Mason & Walsh broke the world record, drilling through 1,508 feet of rock in Tunnel No. 3 in one month. The spillway was down to 130 feet deep, 70 feet below the river. Workers went from four five-hour shifts to three seven-hour shifts per week.

Emp. April 1 (5,689); April 15 (6,223)

Floodlights were turned on. Equipment and dredge crews were ready for work but the river was still frozen. Two more tunnels were holed through. Crews celebrated with a dance in the Recreation Hall.

Gravel shipments arrived from Cole. Dredges, derrick barges, and ferry cars were launched. Government shops operated 24 hours a day. Work began on the spillway gates.

In May the marine diver dove into the cold, muddy Missouri to check underwater conditions. Great Northern officials came by special train, noting their welcome revenues with "we need it."

The 200 engineers and workers at the cutoff wall celebrated their accomplishments with a party at the Nite Owl and breakfast at the Los Angeles Club, claiming it rivaled the "hatchet burying" event of the boatyard and dredge workers.

A ten minute spillway break was ordered so photographer M.A. Ellis could shoot a photo. The shutdown cost the government $284.

The Corps' towboat *John Ordway* arrived from Missouri.

On May 23, the *Fort Peck Press* reported: *Army Engineers Make Best Safety Record while placing 150,000 cubic yards of fill in the dam daily. Man hours, 1,877,621; no-lost-time injuries 59; lost-time injuries 30; fatalities 0.*

Dredges pumped 100 cubic yards of fill a minute into the dam. Washington allocated $15M more for the project.

Emp. June 1 (7,035)

The first piles were driven through the river to firm shale for the cutoff wall. More railroad track and trestles were built. The mile-long dam was rising as dredges pumped in fill. Government contracts were awarded for more than $13,000 worth of electrical supplies, rubber tape, soap, cups, mattresses, honey, raisins, and other items.

Dredge crews were surprised to find seven rattlesnakes on board a dredge surrounded by water. They asked, "Can rattlesnakes swim?"

By mid-June Corps officials noted the project had provided work "directly and indirectly for 16,000 to 25,000 men."

In one June week, deliveries to Mason & Walsh were: 9,000 tons sand, 1,200 cubic yards fine gravel, 5,000 cubic yards coarse gravel, 5,000 pounds of bulk cement, 2,000 bags of cement, 14,000 gallons of bituminous sealing solution.

June had good days, the Jefferson dredged 51,540 cubic yards of materials in 24 hours; and bad days, a burst pipeline sank a big barge.

Emp. July 1 (approx. 7,300)

Rail cars on the Wiota spur delivered 123,000 tons of freight. Approximately 1,607 cars delivered gravel. By mid-July work to enlarge the four holed-through tunnels was underway. Stockpiles of glacial boulders were moved from Phillips and Valley counties to the dam. The first tunnel outlet retaining walls were cemented.

Supplies of waxpaper, sugar, ground alum, flour, copper wire, cups, and other items were received and stored. Bids were let for gate valves, pickup trucks, and cheese and canned goods.

Emp. Aug. 15 (7,236)

The spillway approach was concreted. More than 12,000,000 cubic yards of fill were recorded at the dam. The dredge Madison was pumping fill through a record three-mile pipeline. Another world record was broken when Frazier-Davis drove 163 feet of sheet piling at the west end of the cutoff wall. Several of the common and skilled laborers were promoted and received raises.

Emp. Sept. 1 (6,718)

The Corps reported net tonnage of 140,000 of freight on the Wiota spur the first week of September, making the Wiota-Fort Peck railroad one of the busiest, in ton miles operated, in the country. The progress report noted, "A total of 434 carloads of glacial boulders came in for dumping ... first 34 batch of cars were unloaded in nine minutes flat."

At the spillway, saws and augers were slicing and boring shale *like cheese*. The dredges were continuing their assault on the river's big bend. The first of the two huge 190-feet pile drivers (gantries) was dismantled while the other worked on the river's west side.

Emp. Oct. 1 (7,110)

The project was two years old October 23. The dam fill was fifty-five feet high, one-fifth of the fill was in place.

Emp. Nov. 1 (6,932)

Frazier-Davis Construction Company completed its section of the Spillway and threw a party at the McCone City Bar for all of their employees and friends, before shutting down for the winter.

Emp. Dec. 1 (5,451)

Dredges entered winter harbor for overhauls. The cutoff wall was finished and both gantries dismantled. Projects cut back or closed for winter. Cold weather was forcing layoffs. Men still on the job were cut to 28 hours in five days. Married men living outside the barracks earned $14 a week. Unemployment and cut-backs created hardships.

Winter 1935-36 Layoffs

Employment was 6,953 when the layoffs began in October. By the end of December, some 2,100 men had lost their jobs. Once again families returned to their home farms, lived with relatives, struggled through the winter in the boomtowns, or permanently left the area.

In early November the Fort Peck Women's Guild sponsored food, clothing, and money drives to "make a genuine Thanksgiving" for everyone. They held teas and waffle suppers to raise funds. They earned $76.50 with Bridge parties to buy shoes and warm clothes. During Thanksgiving Fort Peck residents assisted more than twenty-five unemployed workers' families living there and in the boomtowns.

Churches and organizations in Fort Peck townsite, the boomtowns, Glasgow, and Nashua helped provide food, clothing, medicine, and money for fuel. Hospital nurses donated Thanksgiving dinners.

The Fort Peck Relief Association was formed in December by the pastors of Fort Peck Lutheran Church and the Community churches, and representative from several Fort Peck organizations. Their mission was to "Canvas project towns to determine relief needs, bring them to the attention of the proper authorities ... to assure that no one shall suffer unduly from lack of adequate resources."

All townsite owners opened registration centers in their homes. Applicants were screened to ensure help went to those truly in need.

The *Fort Peck Press* noted that Fort Peck townsite residents "Have a sincere regard for project families found in unfortunate circumstances. Social and fraternal groups have curtailed their activities to devote themselves so families have happy holidays."

Glasgow Courier editor Sam Gilluly wrote: "The behavior of the needy ones themselves was a revelation to some of the people who have experience in welfare work." He noted how grateful the people were and how they refused help unless they had great need.

1936

Emp. Jan. 1 (approx. 3,896)

In January, Major Larkin's physician ordered him on a month's leave and rest. His seven years of "high pressure without a leave or break" were taking a toll. He took a break, then returned in February to plan the project's peak employment in July.

The *Engineering News-Record* recognized Corps engineers at Fort Peck for their innovative procedures being used in the spillway construction, many of which were attracting international attention.

Where are the authorities? Pleas continued for jobs for project workers unemployed by winter layoffs. But the Depression was still on, there were no jobs, and little government help was available.

Glasgow Courier editor Sam Gilluly wrote, "It has been six weeks since the attention of national authorities was called to the unfortunate situation of many men laid off because of winter weather."

He noted "vigorous and frequent appeals" to change the WPA's ruling that PWA workers had to have been on relief lists by November to be eligible for other works progress jobs. He pointed out most PWA workers were laid off after that date, "because they had worked and attempted to gain an honest living, they were penalized."

Gilluly noted the lack of response from Washington and Helena, suggesting WPA use common sense and politicians stop bickering. "Playing politics ... with human misery is, at best, a dirty deal."

Change in the Tunnels

On January 15, after a disagreement with the contractor, the Corps made design changes and took over enlargement of the four diversion tunnels. The contractor's equipment and plant were turned over to the government. Several employees stayed on with government workers to finish the job. Under the Corps' plan and its supervision, tunnel employment increased from 1,000 to 4,000 by July 1936.

Emp. Feb. 1 (4,119); Feb. 15 (4,541)

Tunnel activity was stepped up. Plans were made to have all four enlargements finished by July 1937. Project workers returned to their jobs as winter weather allowed.

Record cold – 60 degrees below zero

On February 15, Fort Peck Weather Station recorded 54 degrees below zero, followed by a record 60-below. Men went to work but said it was impossible to operate combustion engines. Most work in the tunnels, where average temperatures were warmer, continued.

Emp. March 1 (5,031)

Work progressed at the spillway. Spillway Builders working on the upper main channel overhauled trucks and built a new central concrete mixing plant. Two-hundred additional workers were hired for three regular shifts and a swing shift.

Addison Miller & Fielding & Shepley, contractors for the spillway gates and cutoff wall, were operating two shovels and ten trucks.

The spring thaw brought the river to its highest flow since 1890. In spite of dangerous debris, the high water assisted dredging.

Bulldozers cleared snow off the roads so trucks could run.

On March 20, the NRS sent notices: *All classified laborers and semi-skilled men eligible in Valley and McCone counties registered with the NRS are notified to report to work.... Everyone in Valley and McCone counties of whom the NRS in Glasgow has record, has been called for employment at the dam.... There is not an eligible man in McCone or Valley counties in the laborer or semi-skilled classes who cannot go to work now.*

In a last call the NRS stated, *If any man has been overlooked, notify us.* Signs were placed in project towns, notices were mailed, and the NRS made personal visits.

Emp. April 1 (6,072). April 15 (6,476); approximately 481 of the workers received promotions and raises.

The dredge Gallatin began pumping fill. Aerial surveys showed a few jammed ice cakes, otherwise the river was clear. The first train loads of sand and gravel arrived from the J.L. Shiely plant at Cole.

In April the Corps placed a tentative work order with the NRS for up to 1,800 more men: 90-percent common labor with a 40-hour week at 50 cents an hour and promotions for qualified workers.

By mid-April the NRS reported that more than 600 Montanans had been hired, and there were "plenty more" to fill requisitions. There would be "no jobs for out-of-state laborers."

These men must be physically fit; youths cannot be employed unless properly referred by the county manager of the NRS in the county where they are registered and are bona fide citizens.

During talks to local chambers of commerce, Major Larkin spoke of the many new jobs and worker promotions, "A large number ... untrained in construction work ... received a certain amount of knowledge, depending on their ability and willingness to work, a great many will have better skills with which to find work."

Major Larkin was promoted to lieutenant colonel in April.

Emp. May 1 (7,755) with 3,275 workers in the tunnels; 1,597 on the spillway; 1,803 at the dam; and 1,080 on other projects.

The Beaver

May 5, the *Glasgow Courier* reported one of the greatest dam builders of all, a beaver, "took a two mile ride from a dredge through five centrifugal pumps and a pipeline before being dumped with the fill into the dam." Workers found the beaver stunned but "unharmed."

Records were being set. In mid-May engineers reported a new world's record, "driving Fort Peck sized tunnels ... enlargement advanced 103 linear feet, an average 25 and 3/4 feet for each tunnel."

An unequaled mark for "driving through shale rock where continuous supports are required."

Dredges set a new record pumping 3,374,000 cubic yards of fill.

Emp. June 1 (9,199). June 15 (10,222) Government workers 7,899, contractor laborers 2,323. *Fort Peck was the largest employer of any single federal project underway in the United States, almost doubling the peak for Boulder (Hoover) Dam, previously the largest.*

Chicago Bridge and Iron Works began work on a fabricating plant to furnish 14,799,000 pounds of steel plate penstock lining for diversion Tunnel No. 1.

In mid-June another record was set at the tunnels, 616 lineal feet excavated in one week. Dredges put 30-million yards of fill into the dam, averaging more than 3,500,000 cubic-yards each month.

The Corps stated the "miniature dam" was no longer a "swimming hole." It was built for "scientific purposes" and "undue interfering" with the sensitive instruments by swimmers defeated its purpose.

During the summer of 1936 a bit of the past surfaced when dredges cut a new channel south of the dam "exposing the original Fort Peck site." Artist and dam worker Arthur H. Buckley sat on the dredge-made island and created a "true-to-life scale drawing" from the exact spot where a traveling artist sketched the site years before.

In July 1936 the Fort Peck Project got a transfer from the United States War Department to the U.S. Rivers and Harbors Commission.

Peak Employment

From a distance the dam and spillway sites resembled a well choreographed dance in the dust of men and machines, the music a cacophony of sounds directed by silent hand signals.

Emp. July 15, 1936 (10,546)

The project was moving full speed ahead when it reached its peak employment of 10,546 (4,600 in the tunnels). The work sites were a "beehive" of activity. It was crunch time for housing, overtime for businesses, and a great time for tourists to view the 24-hour action.

Officials in Washington, D.C., decided it was a good time for the Corps to conduct a *surprise fingerprinting* of government employees. Workers were instructed to line up at the Administration Building.

An estimated couple of hundred left town when word of the event got out. Others left soon after, some without even picking up their paychecks. Men back on the job could only wonder who they had been working next to the day before.

Emp. Aug. 1 (10,383). Aug. 15 (10,241) 80 percent Montanans, and 20 percent contractor key personnel mostly from the Midwest.

Spillway employment was at its peak with 1,560 workers. The first concrete pour was made at the gates, and the gates were assembled. More than eleven acres of the spillway floor were lined with concrete.

A shale slide near the lower end of the dam, damaged the Spillway Builders concrete mixing plant and delayed some work.

The Tomlinson-Arkwright Construction Company moved the last stockpiles left along the railroad in Phillips County: 24,000 cubic yards from Hedges and Spur, 100,000 from Tatnall. About 500,000 cubic yards had been stored, with 270,000 already at the dam.

Emp. Sept. 1 (10,235). Sept. 15 (10,472)

Bartlett-Hayward Company erected steel framework at the top of the Tunnel No. 1 emergency gate shaft. Work continued at the other shafts. Trainloads of materials were dumped to form a blanket over the dam. Shale was dynamited at the spillway. Engineers improvised unique equipment like the "Sky Hook" and "Goldbergig" which nearly doubled the amount of concrete handled at the spillway gates.

Emp. Oct. 1 (10,013). Oct. 15 (9,466)

Dredges were pumping fill at a record 3.4 miles before shutting down for winter. The dam now stood 100 feet above the river valley. Pipelines, trestles, and draglines were removed. The last concrete pour was made in Tunnel No. 1. Sand and gravel delivery shut down.

The Project was three years old October 23, 1936.

Construction was on schedule. Nearly a mile of spillway floor and half of the dam's hydraulic fill (50M cubic yards) were in place. Thousands of jobs had been created at Fort Peck, and in mines, mills, refineries, and material producing plants all over the country.

Cold November weather created problems with concrete work. Three dredges entered winter harbor. The Missouri was the last one in, leaving winter work to shovels and dump trucks.

November 11, Glasgow Courier headline: "LAST DIVERSION TUNNEL HOLED OUT." Workers had successfully built more than four miles of tunnels through Bearpaw shale. Lt. Col. T.B. Larkin placed the last steel ring beam bolt in Tunnel No. 4 at the inlet portal. It was noted that 406,730 pounds of explosives had been used in holing out the tunnels. A celebration dance was held at the Recreation Hall featuring the "Grout Mix" and "Larkin Waltz."

Emp. Dec. 1 (6,167) 1,800 working on the dam and 4,367 at the diversion tunnels and in other projects.

Emp. Dec. 15 (5,351)

The Corps scheduled overhaul and repair work to retain as many workers as possible through the winter of 1936-37, still 976 men were without paychecks during the two coldest months. Many workers left to find new jobs, knowing the project was already winding down.

The Fort Peck Relief Association, churches, organizations, and businesses collected food, clothing, and money for the unemployed.

Fundraisers included the sale of illustrated booklets of the dam.

The Eastern Star, Nashua American Legion Auxiliary, Fort Peck American Legion, Green Hut Cafe, and Vornholt's Drug in Fort Peck donated money to buy groceries wholesale. Some help came for fuel and shelter needs from new public assistance programs.

1937

Emp. Jan. 1 (5,191)

Lt. Col. T.B. Larkin, Maj. Clark Kittrell, and Capt. John B. Hardin attended the opening of bids for spillway gate operating machinery in Kansas City. They had just accepted a $114,479 bid from General Electric, Schenectady, N.Y., for pump motors.

The Corps reported 250 workers cutting timber in the river bottom above the dam for poles, piling, lumber, and stove wood. Materials were being hauled across the river ice.

Emp. Feb. 15 (4,501)

Early in February the Chicago Bridge & Iron Company completed its contract for tunnel steel, and dismantled its plant. The conveyor trestle over the aggregate piles was dismantled. The Corps reported Fort Peck had the largest electric welding plant in the world.

Crews sawed through two feet of Missouri river ice to create a channel so the Corps' marine diver could attach plank braces on the trestle piles. He stayed down in the icy water up to an hour at a time. Safety equipment for his cold, dangerous work included air pumping apparatus and a changing room with a stove and first aid equipment.

Emp. March 1 (4,157) 3,853 government labor, 301 contractors.

Aerial surveys targeted ice-jams between the Fort Peck dam and Fort Benton to be blasted so the dredges could go to work.

Emp. April 1 (4,152). April 15 (4,501) about 500 at the spillway.

Lt. Col. T.B. Larkin spoke to the Glasgow Chamber of Commerce about coming employee reductions after the tunnels were completed in June and the spillway in the fall. He stated, "Workers and work to date (36-million man hours) have provided about two and a half times that amount of indirect employment throughout the country."

Spring jobs were offered first to former employees still living in the area. An additional trestle was built across the river near the dam. Dredging resumed, with the Gallatin out first. Several barges were built for pumping water out of the core pool. Boatyard crews completed the hulls of four large pump barges to remove waste from the core pool. Engineers planned on June for the river closure and diversion of the Missouri river through the tunnels.

Porcupine Creek Landslide

In April authorities reported an "enormous landslide" on the John Ihnot property north of Nashua. The slide had stopped the flow of Porcupine Creek and raised its bed from six to twenty-feet in the air. Ihnot had previously seen steam rising from fissures.

Spillway activity increased. Three shifts of workers with electric saws were "slicing down the sloping side walls" at the main channel.

The first train, pulling 55 cars loaded with toe gravel, arrived from the J. L. Shiely gravel plant at Cole. Gravel was dropped from the sides of railcars and spread under the bridge and upstream slope. The spillway concrete mix plant was dismantled after turning out 525,000 cubic yards of concrete. The first 80-ton gate was set at the spillway piers, the others were waiting. All work was progressing as planned.

Emp. May 1 (5,827). A report noted 81-percent of project workers in 1936 were Montanans. Engineers reported welders used more than one-million welding rods for the diversion tunnels and dredge pump repair. The Barrett Company of New York began applying 130 tons of interior tunnel enamel, giving a smooth patent leather-like coating.

Emp. June 1 (6,881). June 15 (7,348)

Records for dredging and other work were broken and new goals set. Dredges placed 238,540 cubic yards of fill June 3. The Missouri pumped materials equal to 18,000 average truckloads of fill into the dam in twenty-four hours.

The U.S. Civil Service Commission offered exams in Glasgow and Fort Peck for a striker electric dredge engineman. Pay to be $1,800 a year, less $37 a month subsistence and quarters.

The First and Only Missouri River Cruiser Race

In March 1937, Kiwanis clubs in Great Falls, Glasgow, and Fort Benton began planning a 2,300-mile cruiser race to commemorate the last possible boat trip from St. Louis to Fort Benton. Boat traffic would end with the Missouri river diversion, scheduled for June.

Entries came from Malta, Great Falls, Fort Benton, Glasgow, and Fort Peck. During the race, the racers would be joined periodically by cruisers in states they were passing through. The Corps provided a skiff and two-man crew to escort them from St. Louis to Fort Peck.

Glasgow and Fort Peck joined forces to enter a "25-foot, 85-HP, six-cylinder cabin cruiser with berths for four, lavatory, large galley, frig and stove." It was officially christened *The Glasgow-Fort Peck*. Like all the other entries, its crew was made up of experienced local boatmen, and a few others who rode along for short lengths of time. Every town got into the fun and fund raising for the event.

On May 23, after a "rousing send off" from St Louis, the cruisers sped up the river at 16 mph. For the next 26 days they steered through springtime-high water, wind, rain, snags, and sandbars. Crowds on the shore, some waiting there all night, welcomed them along the way.

June 15 the boats maneuvered through dredge lines and deep water to get into Fort Peck harbor. A thousand people were waiting.

Before the racers arrived, the boatyard crew had built a 20x5 feet, two-man boat to accompany them the rest of the way to Fort Benton. Two project workers were ready and waiting to act as guides.

The racers bid farewell to their Kansas skiff crew, and in the wake of their new escort boat headed west on the last leg of the race.

On Saturday, June 19, more than 10,000 people were gathered in Fort Benton for a summer celebration. They gathered by the river and cheered as the boats roared in under the bridge.

Then, just before the big finish, disaster struck. As the cruisers sped forward, the *Great Falls* hung up on pilings hidden beneath the high water under the bridge. The race leader, the *Glasgow-Fort Peck,* swung around and pulled the *Great Falls* free, stressing and killing its motor in the process. Without hesitation the *Great Falls* turned back and assisted the *Glasgow-Fort Peck* to shore.

At 3:04 p.m. the *Glasgow-Fort Peck* was declared the winner, presented a trophy, and given a $600 check for Kiwanis projects.

Ticket drawings had already been held in most of the sponsoring towns. The historic little cruisers would soon be off to new homes.

Missouri River Diversion, June 24, 1937

The Missouri River diversion was one of the most significant undertakings in the Fort Peck dam project. Glasgow Courier.

At 4:30 a.m., during the dark and early hours, men and machinery were rushed into position to roust the Missouri from its bed and send it surging through the four mile-long tunnels under the dam.

The early hour was prompted by some concern over a slippage at the railroad bridge pier. The bridge had suddenly been closed June 23 to sightseers, to allow the passage of trains and dump trucks. Work in the tunnels was pushed ahead and completed that night. Pieces from the dredge maintenance section, a barge, the John Ordway, and small boats were moved in. Trucks and caterpillars waited along the shore.

Lt. Col. T.B. Larkin and Major Clark Kittrell set up their field headquarters in a small building on the Missouri River bridge. Corps engineers and Great Northern officials joined them. Photographers, newsmen, and an aerial photographer were called in and strategically stationed around the dam to record the channel closure.

After everyone and everything was in place, Lt. Col. Larkin gave the order to blast the earth dike that held the river at the tunnel portals. Trains filled with rock rolled across the bridge at a rate of one per minute, stopping long enough for each car to dump its load into the downstream toe where bulldozers waited to push the 20,000 cubic yards of stone into place.

Photo by Paul McFarland

The sun rose on a scene of constant, choreographed movement of men and machines hurling rocks at the wild river to force it from its centuries old course to run through the four tunnels and into its new channel on the north side of the dam. Final closure came at 7:05 p.m.

The men who took part in the historic event paused to breathe a sigh of relief and to gaze in awe at their monumental accomplishment.

Emp. July 1 (7,186). Lt. Colonel Larkin leaving

In July it was announced the highly respected district engineer and his family were leaving July 16. After a short vacation in Cape Cod, he would attend Army War College in Washington, D.C.

Major Clark Kittrell, who had worked beside Larkin as chief of operations for almost four years, would succeed him as the district engineer. Major C.N. Iry was named to replaced Kittrell.

Maj. Gen. Edward Markham, chief of the Army Engineers, came for his fourth and final inspection of the dam during July. He retired in October and was succeeded by General Julian L. Schley.

"Blue Hole" fishing

A small pool formed downstream from the dam, landlocking fish from 2-pound goldeye to 40-pound sturgeon. Pool fill was planned, but first the Corps invited area fishermen to enjoy a few days of "no quota" fishing so as not to waste the fish.

Paint, Pictures, Rock, and Owls

All four dredges were beautified in July. Their scuffed, worn, weathered, white exteriors were painted in colorful combinations of scarlet, buff, gray, and black. Their new look was a hit with everyone.

Aerial photographs showed that the Fort Peck Lake was forming south of the dam and spreading out over the old river bed, covering approximately 106 square miles.

Shipments of big boulders from Snake Butte began in July. All phases of the project were in full operation.

Owls hunting mice in the mile-long stretch of concrete spillway were menacing workers, especially the graveyard shift. The big-eyed birds were attracted to, or blinded by, floodlights and crashed into everything. Occasionally they attacked workers, rattling the nerves of the men on narrow steel beams atop 85 feet piers. During the day, the owls flew below ground at the cutoff structure to rest in the cool, dimly lit sections. Here they annoyed the "rats" (tunnel workers).

The Swing Bridge

In July a 310 feet wide channel was dug on the south side of Park Grove, connecting the west side dredge cut to the Missouri river on the east side of the Nashua highway.

A temporary swing bridge was built to carry supply trains on the Wiota spur, vehicles on the highway, and pedestrians. Signals were manually operated around the clock to control the endless stream of traffic. When dredges or their floating plants needed passage through the channel, the attendant stopped road and rail traffic, and swung the bridge open from its center piling so boats could pass on either side. The "swinging" bridge was ready when dredging began in August. Thousands of visitors came to see it in action.

Emp. Aug. 1 (5,961) about 1,560 at the spillway.

The Corps announced additional hiring was highly unlikely. Many workers left in search of new jobs while the weather was still good.

Some 2,100 yards of concrete were poured at the spillway cutoff wall in two days, completing the discharge end.

Emp. Sept. 1 (5,137)

The last carload of glacial boulders arrived from the Phillips County stockpile. Over 15,000 carloads of rock had been placed.

Gen. Julian L. Schley, newly appointed Chief of Army Engineers, and Gen. Max C. Thyler, assistant chief, toured the dam. They would stay on until after President F.D. Roosevelt's visit in October.

Emp. Oct. 1 (4,914)

President Franklin D. Roosevelt's Second Visit

More than three-fourths of the project had been completed by the president's second visit October 3, 1937. He was again greeted by huge crowds in Glasgow. People waited along the highway past the boomtowns and at the construction sites to wave and cheer.

From the train platform he shared with Governor Roy E. Ayers and General Schley, Roosevelt gave an inspiring speech affirming the "useful work" being done at Fort Peck. His speech was heard by thousands of radio listeners and read in most newspapers.

Roosevelt was presented with a special bust of himself, carved by project worker-artist Frank LaFournaise from a cottonwood dredged from the heart of the dam. He received a moss agate watch charm, presented by Glasgow Gold Star Mothers, and flowers from students.

Emp. Nov. 1 (4,510). Nov. 15 (4,301)

Five-hundred men were at work on the spillway cutoff. Favorable weather delayed the winter layoffs.

Emp. Dec. 1 (4,031)

Approximately 3,223 government employees were able to stay on their jobs through the winter. The other 808 worked for contractors, mainly Addison Miller, and had jobs until spillway work shut down.

The dredges moved into winter harbor, boasting of more than 30M yards of fill placed in the dam in 1937.

Records were again made in tunnel and spillway construction.

Emp. Dec. 15 (3,695)
With the project winding down and spillway work halted for the coldest months, several workers returned home in search of new jobs.

1938

Emp. Jan. 1 (approx. 3,000)
Favorable weather allowed unprecedented progress in all areas.
Emp. Feb 1 (3,029)
Many projects were completed. Equipment was moved out. The Missouri river bridge and its appurtenant works were removed by engineers. Railroad trestles and ramps were dismantled and stored.
Emp. March 1 (3,362)
One of the worst snow storms in years hit the end of March. Zero temperatures stopped excavation at the spillway.

Elevators were installed in the tunnel shafts. Dredges pumped fill more than three miles to the berm of the dam above the upstream toe.
Emp. April 15 (3,754). May 1 (3,944). May 15 (4,110)
Spillway heating units were tested. The pump barge was moved out of the core pool. Spring work was proceeding as planned.
Emp. June 1 (4,104)
Final acceptance tests were made on eight of the sixteen spillway gates. Addison Miller and Fielding & Shepley, contractors for the gates and cutoff structure, finished their jobs, dismantled the concrete plant and moved their equipment. The spillway was done.

It was an impressive structure with its 16 vertical lift gates, 25 by 40 feet, weighing 80-ton each; and the mile-long ribbon of concrete running north to the river. Later, a huge spillway building would be built to stand above it all.

Emp. July 1 (4,167). July 15 (4,297)
Installation of the control gates began in Tunnel No. 2. The Fort Peck Lake continued to fill with water, some of which was released for downstream navigation as far away as Sioux City, Iowa.
Emp. Aug. 1 (4,241)
The foundation for the tunnel control shaft was poured.
Emp. Sept. 1 (Approx. 4,240)
A record 4,000 tons of rock were placed on the upstream face of the dam in one day. An average of 100 railcars a day arrived from the quarry at Snake Butte. An emergency signal system with boxes every two-hundred feet was built along the upstream face of the dam.

The Slide

Army Corps of Engineers, Fort Peck, Mont., Sept. 22, 1938:
A partial failure in the upstream face of the Fort Peck dam near the east abutment occurred at 1:15 today, moving a quantity of fill material into the lake upstream. The cause of this failure has not been determined. The movement of material has apparently practically stabilized, leaving still over 100 feet of freebroad at the point affected. No damage was done to the tunnels and the flow of water through them continues normal.

The casualty list has not yet been determined.... A preliminary survey of the damage done indicates that no reason for alarm should exist regarding the security of the main dam.

The Corps issued a second statement September 23: *The water level of the reservoir is below any portion of the dam which may have been weakened by the movement.*

Courtesy Army Corps of Engineers

Although there had been some indication the night before, the "earth movement," known as the "Slide," came suddenly with little warning. According to eye witnesses, in less than five horrendous minutes it was over. A 2,000 feet long section on the upstream face of the dam, west of and below the four tunnel gate shaft buildings, had slid out into the 90 feet deep lake, taking sections of railroad track, work trucks, heavy equipment, and tools with it. A pump barge and draglines were pulled down into the tangled mass with all the rest.

Workers were violently thrown into the water. Gasping for air they swam up and desperately grabbed onto anything that was floating. They fought to save themselves in the churning water, mud, and whirlpools, and to swim away from the rolling rocks and fill.

Men working on top of the dam ran faster than they had ever run before, in spite of their heavy, steel-toed work boots. They jumped over cracks and shifting fill to reach solid ground on the east side.

Engineers and workers in the safe areas rushed to rescue the men struggling out in the water and the ones trapped on unstable ground. Shocked by what had happened, they tried to mentally process the tragedy while making split second decisions on how to help their co-workers and save themselves. A motorboat crew jumped into a boat and sped through debris to rescue 30 shaken, but mostly unharmed, workers who had ridden out into the lake on the sliding fill.

Supervisors immediately began an accounting of the "upwards of 160 men" on crews working in the area. Engineers quickly assessed the damage and calculated the possibility of further earth movement.

Wet, muddy, shocked crews gathered with their supervisors on solid ground. Injured workers were rushed to first-aid stations where ambulances waited to transport them to the Fort Peck Hospital. There, doctors and nurses cleared mud, sand, and water out of their eyes, ears, noses, and lungs, and treated them for cuts and bruises.

The Corps detained slide survivors and workers who witnessed the earth movement long enough to record their statements before crew trucks took them home to their worried and frightened families.

By late afternoon all but seven men had been accounted for. One seriously injured man was found shortly after the slide and rushed to Fort Peck Hospital where doctors tried in vain to revive him in an iron lung. After the final count it was determined that eight men had lost their lives, six of them would be forever entombed in the dam.

There were many acts of heroism during and after the slide as workers helped care for other workers. Stories of their compassion and courage that day would never be forgotten.

One story was told about Gene Tourtlotte who was driving three executive engineers from Omaha, and Maj. Clark Kittrell, Fort Peck district engineer, on an inspection tour when the slide began. Yelling "Hold on!" he threw the car into reverse and with the ground cracking beneath it, he sped backward some 1,500 feet to solid ground.

Later when Tourtlotte received a special citation for his quick thinking, he responded "I was saving my own skin, too."

Warning the towns

Immediately after the slide the Corps dispatched vehicles with loudspeakers to inform boomtown residents of the earth movement. As a precaution, people in the lower towns of Park Grove, Midway, and New Deal were warned to go to higher ground.

Before the Corps arrived, some frightened workers had driven through the towns shouting that the dam was "going" and residents should get out. Parents rushed to the schools to pick up their children. One father jumped over the high wire fence surrounding Park Grove School to get his son and to warn the teacher and students.

Hundreds of boomtown residents living on the flats threw their belongings on top of their cars and left. Neighbors helped neighbors without transportation get away. Several people ran to the top of the hills at New Deal and McCone City. Park Grove and Parkdale were turned into ghost towns. Workers returned to find their families gone.

The *Glasgow Courier* reported, "A steady stream of traffic began pouring out of these towns...." Several cars drove through Nashua during the afternoon "apparently leaving the project for good."

Word of the earth movement left many families desperate for news of their workers. Women and children stood in the streets of towns on higher ground and anxiously waited and prayed.

Dozens of off-duty workers and family members gathered outside the Corps Fill Office where engineers were checking crew sheets. A worried 13-year-old boy tearfully sought information about his father.

The slide was indelibly marked on the memory of every man there that day. They were saddened by the loss of life, heavy-hearted at what the slide had done to their dam, and concerned about their jobs. Most of all, they were humbly grateful to have survived.

Several workers who would have been on the dam had the day off. Others were working elsewhere at the project. Railroad workers east of the dam shaft buildings heard and felt the rails move, others saw the core pool going down. Workers at a welding shop felt an unusual tremor and stared in disbelief at the chunk of missing dam. Other crews watched from a distance as machinery went down in the water.

Some workers were unaware of what had happened and wondered at the many cars loaded with luggage leaving the boomtowns.

Residents of river-bottom communities several miles below the dam were unofficially told it was "going out." The Frazer community was warned to "take to the hills." Residents grabbed what they could and left. Most stayed away through the weekend.

News and rumors spread. Calls poured into Corps headquarters and newspaper offices from worried family and friends of the workers and boomtown families. Media from around the country rushed for stories. They received official Corps reports but, as in many disasters, sensationalized accounts were printed and broadcast around the world.

Rumors were more slides had taken place and the dam would not be finished. One rumor, persisting for years, was that more workers than were counted were buried in the dam. Major Kittrell stated that lists were cross referenced and more than 100 men had gone over and over the area again and found all men except the eight known dead.

The blame. The *Havre Daily News* editorialized: "Let's suspend judgment on the Fort Peck Mishap." In response to "rumor mongers" criticizing the Corps, the editor suggested comments be withheld or confined to "expressions of sympathy" until the investigating board of expert engineers issued a report. "We deplore any effort to bring partisan politics into the picture...our stack is still on the engineers to win...let's not jump to hasty and possible erroneous conclusions."

Maj. Gen. Julian L. Schley, chief of the Army Engineers since October 1937, arrived at Fort Peck to study reports of the slide. By November a chairman and an eight member board of "blue ribbon engineers" had started an inquiry.

Rebuilding the dam

Recovery of the lost quarry stone began October first. The railroad section was replaced in three days. By October 15, salvage operations had raised nearly all of the downed equipment and machinery.

Extensive core drilling was done and a dike built around the slide area. The dredges were already pumping in new fill. The project was moving forward. Construction was reported to be in "high gear."

Emp. Oct. 15 (4,300)

The project's Sixth Anniversary, October 23, 1938, passed quietly in the shadow of the slide. But there *was* cause for celebration; the two-mile dike section on the main dam's west side was completed, and employment was still 4,300 due to good weather and repair work.

Emp. Nov. 1 (3,379)

The Harlem quarry shut down for winter. Dredges had the longest season on record. The Madison and Gallatin went into winter harbor.

Emp. Dec. 15 (3,134)

The Jefferson and Missouri worked through December before they entered winter harbor. Only 65 men were affected by winter layoffs.

1939

Emp. Jan. 15 (3,080)

Cold weather limited all work except in the tunnel shafts.

Miles of pipeline damaged in the slide were repaired.

Emp. Feb. 15 (3,140)

Rip-rap work to protect the dam from erosion began with 30 trucks hauling field boulders and quarry stone 24 hours a day to the dam.

Emp. March 15 (3,215)

River ice-breaking operations began. The John Ordway started new dredge cuts below the dam. Two small boats were added to the "Fort Peck Navy." Jobs opened again as boulder placement got underway. Concrete was poured at the tunnels.

Emp. April 1 (3,278)

By May the dredge Missouri was pumping fill from five miles away into the dam. May 25, a storm with 42 mph winds suspended work for twenty hours and shut down the Jefferson and Missouri. Heavy rain turned roads to sticky mud, and stalled trucks.

In June dredges finished filling the area damaged by the slide. Materials were placed up to ninety feet above the reservoir.

Placement of rock was progressing. Dredges moved over to work on the cuts near the swinging bridge south of Park Grove. The field office was moved downstream to be centrally located. More concrete was poured in shaft No. 3. A new steel derrick barge was installed in July. Bids were let for the two power turbines to be used at the dam.

There was a tragic accident at Snake Butte Quarry in July. During the routine blasting a 26-ton charge of dynamite escaped horizontally through a fissure and blew out a wall of rock, sending chunks 200 feet in the air. Eighteen workers were injured. Sections of the railroad were twisted, fourteen flat cars and two of the camp buildings were destroyed and others damaged. Fifteen rail cars were wrecked.

Just before the accident, a supervisor, accompanied by his 14-year-old son, had stopped at Snake Butte to say goodbye to his crew before his transfer to Oklahoma. The boy was standing by his father's side photographing the blast when he was hit by debris and killed.

Captain Plank leaves. Work continues

In August, Capt. Ewart Plank, whose duties included management of the town of Fort Peck since January 1934, left to attend a command and general staff school in Fort Leavenworth, Kansas.

Workers began rebuilding an inlet portal at the tunnels. Dredges shut down for the winter in November after placing approximately 122-million yards of fill in the dam. The dam's berm was graded and scheduled to be "topped off" with rolled fill in 1940. In November an accident killed one man and injured five others at the intake portals.

One of the last projects for the year was to paint a coat of coal tar enamel on the steel shaft works to protect them from the water.

The project was winding down. Progress reports and employment numbers printed in local newspapers were discontinued in mid-1939.

Jobs ended for about 650 workers at the dam and Snake Butte Quarry after boulder shipments ceased. More layoffs came with winter.

1940

In January engineers reported their plans to complete the project were on target. The intake structure at the diversion tunnels needed a few finishing touches and some work remained on the main control gate at the spillway. The dam would be topped off in the spring, and dismantling the dredging fleet would begin when warm weather freed several hulls encased in eighteen inches of ice.

Major Kittrell leaving, Major Iry takes over. More layoffs

The Corps announced that Maj. Clark Kittrell, at the project since 1934, and district engineer since July 1937, would leave in July to attend Army War College in Washington, D.C. Major C.N. Iry, chief of operations since July 1937, would serve as his replacement.

July 4, the Glasgow Courier noted "the big layoff on the project last week has put a number of Wheeler residents out of work."

In August an 18-inch coat of gravel was spread on the upstream face of the dam to protect it from waves. In September quarry stone was placed. In October spillway lights were installed, the last concrete poured, cables buried, and remaining projects completed.

In November J.A. Terteling & Sons hauled in the last load of sand. A rock and gravel facing was spread across the upstream face and downstream slope of the dam.

The Dam is Done

The nearly four-mile long dam (two miles of main dam) crested at 250.5 feet above the old river bed, making it the largest hydraulically filled earth dam in the world. The Slide in September 1938 delayed completion slightly more than a year, but Project No. 30 was finished.

A small crew of workers stayed to operate the dam after the others moved back to their farms and ranches or on to new jobs elsewhere.

1941

In June 1941, a temporary road over the dam was opened. Plans were made for a permanent bituminous road after the fill settled.

In October the Corps transferred ownership of two houses and six barracks to the Fish and Game Commission for use in the new Game Farm below the town of Fort Peck. The first Power House was built by Woods Brothers of Lincoln, Nebraska, the second in 1961.

Equipment Disposal

Hundreds of structures were built and thousands of pieces of equipment brought in for use at the Fort Peck project. When the job was done they were removed, recycled, or stored.

In December 1937 the Works Progress Administration (WPA) in Washington, D.C., announced that half of the machinery no longer needed at Fort Peck would be passed on to Montana WPA projects.

In April 1938 the Corps called for sealed bids on the mess hall appliances, cabinets, and even the kitchen sinks. Worn out items were disposed of. In January 1940 sealed bids were opened on six RD8 tractors, four crawler type D8 caterpillars, and other equipment.

The Dredges

Construction of the Gallatin, Jefferson, Madison, and Missouri began in October 1934. Boatyard carpenters worked non-stop to get them out pumping fill and digging a 200 by 4,000 feet winter harbor.

Each dredging plant consisted of a wood-hull dredge and pumps, electric motors, and 28-inch pipelines; a floating booster plant with two pumps; and a land booster plant on rails, with one pump. The accessory plant included 375 pipe pontoons, 16 elbow pontoons, 200 power cable pontoons, two 25-ton derrick boats, one 210-hp diesel towboat, seven gasoline motorboats, four landing barges, four anchor barges, and two car ferry barges for moving land boosters.

On April 14, 1935, the fleet moved out through the ice into the spring-high river water. Progress was slow without their towboat John Ordway (stuck in South Dakota ice until May). Small tugs struggled on sandbars. Dredges were forced to cut their own way. At the upstream borrow pits the Jefferson and Madison dredged slips on both sides of the river. The Missouri and Gallatin worked in the channel.

Most dredging was done by 1939. Dismantling the fleet began with the Gallatin, Missouri, and Jefferson. By February 1940 more than 17 miles of pipe had been classified and stored. Equipment from the lower fleet was moved into the government warehouse. Further dismantling was delayed until two hulls, two floating boosters, and a lower fleet pump boat could be freed from 18 inches of river ice.

The Madison was retired in 1940 and stored downstream from the dam. Its dismantling began in August 1941. The huge dredges were taken apart by some of the same workers who had assembled them. They held out hope until the end that at least one of the hard working dredges would be preserved. But it was not to be.

The John Ordway, flagship of the Fort Peck fleet, was built in Gasconade, Missouri, one of the Corps' seven vessels in the Missouri River System named for Lewis and Clark expedition members.

Piloted by Captain Joseph Leach, one of the very few remaining "Mountain Pilots," the Ordway was the last large boat to travel up the Missouri River before the dam was built.

Its 1,875-mile trip to Fort Peck began in late summer 1934. After wintering in South Dakota, it arrived at the project in May 1935. For four years it moved heavy equipment from the floating plant, and was used during many inspections and surveys. It also moved personnel and supplies. The crew lived on board.

After its work was done the Ordway spent the winter of 1939-1940 at Fort Peck. It left in April for a new assignment in Nebraska.

The Milk River Railroad Bridge was built in January 1934. It carried a steady stream of trains loaded with supplies, materials, and stone across the Milk River for more than three years. Rail cars were switched off the Great Northern main line at Wiota and picked up by smaller engines to cross the bridge and travel to the dam and spillway.

The depot closed when the trains stopped running. The track was purchased by the Great Northern Railroad in 1940. It was dug up and moved to other branches. The bridge had served long and well.

The 200 feet long Missouri River Bridge was part of the six miles of trestle north of the dam encircling the valley. The bridge opened for train and vehicle traffic in October 1934. During its three years of service, more than 2,376,219 cubic yards of gravel aggregates were dumped out of railcars and over its sides. The bridge played a major role in the river diversion. Workers and visitors drove across it daily.

In September 1937 the Corps announced the bridge was of no further use and its dismantling began. The steel girders and trusses were put up for sale. In October the Great Northern railroad bought and removed 40 pairs of steel plate girders and a deck girder span. By February 1938 the Corps had removed the trestle and ramps. All parts of the bridge were hauled away.

The Swing Bridge, built over the channel dug on the south side of Park Grove between the Missouri River and the west side dredge cuts, opened in August 1937. When the dredging was done the "swinging" bridge was closed and dismantled August 24, 1939. Within three days the Corps had built and opened a new, permanent, vehicle bridge.

Eight freight cars full of boilers, booms, oil tanks, and parts of two barge derricks were sitting in Portland harbor in November 1941, marked: "From U.S. Engineer Warehouse, Fort Peck, Montana: To the District Engineer, Portland, for District Engineer of North Africa, Port of Massawa, Eritrea." The equipment was part of a new Lend-Lease program, for use by British engineers in their Red Sea port.

In July 1940 and August 1941 the first and second 20,000 K.V.A. synchronous condensers were dismantled and sent to the Corps of Engineer's Bonneville Dam project between Washington and Oregon.

Five barracks buildings and mess halls were sold and moved in 1938. Twenty buildings, including other barracks, were transferred to government agencies at the Bureau of Reclamation in Malta, the Indian Irrigation Service in Wolf Point, the Department of Agriculture in Glasgow, and the Bureau of Biology Survey in Medicine Lake.

In 1940 ten barracks were razed and the lumber used for buildings by the seven farmers who formed the first cooperative to secure a Farm Security Loan for land leveling and building improvements.

Most temporary building and landmarks were gone by 1941.

Private contractors provided their own equipment and built most of their own buildings. When their work was done they dismantled their plants and hauled the machinery away to their next job.

Labor Unions

Union organizers generated heat but little fire at the project. Workers were short term and many objected to some union tactics.

Nationally labor union membership was at its lowest point in 1933, representing mostly skilled workers. An internal shakeup resulted in a membership drive and movement to organize unskilled labor. A few organizers, familiar with Butte, moved into the project area in 1934 to stir up interest in joining a union.

An August letter sent to the *Fort Peck Press* stated that damsite conditions "disclose the crying need for organization by the workers and farmers." The writer urged laborers to "struggle against those who profit from the sweat and blood of the workers and farmers."

Most workers were not interested in joining a union. Their jobs had been created when they desperately needed them and they did not want to protest their wages while thousands of other Montana men still stood in reemployment lines.

Meetings attracted foodservice workers, barbers, and a few others, but most laborers did their job, accepted their pay, and moved on.

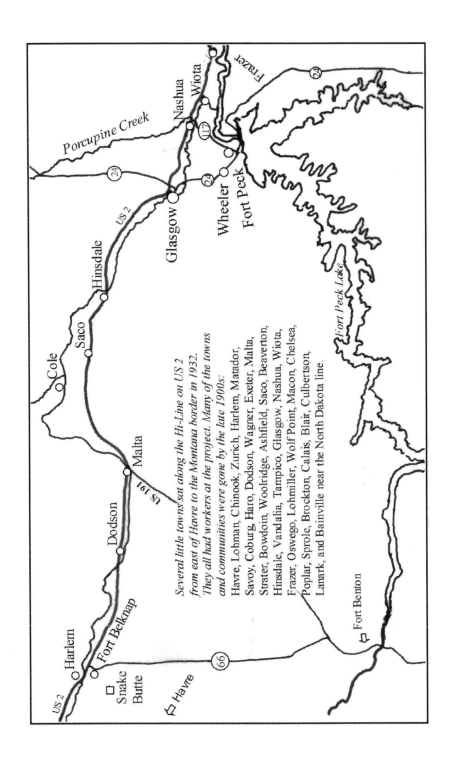

Several little towns sat along the Hi-Line on US 2 from east of Havre to the Montana border in 1932. They all had workers at the project. Many of the towns and communities were gone by the late 1900s: Havre, Lohman, Chinook, Zurich, Harlem, Matador, Savoy, Coburg, Haro, Dodson, Wagner, Exeter, Malta, Strater, Bowdoin, Wooldridge, Ashfield, Saco, Beaverton, Hinsdale, Vandalia, Tampico, Glasgow, Nashua, Wiota, Frazer, Oswego, Lohmiller, Wolf Point, Macon, Chelsea, Poplar, Sprole, Brockton, Calais, Blair, Culbertson, Lanark, and Bainville near the North Dakota line.

53

Cole, home of the J. L. Shely gravel plant.

Courtesy of the Phillips County Museum

Part 3

Rocking the dam
Hinsdale - Cole - Saco - Snake Butte – Harlem

Processing rock for the Fort Peck dam provided jobs for hundreds of men and brought a brief economic boom to some Hi-Line towns.

Big dam bringer of good times.... Saco, just across the county line in Phillips is also experiencing a mild boom due to the opening of two gravel pits at Cole and Tatnall, north of Saco. Several hundred men are stationed within a short distance of that town and employed in getting out hundreds of tons of rock and gravel. Other towns – Hinsdale, Opheim, Frazer, and Oswego while not benefiting so directly, have been helped.... Crop failures due to dry weather and insect invasion plus the Depression had nearly ruined Valley County, that all changed now. The county is decidedly on the map and in line for a few good years at last. Hinsdale Tribune 2/9/1934

One-thousand men were hired in the winter of 1934-1935 to start stockpiling rock for the Fort Peck project. Picking stones from the frozen ground, they created seven piles of 20-pound to 2-ton boulders, one each at Cole, Hedges, Spur, and Ashfield, and three at Malta.

Hinsdale "rock pickers"

In August 1934 the R. Newton McDowell Company established its headquarters near Hinsdale and hired 300 men for three months to pick rock. Thankful for jobs, short-lived as they would be, the men and many of their families traveled to Hinsdale to live any place they could while the jobs lasted. The little town welcomed them.

Hinsdale was settled in 1887 near to the Milk River twenty-nine miles northwest of Glasgow, one of the several little Great Northern railroad sidings. It grew from a side-tracked boxcar depot to a thriving town with a post office, newspaper, and several small businesses. It lived well as a center for homesteaders and ranchers, and nearly died when most of the homesteaders left during the first dry years.

Hinsdale families shared their homes with as many of the workers and their families as possible. Tents and "private domiciles" were set up in the city park. An old school was opened for sleeping quarters. A contract was let to provide food services. The grade school made room for the workers' children for as long as they needed to attend.

October 12, 1934, the *Hinsdale Tribune* reported, "The company's crew was considerably reduced this week."

The job of stockpiling 45,000 yards of materials was almost done. The barring gang was laid off, leaving 225 workers for another week. Company crews finished the job. Hinsdale went back to surviving the hard times. The little town is still there today along the Hi-Line.

Saco-Cole gravel

During their search for rock and gravel for the project, the Corps was told of a field of glacial rock at Saco and Cole. More than enough to supply the "5M cubic yards of material for concrete aggregate, and for the gravel toes and upstream face blanket of the dam."

A survey was made and options taken on 400 acres owned by the Palm and Knight families. Contracts were awarded to Becker County Sand & Gravel Co., Crosby, Minnesota, for the dam toe and blanket gravel; and to J. L. Shiely Company, of St. Paul, for screened and washed gravel delivered to the dam from their new plant at Cole.

The J. L. Shiely gravel plant was built in the spring of 1934 at the confluence of Whitewater Creek and the Milk River about ten miles northwest of Saco. Machinery was operated with power from a 50-kv transmission line. Wash water used to process the gravel was pumped through thousands of feet of pipe from the creek and river.

Contractors built a Monighan-Walker dragline with an eight-yard bucket and 150 feet boom "the largest in the world." The dragline and its companion delivered rocks to the hoppers for screening, washing, and dumping into storage bins; with anything larger or smaller than 1/2 to 6 inches wasted (stored) in stockpiles for later use.

Processed rock and gravel were loaded into gondola bottomed rail cars at the rate of three an hour. The trains traveled from Cole down the southern six miles of the old Saco-Hogeland Great Northern branch to Saco, where they joined the main line east to the project.

The first train left Cole October 5, 1934, followed by 70-car trains every 24 hours. Cars were weighed as they passed over an automatic track scale at Glasgow on their 55-mile trip to Wiota and the dam.

Shiely provided rock for the Fort Peck townsite, Wiota-Fort Peck railroad, tunnels, water-filtration plant, and more. Work continued the winter of 1934-1935. By mid-January an estimated 200 cars of toe gravel had been loaded every 24 hours by 200 men on three shifts.

March 28, 1935, the *Saco Independent* reported, "Last Sunday marked the starting point for much bigger operations at Cole when a second dragline started operation for A. Guthery & Company.

The third dragline, which is steam propelled, was put to work. The J. L. Shiely Company successfully tested out their gravel washing plant Monday when they loaded out five cars of ballast for the dam. The company estimates that the maximum output of the plant can be five-hundred ton per hour of washed gravel."

In mid-April an overheated stove in the testing lab caught fire and destroyed the $7,000 Cole roundhouse and some of its equipment.

The record cold winter 1935-36 forced a three month layoff of 250 workers. Pleas for WPA jobs to help them went unanswered, creating severe hardships for workers and families. Work resumed in April.

On June 12, 1936, the *Hinsdale Tribune* numbered the Cole work force at 155. In October the plant shut down for the winter 1936-37.

June 24, 1937, the day of the Missouri River Diversion, workers sent a steady stream of traincars full of rock to the dam and onto the Missouri River bridge. Load after load was dumped down into the channel until the river turned and ran through the four tunnels.

In December 1937 all toe gravel shipments shut down. The Shiely plant had processed more than the Corps' estimated 5M cubic yards of material and carried it out in 3,000 trains averaging 40-50 railcars each. It had successfully filled the "world's largest gravel contract."

The last Cole train finished in 1937, in time for trains from Snake Butte to start moving boulders to the dam. Hundreds of acres of rock had been hauled away. Teepee shaped rows of waste remain today.

Cole

In 1934 Cole was but a few deserted buildings sitting beside the once busy Saco-Hogeland railroad spur, about ten miles northwest of Saco. Its glory days of the homesteading era were over.

Cole sprang back to life when J. L. Shiely built its gravel plant. Railroad crews came to lay a passing track to the gravel pits. They sidetracked rail cars for offices, mess halls, and bunks for workers.

Five-hundred workers were hired. Most brought their families and built shacks or pitched tents. Cole had a thousand residents.

Grocery and clothing stores opened, also a butcher shop, cafes, a book store, filling station, garage, dance hall, tavern, and more. A school was started. Clubs were formed for all ages. Church services were held in the town theater.

Trains ran non-stop for the four-plus years the Shiely plant was in operation. So did the friendly little town. Residents left when the work was done and the plant dismantled. Cole was again deserted.

Saco

Saco started as a railroad siding in 1887 about 45 miles west of Glasgow. Some say it was named for Sacajawea; most likely it was named by a Great Northern railroad clerk with a globe, in St. Paul.

The depot agent opened a general store, followed by a saloon and post office. Twenty more businesses were established, including a contractor's office, barber shop, baths, laundry, millinery, gift shop, "thirst store," ice house, creamery, and livery barn.

When Saco incorporated in 1918 it had electric lights, a school, library, churches, a ballroom, city band, and a doctor and nurse. The *Saco Independent* published legal notices and news from 1909-1975. The population dropped to 425 in 1920 and increased to 506 in 1930.

When rock picking began in the Saco-Cole area, several workers and their families moved to Saco and built their homes. A company camp grew up with five small houses for foremen and engineers, a mess hall, office, supply house, machine shop, and garage. The town added new businesses. Residents called Saco a "great place to live."

Trains hauling gravel from Cole, and boulders from Snake Butte, rumbled by day and night into 1939. Vehicle traffic was heavy on US Highway 2 past Saco's door. Things changed when the workers left; the population dropped to 452 in 1940. The town continued on.

Saco gas field: In 1928 two gas wells were drilled at Bowdoin, northwest of Saco, with a municipal system in Saco. Some of the gas was used at the project. The system is still in operation.

The Plunge. In 1922 a wildcatter drilling for oil ten miles west of Saco tapped into an artesian well of hot mineral water at 3,200 feet. The site was developed during the 1930s with WPA assistance and a partnership between the Phillips County American Legion and Soil Conservation Service. The "Saco Health Plunge," "American Legion Plunge," or simply "The Plunge" was popular with project people.

Snake Butte Quarry – Harlem

In 1934, boulders were needed to cover a 16-inch bed of gravel on the upstream face of the dam. Plenty were found at Snake Butte on the Fort Belknap Indian Reservation fourteen miles south of Harlem.

In September 1936 the Tomlin-Arkwright Construction Company of Great Falls prepared sub-grade for a railroad spur between Harlem and Snake Butte to the blasting site.

In May 1937 the Great Northern railroad completed the 14-mile spur, added switches, and placed a siding track at Harlem.

The Montana Power Company strung a 50,000 watt line to provide electricity for tools and the 110 feet high derricks. Carpenters built supply sheds and crew quarters. A crew of 250 supervisors and workers skilled in the use of dynamite and drilling equipment were hired for three shifts, 24 hours a day, with night work by floodlights.

Blasting began in May 1937 dislodging 6,000 yards of rock. In July the first five rail cars of boulders left for the dam. By September officials counted 15,000 loads of boulders, plus the last glacial rock from a Phillips County stockpile, dumped at the project.

Approximately 36 tons of stones, 2-10 tons each, were loaded on flat cars in 50-60 car trains that ran the 130 miles to the dam day and night. In September 1938 officials reported some 4,000 tons of stone, carried by 100 cars, had been placed on the dam in one day.

During blasting in May 1939 about 70,000 solid cubic yards of rock were dislodged and 800 tons dropped on the quarry floor. It was part of the million or more tons of stone taken from Snake Butte to the Fort Peck project, and part of a stockpile created for later use.

An accident during routine blasting in July 1939 heavily damaged the facility, injured eighteen workers, and killed a teenage boy.

The last load of quarry stone was hauled out in August 1939, and the quarry shut down. A few key workers stayed long enough to clean up the site and move the machinery. In October 1940, Snake Butte stone topped off the dam at 250.5 feet. The last boulder was set in November. The job to cut 475,000 cubic yards of stone was done.

Snake Butte stands out on the prairie southwest of Fort Belknap. Nomadic Indians once camped by its spring and used its rims for vision quests. Legend tells of a "huge snake with evil powers" that slithered up from a crevice and stole the body of an Indian baby. A medicine woman said it was "a warning not to linger too long on the rims."

Quarry workers saw several snakes when blasting began but the snakes were soon gone. The longest rattler measured five feet and the longest bullsnake was seven. Workers stocked rattlesnake bite serum in their first aid kits, but there is no record it was ever needed.

Harlem

Harlem is located on the north side of US 2 in Blaine County, 122 miles northwest of Fort Peck. It was an 1889 railroad siding named by a Great Northern clerk. It served as a trading post for the Fort Belknap Indian Reservation and for early 1900s homesteaders.

The population was 708 in 1930. Workers from the Snake Butte Quarry and their families lived there in 1937-1939. The population boomed to approximately 1,500, with 1,166 still living there in 1940.

The neighborly little town of Harlem still greets visitors traveling along the Hi-Line.

Fort Peck Project On The Job Accidents and Death

On Sunday, September 1, 1935, Spillway Builders Inc. shut down their machinery and workers stood for two minutes of silence to honor workers killed on the project.

Although the Corps of Engineers, private contractors, and workers themselves observed strict safety rules, sixty workers died during the course of the project as the result of job related accidents.

Worksites were an anthill twenty-four hours a day, seven days a week, for nearly six years. The work was dangerous and few laborers had experience working at great heights or depths, or on large crews. There was continuous loud noise, and the constant movement of men and machines. Sand, gravel, boulders, and fresh banks of earth were subject to slides. Temperatures ranged from 60-below to 119-above zero. Conditions included slippery shale, sticky gumbo, high winds, clouds of dust, and drifting snow. Added in were the inevitable freak accidents. Workers were small and vulnerable in the midst of it all.

"Safety First. Make sure you get home safely," *worksite sign.*

There were frequent inspections and all safety rules were enforced. Disregard for safety, endangering others, and drinking on the job were causes for prompt dismissal. Supervisors were trained in first aid to ensure every injured worker received immediate attention.

A 1936 report noted most accidents were caused by inattention, disobeying rules, poor planning, haste, and defective equipment.

Corps Report Nov. 26, 1936

Deaths under average in tunnels: Fourteen lose lives during work ... one fatality recorded for every 730,000 man hours of labor (below U.S. average).... Many of the world's best engineers who have visited Fort Peck have acknowledged that tunnel driving through the blocky, faulted Bearpaw shale in this locality is a difficult and hazardous undertaking ... fatal accidents at Fort Peck tunnels have occurred on operations where they should not have happened or under freakish circumstances or through careless disregard of express safety instruction.... A first-aid station with trained attendants and a waiting ambulance has been maintained near the portals giving 24-hour service. ... Prompt attention to all injuries ... has been available.

In addition to the fourteen workers killed in the tunnels, fifteen had died at other work sites or in hospitals by the end of 1936.

Reports of their accidents and deaths listed the causes as: crushed under rock, hit by shale, struck by equipment, caught in a conveyor belt, buried under a crane, crushed between two trucks, fell from an 85-foot tower, fell to the bottom of a gatehouse shaft, pinned under machinery, suffocated in a cave-in, drowned, and electrocuted.

A Corps surveyor on the first survey crew suffocated in an earth bank cave-in. Two engineers died of heart attacks.

Injuries on the job

Injuries included broken fingers, legs, arms, backs, pelvises, jaws, and noses; skull fractures; sprains; crushing injuries; cuts, lacerations; severed arms, fingers, and toes; burns; and infections, gangrene, and blood poisoning from untreated or improperly treated wounds.

The visiting president of a Minneapolis firm was injured when a worker dropped a pipe on his foot. A welder was hurt when his machine jumped out of control, dragged him eighty feet and dropped him into a fifteen foot pit. Many men suffered the rest of their lives from their injuries; most received some compensation and retraining.

Close calls

A crowbar, accidentally dropped from above, hit a worker's hard-hat, shot down between his heavy coat and underwear, and pinned him to a plank. He escaped with scratches. A pipe-smoking dredge worker, fell through an ice hole. He was pulled out with his pipe still in his mouth. A worker was stranded when his barge broke loose and headed down the river. Ferry landing workers caught the barge and brought it back to shore.

A worker being lifted from the bottom of the 130-foot spillway cutoff escaped death when the elevator bucket leverman lowered the bucket after feeling an "unfamiliar tug" on his cable and found the worker's head was caught in the machinery.

Heroism

Hundreds of workers were saved from injury and possible death by the quick thinking and extraordinary actions of their co-workers. Men risked their own lives saving others from cave-ins, sand and gravel slides, rolling boulders, and machinery. Often their bare hands were their only tools. Sometimes the victim was their father, brother, or a close friend; but they didn't take names, every life mattered.

When a worker died in an accident, his crew took up a collection and did what they could for his family, then grimly went back to work.

In Memory of the sixty workers who lost their lives in work related accidents at the Fort Peck Project.

Raymond Hagen, 19, was hit by a spreader jack and fell from a scaffold at the top of Tunnel Shaft No. 3, to the bottom.

Emerald Wheatley, 23, on his night shift, fell from a pontoon being moved down the river. His body was never found.

Eight workers lost their lives in the Slide, September 22, 1938.
Six are forever entombed in the dam:

Oliver Bucher, 55, worker; *John I. Johnson*, 25, motorboat operator; *Walter Lubbinge*, 29, drill runner; *Archie R. Moir*, 26, deckhand; *Dolphie Paulson*, 51, worker; *Nelson P. Van Stone*, 31, foreman.

Albert V. Stoeser, 23, deckhand, was found in the slide and rushed to the Fort Peck Hospital. Doctors tried to revive him in an iron lung.

Douglas J. Moore, 35, associate superintendent. His body was found about a mile from the dam a week after the slide.

A monument for slide victims stands by the dam on a hill above the powerhouses.

The following list of workers who died on the job or in hospitals from their injuries, was prepared from their newspaper death notices, by the author.

In Memory of:

1933: *Victor Carlson*, 35, core driller.

1934: *Martin Risa*, 50, gravel pit worker. *Neil McNeil*, 52, tunnel portal worker. *Russell Taulbee*, 26, rodman. *Lloyd Burke*, 22, drill runner. *Oliver Spracklin*, 31, rig oiler. *Clarence Eggum*, 23, crane operator helper. *Oliver Winsky*, 56, crane operator. *Adolf Berg*, 41, dump truck foreman. *Wayne McMillan*, 19, jack hammer operator. *Dan Anderson*, 45, excavation crew. *Joseph White*, 40, trestle crew.

1935: *Lewis Davis*, 35, tunnel worker. *George Peart*, 36, electrician. *Emerald Wheatley*, 23, deckhand. *George Boston*, 22, dam worker. *Norman Olson*, 24, Cole gravel pit worker. *Donald Swartz*, 25, lineman. *George Rush*, 39, dump truck driver. *Ray Berube*, 41, dam worker. *Clarence Livingston*, 24, tunnel worker. *Arthur Kveseth*, 43, oiler. *Clarence Fly*, 24, paint sprayer.

1936: *Herbert Young*, 37, steam boiler fireman. *Frank Torres*, 35, dam worker. *William Stevens*, 31, tunnel driller. *Sydney Conyers*, 26, shovel runner. *John Hunewell*, 57, tunnel worker. *Wyatt Jones*, 31, welder. *Ferdinand Hickel*, 40, driller. *Clarence Bernau*, 24, steel worker. *Purl Dickson*, 46, brakeman. *Worker*-control gate shaft.

1937: *Maurice Weinrich*, 27, steel worker. *Charles Reed*, 29, Corps member of first survey party. *Leonard LaJoie*, 26, watchman at Cole gravel plant. *Raymond Hagen*, 19, rigger. *Louis Eibon*, 27, crane operator. *Roland Schumacher*, 25, electrician. *Elmo Bailey*, 24, spillway crew. *Glenn Cummings*, 20, oiler. *Henry Annan*, 32, lineman. *Harry Christianson*, 28, welder. *Fred Amon*, electrician. *John "Al" Lindgren*, 40, gravel train worker injured during Missouri River diversion, died in the Deaconess Hospital two weeks later.

1938: *Oscar Bilstad*, 45, brush cutter. *A. E."Bud" Phares*, 24, drill helper, Snake Butte Quarry; *William Chamberlain,* 24, Snake Butte Quarry worker. *Gregory Leichner*, 31, oiler. *Howard Brown*, 54, truck driver. *Eight Workers* lost their lives in the Slide.

1939: William Mackey, 26, intake portal worker.

Many of these men were married and fathers of small children.

Six or more workers died of pneumonia in 1935, including a pay master, iron worker, boatyard foreman, carpenter, and two laborers.

Montana was hit with an influenza and pneumonia epidemic in the winter of 1936-1937. At least thirty-six project workers, a Fort Peck Hospital nurse, and many townspeople died of what was referred to as a "quick" pneumonia. Most of them died at home. Death notices read, "taken suddenly ill, developed pneumonia ... died within three days."

Wives and mothers rushed to the project but often arrived too late. Glasgow funeral directors sent bodies home to families in Montana, Minnesota, Oregon, Iowa, the Dakotas and other states. One worker was survived only by his mother in Norway. A 23-year-old worker was one of several for whom no living relatives could be found.

Wives and children, themselves sick with flu and pneumonia, were left alone in sorrow and needing help through the cold winter.

*"Another suicide...*26-year-old tunnel worker....*" Fort Peck Press.* Seven or more workers, and other men who failed to find jobs, found their despair and loneliness unbearable and ended their lives.

Accidents off-the-job, took the lives of ten or more workers from 1935-1940. A welder and a dredge chief died of heart attacks. A 22-year-old truck driver was the first of several to drown in the lake.

A worker died after accidentally inhaling the fumes of gas used to fumigate his barracks. His fingerprints revealed several aliases and fugitive status from McNeil Island prison in the state of Washington.

A few workers were killed in vehicle accidents, some were drunk. One was killed when he swerved to miss a horse. Another was hit by a gravel train in Nashua, another was killed by a truck in Wheeler.

Looking for loved ones. The Corps and county agencies received calls and letters from families looking for loved ones who had left home to find jobs at the project and had not been heard from since.

An Iowa mother begged newspapers to run a story about her son: he and a friend left home to find work, his car was sold in Billings but the transfer signature was not his. A Washington man was searching for his father and feared foul play. A woman looking for her husband said she and their children had not heard from him in over a year.

Missing persons were seldom found. Most were not eligible to be hired for project jobs. Some used aliases so as not to be found.

A number of men, unemployed and desperate, believed welfare would care for their families if they simply disappeared.

Part 4

Fort Peck "The Government Town"

Only a single tree grew in the city of Fort Peck, Montana.
Ripley's Believe It or Not, 1936.

Due to the isolation of the area in which the Fort Peck dam and spillway would be built, the Corps deemed it necessary to construct a government town with housing for Corps personnel, the men "in positions of responsibility," and their families. Rows of barracks and dorms would be built outside the town for workers and supervisors.

Corps spokesmen later stated that "providing facilities for housing and feeding all of the required employees in an area with no nearby accommodations was in itself a task of great proportion."

Plans for the government town were drawn at the Army Corps of Engineers Headquarters in Kansas City in 1933. The chosen site was a benchland and rolling hills overlooking the Missouri River Valley, high above the west side of the river, less than a mile northwest of the dam. The town would be named Fort Peck, a name taken from the nearby, long deserted 1870s Fort Peck trading post.

The nearest neighbors were the incorporated towns of Nashua, 14 miles to the north, population 351; and Glasgow, 22 miles northwest, population 2,200. Several little boomtowns were already springing up to the west and north, and across the river to the east.

Building Fort Peck and the several structures in it, including the Administration Building, Employees Hotel, and hospital began in the spring, 1934. Twelve contracts were let for construction of buildings, utilities, and roads. Work to finish the "model city" was continuous.

Operation of the town was one of the responsibilities of Maj. T.B. Larkin, district engineer. Captain Ewart G. Plank was town manager.

Townsite report: *The town includes four hundred and three houses and apartments, an employees' hotel, three blocks of foreman's dormitories, nine blocks of laborers' barracks, town hall and post office, recreation hall, theater, store building, hospital, school building, laboratory, garage, commissary warehouses, cold storage warehouse, and laundry.... There are 15 miles of paved streets, 18 miles of sidewalks, a water filtration plant, sanitary and storm sewers, and usual water, gas, and electric distribution systems.*

Houses. A dozen stylish, three or more bedroom permanent houses with garages were built along East Kansas Street on the northeast side of Fort Peck for ranking Corps officers.

Nearly twenty temporary houses and garages lined West Kansas Street next to the tennis courts, for Corps officers and their families.

Another 298 temporary houses, constructed from seven different floor plans and ten unlike exteriors "to avoid monotony" were built on the south-southwest end of town on Missouri Avenue. The houses were small with an in-door bed in the living room, a kitchen/dinette, vestibule, bathroom, and screened porch; 188 had garages.

Residents paid monthly rent which included gas, electricity, water, and garbage collection. Rent, by home size, ranged from $28 to $50.

Housing assignments were made by the district office from a long waiting list. Applicant eligibility was determined by the division chief, with approval granted in accordance with "relative needs and interest of the government."

The first three blocks of homes, one block of dorms, and three blocks of worker barracks opened in September 1934.

Fort Peck residents were mostly Corps personnel, key contractors, inspectors, some skilled workers, concessionaires and their families from several different states. They soon formed a productive and busy community with organizations, clubs, and churches.

News of Fort Peck people and their activities appeared in the local newspapers along with Corps promotions and assignments. Columns noted: "Pastel shades predominated in floral arrangements for the bridge club luncheon. Covers were laid for eight." "Miss H. gave an after-dinner concert of Schumann and Debussy." "Mr. K. presented a selection of African-Cuban and modern-impressionistic rhythm and dances." Dancing, bridge, and the game "Easy Money" were popular.

*A **Do/Don't list*** was posted by town management. Major Larkin sent out "circular letters" on issues such as vehicles on sidewalks, and prohibition of unauthorized persons sharing residential housing.

In spring 1935 residents planted lawns, shrubs, and flowers. Major Larkin sent out How-To tips and offered cash prizes for the best appearing lawns.

Clean Up Weeks were held spring and fall. Trucks picked up trash and ashpiles. *Notice: Do not throw your slops around promiscuously. Let us cooperate by keeping our towns as sanitary as possible.*

In January 1935 a high, wire fence with pedestrian and vehicle gates was built around the government town. Roads down the hill south of the Administration Building and East Kansas Street were closed. Fort Peck town was a safe, modern, "desirable place to live."

Utilities. By September 1934 the first million gallons of water had been pumped from the Missouri River and processed through the new filtration plant a mile and a half west of Fort Peck.

Natural gas for heat, and other project purposes, was supplied by the Montana-Dakota Utilities Company from the gas fields near Saco. Electricity was provided by Montana Power Company's Rainbow Falls station in Great Falls, via a substation at Fort Peck. Street lights were turned on in October. Telephones were installed by Fort Peck Telephone Exchange from Mountain States Telephone & Telegraph.

The town's utilities section was responsible for utility distribution; sanitary and storm sewers; and the maintenance of streets, sidewalks, buildings, and grounds. It also managed the services of electricians, carpenters and plumbers for residents and concessionaires, and kept records and stocked supplies.

In June 1934 a temporary post office was established to provide workers and Fort Peck residents with general delivery mail service. In December 1935 authorization of a Second Class facility was granted, and a new post office was built in Fort Peck.

Government housing for workers

Apartments: Initially one apartment building was built for married workers. By 1935 requests exceeded availability. Fifteen barracks and three mess halls were turned into an additional eighty-two apartments.

Gas stoves, and a kitchen sink with running cold water (carried to the bathhouse for disposal), were installed. Partitions served as room dividers. Bathrooms, showers, and laundry facilities were available in nearby bathhouses. Monthly charges for rent, gas, electricity, water, and garbage pick-up averaged $23.

Employees Hotel: A three story, 55-room hotel was built on a hill west of the Administration Building for a few "transient guests" and government workers. Rooms were designed with a large closet and a choice of a private or two-room shared bath. Official guests and the "men and women with positions of responsibility," whose dependents were not with them, stayed for varying lengths of time.

Single occupancy rooms ranged from $15-$40 a month. Transient official guests were charged on a daily basis at standard hotel rates.

Two 20-room wings were added on the hotel, the east wing for men and the west wing for women. Monthly rates were $13 each for two in wing rooms, $28.50 for two in larger rooms with private baths.

Daily meals and special dinners were served in the hotel dining room on the main floor. The dining room and adjoining lobby with a fireplace were "comfortable but not extravagantly furnished." Known today as the Fort Peck Hotel, the Employees Hotel still welcomes guests and serves meals in the original dining room.

Women's dormitories. Two dorms were built south of the hotel for single female employees. Rooms were $12 each for two, $15 for one. There were no closets and space was limited, but residents had only a short walk to work in the "Ad Building" and other offices.

The dormitories and barracks for men were built a half mile west of Fort Peck on both sides of Marias Avenue. Captain Plank noted they were "grouped together and separated from the residential and business sections." Big Horn Street connected the dorms to town.

Three Dormitory blocks, each with eight 30x70 feet dorms and a mess hall, were built for foremen, inspectors, and skilled labor of the "higher brackets." Each dorm had fifteen private rooms, a bathroom, lobby, and screened porch across the front. Rooms had desks, chairs, and single bunks. There were two 26-vehicle garages in the blocks.

Barracks. Nine blocks of wood frame "bunkhouses" were built for laborers. Each block had sixteen 23x70 buildings; each building had one large open room with 24 single or double-deck bunks, for $10 per month. The barracks were lined up in two parallel rows of eight buildings each. A large bathhouse sat between them at each end. A section in the middle of each block, shaped like an "H," had a kitchen on the crossbar and dining rooms on each side with mess hall space to feed 384 men at one time. Seven barracks opened in January 1935. By October there were six men in double bunks in a space 10x17 feet. To relieve overcrowding, 24x84 feet of space was opened in the fire hall.

Cleanliness was emphasized in all government housing. It did not rule out the periodic fumigation of bedbugs, but it helped.

Charges. Rent for hotel rooms, dorms, and the barracks included linen, towels, and janitor service. The town management Billing and Collection Department handled all worker financial obligations to the government. Payroll deductions were made for rent and meals.

Monthly statements were mailed to concessionaires and private contractors for their rent and expenses, payable at the town hall.

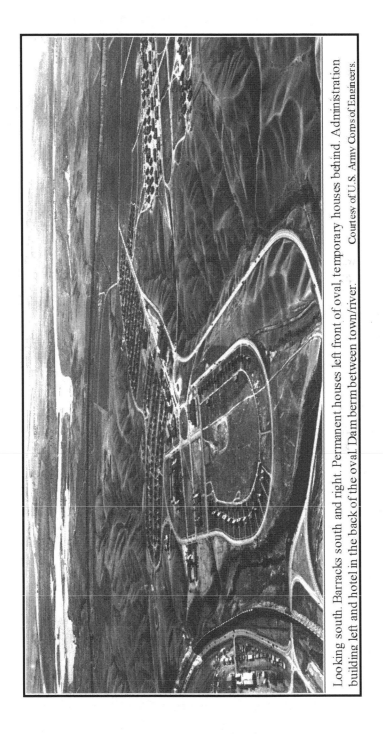

Looking south. Barracks south and right. Permanent houses left front of oval, temporary houses behind. Administration building left and hotel in the back of the oval. Dam berm between town/river.　　Courtesy of U.S. Army Corps of Engineers.

Government orders workers into the barracks
In February 1935 notices appeared in project work sites:
All single men are to report to the barracks by Tuesday.

All single males working directly for the government and private contractors were ordered to move out of their boomtown homes and into the barracks. Failure to comply could result in the loss of jobs.

"Single" included married men whose families were not at the project. Most government workers and an estimated eighty-percent of the laborers employed by contractors were affected by the order.

Petitions appeared in boomtown businesses. Several hundred men met with American Legion State Commander Hugh Marron, a Wolf Point attorney. He was asked to write a brief protesting the order.

Objections were: No barracks existed when the men came to work so they built homes in the boomtowns, Glasgow, and Nashua. Many of them shared homes with extended family members dependent on them. Most workers preferred living in their homes to save money. And, they felt loyalty for the boomtown businesses that served them.

Arguments were: "This is a free country," and workers should be able to eat, sleep, and spend their wages where they choose; the cost of living in the barracks would not leave enough money to support families back home, and, the regulation could force some families onto relief even though the men were working.

Marron's brief and a petition with 2,000 signatures was sent to Sen. Burton K. Wheeler in Helena.

By February 28, Commander Marron received a telegram from Senator Wheeler, "The War Department just talked to Major Larkin by telephone. He states the order with regards to married men has been suspended. Investigation is to be made of the whole situation."

Larkin added that the revocation order "applies to future married employees as well as those now working."

Unmarried men *did* have to move to the barracks. Some got married. Others who owned boomtown houses and shared them with family members or other workers, managed to stay in their homes.

A boomtown weekly correspondent for the *Fort Peck Press* wrote, "Strommie, a spillway worker who has resided here for a number of months, was forced to move to the barracks to retain his job."

In April 1936 barracks residents protested the announcement that double bunks would be installed in selected barracks for workers hired during the peak employment in July. Meetings, and some labor union involvement, had little effect on the order as thousands of men desperate for jobs came to work willing to live anywhere they could.

By winter nearly a thousand workers had finished their projects and returned home, leaving fewer men in the barracks than when the question of bunks and overcrowding arose in April.

The Merit System gave three of 73 men in Barracks #3232 some 22 project tickets each for "cleanest mess hall during the month."

The Olympic Commissary Company, boarding contractors for the project, provided food in the mess halls, and in buildings and tents at the tunnels, shipyard, and other work sites.

Most of the food was supplied by Montana companies and stored in a 212x50 feet warehouse and a 264x50 feet cold storage unit. The facilities included an ice manufacturing plant with a 300-ton storage; a large creamery; meat cutting room and butcher shop; and a bakery that turned out 3,000 loaves of bread, 800 pies, 350 dozen sweet rolls, and 500 dozen cookies daily.

Commissary staff prepared about 14,000 sandwiches each day and delivered them to mess hall bins. Workers made up their own lunches of sandwiches, pickles, onions, cake, cookies, and fruit. Food cost $25 a month, except for the hotel's "more elaborate $30 service."

Approximately 1,500 meals were served in barracks kitchens and mess halls every twenty-four hours. Workers were allowed to eat as many meals as they wanted. According to Captain Plank, "Checks show this is not abused." But it was known a few workers carried extra sandwiches in their lunches and gave them to boomtown co-workers with large families, whose lunches were "mighty slim."

Fort Peck Businesses Concessions

"Even before the project was authorized, ambitious merchants began soliciting personnel in charge of field investigations.... To avoid fly-by-night boom-town enterprises and to avoid over-building: formal applications regarding reliability, experience, and financial backing were required. Advertisement of the proposed award of certain concessions was made public." Report by Capt. Ewart Plank.

June 15, 1934, concession permits were awarded based on "ability to serve." While stores were being built, concessionaires trucked in groceries and goods from Glasgow and delivered them door to door.

Eight stores opened in October, and a Concessionaires Association met weekly to make plans and compare their prices to local stores.

A large building was erected in the center of town to house a grocery and meat market, a department store, drug store, news stand, shoe store, barber and beauty shop, and dry-cleaners. Permits were approved for a theater, confectionery, three filling stations, a garage, restaurant, and billiard parlor/bowling alley. Great Falls Coach Line, Western Union, and American Railway Express all had offices there.

Owners provided all of their own equipment and paid enough rent to amortize the building within four years.

Most businesses opened in the fall of 1934. The Green Hut Cafe was the area's largest 24-hour restaurant. Vornholt's had the most popular drug store and soda fountain. Buttrey's Department Store opened in 1934, added ten clerks in 1935 and built a dorm for them. Some larger businesses closed in 1937, others operated into 1939.

Most concessionaires, businesses managers, and their families lived in sixteen small homes on space reserved between the barracks and temporary houses on the southwest side of Fort Peck town.

Fort Peck reached its peak population of 7,200 during the summer of 1936. The number dropped to 6,195 in October. From 1937 to the end of the project, vacancies allowed a few selected government workers and their families to move from the boomtowns into Fort Peck. By November 1940 the population was 1,000.

Between 1938-1940 many small homes were moved. Barracks and dorm buildings were razed, or sold to private owners and moved. A few were saved and incorporated into the new plan for the town.

In 1985 Congress authorized the sale of houses, land, and fixed assets to the residents of Fort Peck. The Corps updated the utilities, repaired sidewalks, installed a new water plant, and made several other improvements. The final sale took place August 15, 1986, and most of the government town became private property.

Fort Peck Hospital. Construction of the town's 22-bed hospital and dental office began in mid-1934. In September the nearly completed $70,000 building was destroyed by a fire which started when a pail of tar, heated with a blow torch, exploded.

The hospital was rebuilt with fireproof walls. The fully equipped facility opened in December.

Government employees injured on the job were treated free. Their dependents, and off-duty workers, paid according to an approved rate. Patients needing extended care were taken to Glasgow.

General health care and medical treatment were also available at the Smith Clinic near the Fort Peck Post Office.

A public health officer was appointed from the medical staff. He made bi-monthly inspections of "critical areas and functions in the town," including mess halls, bath houses, barracks, and businesses. He also issued quarantines during outbreaks of contagious diseases.

Hospital doctors and nurses assisted in government-provided First Aid Training for project supervisors, enabling them to immediately respond to the needs of workers injured on the job .

Fort Peck Police Department. Chief of Police G. W. Fleming and his dozen officers protected the town of Fort Peck, directed traffic, and observed or aided the thousands of tourists visiting the town.

They kept an eye on the hundreds of spirited young men from the barracks where card playing was allowed, but not gambling. Beer was sold at five awarded concessions. Hard liquor was not allowed, and "control predicated on improper acts resulting from its intemperate use." In plain words, men would be fired for possession and use.

Captain Plank stated that no major crimes had taken place in Fort Peck. "Minor cases are handled by admonition, reprimand, or discharge." He added, "Some fugitives from justice seek anonymity in the transient population in and around Fort Peck."

In 1936 Captain Plank outlined law enforcement responsibilities in the greater Fort Peck area: *The Acting Secretary of War, by letter to the governor of Montana, assumed ... exclusive jurisdiction over the area on behalf of the United States. ... includes the spillway, dam, tunnel, and town sites and territory adjacent thereto, approx. 23,000 acres. Responsibility for law enforcement ... rests squarely with the government. Because the federal judicial system has as its primary subdivision a federal district court, no minor court comparable to the ordinary police court exists in Fort Peck.*

Fort Peck Fire Department. By October 1934, the Fort Peck Fire Department had been established by Chief Harley Wyatt, of Kansas City. Harry V. Ishum was named fire chief for the next six years. He left when the project ended in 1940 and the fire department was trimmed to three firemen and fifty volunteers.

The department had a well trained staff of up to twenty men. It was fully equipped with a Howe firetruck, 1,800 feet of hose, ladders, axes, and all necessary tools and chemicals. The truck was housed in a Fort Peck garage. Emergency equipment was stored in seven different locations in the area. A fire alarm with 23 call stations was installed. Its wail could be heard in the "mushroom" towns.

73

By 1936 the department had trained 270 volunteers in Fort Peck. Adults and children had been taught to use fire extinguishers. Homes, schools, and all other buildings were inspected regularly for hazards.

Capt. Ewart Plank noted that the fire department was responsible for 600 buildings in the townsite and valley adjacent to the river. All but thirteen of the buildings were temporary wood-frame construction and most had gas burning furnaces, stoves, and water heaters.

In addition to the town of Fort Peck, the department protected the four dredges and all floating equipment, the buildings in the industrial area flood plain below the town, and the contractors' buildings. It responded to highway accidents, and to calls to the boomtowns after their bucket brigades and volunteers had exhausted their resources.

Insurance rates in Fort Peck were comparable to the rates in other Montana towns. Fire loss in 1934 was $2.52. In 1935 it was $59.61: a worker started a fire while smoking in the barracks; a fire flared up in a contractor's building eight miles from town; and fires were started by an electric iron, and a defective water heater.

In February 1936 some $5,000 worth of supplies and records were lost in a fire at the Spillway surveyors' headquarters. The fire started while firemen were at a fire in the tunnel portal. A $12 fire in 1937 started in an overheated barracks furnace. Loss in 1938 was $3.70.

Fort Peck, former "government town" of the project dam days, grew up in a hurry to serve its purpose during the 1930s dam and spillway construction. There have been many changes over the years.

The town has aged well and continues on with enthusiasm and grace, prepared for the opportunities and challenges happening now.

Part 5

The Project and the Media

The Corps of Engineers issued notices to the media

All information for the press from the Fort Peck District is cleared through the Historical Section. Press releases are prepared weekly, mimeographed copies sent to all newspapers and several national technical publications. Releases cover progress of construction during the past week with mention of outstanding performances ... description of work of various agencies ... laboratory, Recreation Association, safety, school, fire, police, etc....

The Corps of Engineers maintained an Information Office and a Photography Department. Most of the technical reports were prepared by district personnel. Several of their articles appeared in national engineering magazines including: *Engineering News-Record, Military Engineering,* and *Excavating Engineer.* In addition to weekly media releases, press releases were sent regarding special events.

In July 1937 government photographers reported more than 4,000 black and white 8x10 photos and 50,000 feet of moving pictures had been taken. They estimated 5,000 "still" pictures depicting every phase of construction would be filed before the project ended.

Hundreds of news stories and editorials appeared in *The Glasgow Courier* about the project. Among them was a *Fort Peck Feature,* December 1, 1933; and *Our Dam* by Major Clark Kittrell, in a special feature in the November 30, 1937, Agriculture insert. Several national newspapers sent their photographers and reporters.

Newsreels: Cameramen in charge of the sound recordings for Fox Movietone News made frequent trips to the project. Their film, with the dialog by noted news commentator Lowell Thomas, was released throughout the United States and viewed by thousands of moviegoers.

In March 1935 newsreel pictures of the dam, taken by a Pathe cameraman, were shown in the Fort Peck Theatre. In October 1935 Universal newsreel cameramen toured the dam several times taking pictures for the WPA. Members of the Corps photo and information staff guided media tours for visiting reporters and cameramen.

Foreign Publications: One of the many foreign articles about the Fort Peck project was *"La Technique des Travaux": Le Barrage Terre de Fort Peck (E.-U.).* The French engineering magazine printed a twelve-page story with fifteen illustrations in its April 1937 edition.

How some saw it: Among the many stories written about the project was this one in a Minnesota newspaper in 1935:

"Minnesota Man Saw Many Strange Sights at Fort Peck: Read 'em And You'll Be Surprised."

The writer was identified as a monument company manager and a "keen observer of things." He had observed the government spending "a vast sum on the dam" and stated "the waste is appalling." He claimed workers loafed on the job so as not to get ahead of schedule, and when timekeepers found them sleeping "they took the time cards out of their pockets and punched them, showing they were on the job." In conclusion, he reported seeing "fine wheat" in the drought-devastated country side.

Others: In February 1937 the *Glasgow Courier* mentioned a letter an Iowa "engineer of science" mailed to the *Fort Peck Dam On the Missouri River, district engineer office:*

"Dear Sir, It will probably rain this spring as the weather is inclined to change every often." The writer went on to ask the engineers to "hold back all the water you can up there until June 1st, at any time there is an excess down here."

Corps engineers remarked the writer forgot one major detail; "the dam will not be finished until 1939."

In June 1937 the *Glasgow Courier* reported a "current rumor" that "Seer Rose Dawn, astrological prognosticator of radio fame," had predicted the partial annihilation of Fort Peck townsite and the dam.

Since she had made "some accurate long-range predictions in natural disasters," there was speculation.

However, the editor noted, the Seer's prediction was "asking a little too much of Mother Nature; Fort Peck (town) as usual still stands on the hilltop."

The Slide at the dam occurred on September 22, 1938.

Ernie Pyle, The *Nation, Life* Magazine

Ernie Pyle "roving correspondent for *Scripps-Howard* news chain" visited the project in 1936 and wrote the most widely read of the many sensationalized columns about the boomtowns.

In his *Washington Daily News* article, September 1, 1936, he made light of the "shantytowns" and houses made of "boxes and tin cans and old boards and tar roofing." He called Wheeler a "slopover" from Fort Peck townsite, the "wildest west town in North America."

He wrote of a "melee of drunken men and painted women." He noted open gambling and alcohol in the face of the law; and prostitution by "thousands" of project women. His colorful distortions painted an 826 word-picture that drew curious tourists and inspired copycat writers to rephrase and reprint his column. A copy of the column was later printed on postcards and sold in project stores.

Pyle's haunting last line motivated serious writers to dig a little deeper: "Wheeler will be gone in three more years, ... somebody had better record it for posterity before it's too late."

The Nation magazine article

An article, *Fort Peck: An American Siberia,* by James Rorty, one of the eastern "social consciousness writers" of the day, was printed in the *Nation,* "America's oldest weekly magazine," September 1935.

Rorty claimed to have spent several months traveling in the West "investigating social and economic conditions." In his article he soundly criticized the government and the Corps. He referred to the town of Fort Peck as "Spotless Town" and the boomtowns as "pitiful towns" a "sprawling, malodorous slum-in-the-desert."

Rorty claimed to have talked to project laborers who spoke in voices "loud, profane, and bitter" about the project, because they considered themselves "exiles ... helpless and desperate," mistreated by the Corps and "profit-hungry" contractors.

He quoted from the *Fort Peck Project News*, a short-lived activist sheet proclaiming itself the voice of the workers, written and, for a short time printed, at the writer's boomtown home.

Rorty's article called the New Deal project a "ghastly joke," and claimed the government violated human rights by telling workers where they "must sleep...and eat." Stating that families had been "torn apart" and spirits "undermined." Rorty ended his tirade by stating the Board of Labor Review acknowledged *some* problems, the Corps was willing to correct them, but workers "don't think so."

Many questioned Rorty's sample group of prevailing opinion.

Life magazine

News that the first edition of *Life* magazine, November 23, 1936, would feature Montana's Fort Peck project was met with anticipation by the Corps of Engineers, the Glasgow Chamber of Commerce, and project workers. It was an opportunity to showcase the construction of the largest earth dam in the world, and to show how the jobs had provided hope and livelihood for thousands of unemployed workers.

Life assigned Margaret Bourke-White to cover the story. A 1927 graduate of Cornell University, she had set up a studio in Cleveland and was gaining recognition for her photos of industrial buildings.

Bourke-White arrived at the Glasgow Airport in mid-October. At the project, Public Affairs officer Capt. Claude Chorpening assigned his media personnel to take her on tours of all the construction sites.

Her photo shoots often delayed workers for more than an hour, and according to her guides, she was "persistent" about seeing Happy Hollow and the boomtowns. It appeared she had her own agenda.

She had apparently been influenced by Ernie Pyle's column a month earlier, as she and her editors at *Life* adopted his "wild west" brand. And it was possible she had read the *Nation* magazine article.

When Life appeared, readers were impressed by Bourke-White's cover photo of the massive Spillway piers (mistakenly-identified as the dam). But the eight-page photo essay inside was a shock and a disappointment to everyone, especially the Corps of Engineers.

There were 16 photos and captions following the lead "10,000 Montana Relief Workers Make Whoopee on Saturday Night." The first photo showed "taxi-dancers" and their "fares," "loping" around the barroom floor, all eyes on the photographer. No mention was made that the dancers angrily demanded the film when they found out what they were being photographed for.

Eleven of the photos were taken inside of bars, with captions that played on the overall "cowtown" theme. Many of them contained errors. Wording in some captions was downright crude.

There was a small mug shot of Lt. Col. T. B. Larkin captioned "is boss," next to a story of project hot spots. A small mug shot of a pipe-smoking Major Clark Kittrell "number 2" sided a story on "all night whooperies," and the "little ladies of Happy Hollow."

One photo showed a "liner" type "apparatus" to carry the river "around Fort Peck dam." The statement was made that "theoretically" the "relief workers" were building things like diversion tunnels, but they were "actually" building "relief-boomtowns."

There was an impressive aerial view of Wheeler, and a good shot of the downtown with a comment that life in the "cowless cow town" was "lush but not cheap." There were two photos of the same children, one by a sign for "hotspot" New Deal, the other with their mom, siding a statement on women's troubles and "hopeless hope."

Bourke-White featured herself in one shot, tossing down a drink.

One photo in particular offended most of the local readers. It was of a little girl sitting on a bar next to three men and two women, her questioning, almost hostile eyes focused on Bourke-White.

Most local newspapers ignored Life's story. *The Glasgow Courier* editorialized and invited letters to the editor. November 19, an editorial by Sam Gilluly appeared on the front page:

"The photographs made by Miss Margaret Bourke-White, who must have spent even more time than we credited her for in the beer halls and hot spots of the project area, are excellent. They are going to sell a lot of copies ... however ... Miss Bourke-White has 'overplayed' the wild west angle of the project towns. There is but one construction picture of the Fort Peck project while those of taxi dancers, beer parlors, and like scenes are myriad.

"Nobody can tell you or I, who have been in the project area, that things are as bad as Miss Bourke-White makes them out. She has indulged in some very clever exaggeration.... The lady may have done us a left-handed favor. Thousands of folks are going to read the first issue of *Life* ... many will want to see ... any publicity may be good publicity.... We'll also bet a good Montana silver dollar these pictures generate a spirited controversy. We don't believe they tell the whole story, even if they tell a sensational story."

The *Courier* commented on the upcoming *March of Time* radio show on which Bourke-White would appear and relate her project experiences: "Valley County residents may expect to hear almost anything about the Fort Peck dam and the surrounding territory."

Most workers heard about the article but didn't purchase a copy. One said, "I just took it in stride and went on and did my work."

A long letter to the editor was printed in *The Glasgow Courier:* "Many felt ... Miss Bourke-White's visit was rather a search for sensationalism than an honest hunt for unusual activity that will have a lasting place in our national scene.... Miss Bourke-White's shot of the spillway piers ... is indeed a fine picture that most of us will be proud to keep and remember. Inside the cover there is little about Fort

Peck and.... The results of Miss Bourke-White's trip makes engineers pause and wonder. It appears to them that with the incredible ability and facilities afforded, this effort should not have gone so wide of its expected mark.... in general comes a not too satisfactory reaction to the first display of Fort Peck.... *Life* now marches on, we hope to better horizons." Signed Project Resident.

Letter to *Life*: A letter titled "Innocent Little Girl," written by New Deal School Principal Erling Voldal was printed in *Life*, and reprinted on *The Glasgow Courier* front page December 29, 1936.

"... you muffed a golden opportunity to get some real human interest and news pictures of life in the shanty towns surrounding the Fort Peck dam .... on the basis of 15 months residence in the heart of a number of these shanty towns I can assure you ... the general view resulting from the editing of your many photographs is false and grossly exaggerated. Night life does not play nearly that big a part in the life of a vast majority of our inhabitants. All credit for having discovered a unique and newsworthy community, ... we are not adverse to publicity, so let's have the other half of the picture....

"For the sake of the little girl who was so innocently and prominently sat on the bar, *Life's* readers do not have to shed tears of sympathy for her. Her looks belie that she is a neglected child. In fact she is a regularly enrolled pupil in one of our first-grade rooms, is healthy, a bright scholar, and has lost two days of school during three months attendance. It was a jolt to discover that the dignified editors of *Life* would exploit a child in order to make interesting news ...."

Bourke-White later referred to this period of time during which she photographed the Fort Peck story as the "rapturous period" of her career, devoted to "industrial shapes" with people "only incidental."

Later in Life: Over the next ten years, *Life* printed a few photos and stories about the project, including a Tenth Anniversary feature.

Still today, many years after Bourke-White's photo essay (with captions probably enhanced by editors), a mention of the project history draws the question from people who haven't seen the article, "Did you know Fort Peck Dam was in the first copy of *Life*?"

Unfortunately, errors in the article have been picked up and used as facts, they can be found in newspaper features, histories, and articles in respected magazines.

The irony of it all may be that Bourke-White's spillway and other photos have also been picked up, numerous times, most often without giving her credit for her excellent photography.

Fort Peck Press

Largest Circulated Paper On The Dam Site (1934-1937)
Continuing the Hogeland Herald, Turner Big Flat News, Chinook News
Published in Wheeler, Montana. Subscriptions $2 a year in advance.

The Fort Peck Press was established and edited by M.D. Eastly, a newspaper man from Wyoming with forty-five years experience. He moved to Bowdoin and taught school for one-year during the time he published the *Hogeland Herald* from 1930-1934.

In July 1934, he moved his antique Washington Hand Press out to Wheeler and set up an office in half of the Norman Jewelry building. His first issue of the *Fort Peck Press* was published August 2, 1934.

Publisher T.J. Hocking of the *Glasgow Courier* made a "fraternal visit" on press day, and editor Sam Gilluly stopped by soon after. Eastly wrote, "The first of a great army of newspaper men whom we expect to see at Fort Peck before it's finished."

Eastly was a charter member of the Wheeler Commercial Club. He met Corps officials and arranged to carry project progress reports. He recruited boomtown correspondents and gave subscriptions for news.

"Items must be of major importance, word of mouth will do, but we prefer written." He added, "People are sending subscriptions to friends ... let us do likewise."

The Press carried school news written by students and a weekly health column by Dr. C.C. Lull. Patent insides (ready print) provided national news, ads, and cartoons. A Bible verse was printed in every edition. During its first three months the paper carried an impressive amount of project news, information, ads, and social notes.

In October, Eastly was rushed to Glasgow Deaconess Hospital for emergency surgery and an extended stay. Mrs. Eastly came from Bowdoin to run the paper and put it up for sale.

On December 13, 1934, J. B. Thomas was introduced as editor. He and his wife, and their five children had just moved to Glasgow where they started the *Glasgow Daily News* and print shop.

In his first issue Thomas wrote: "As the new editor ... I am desirous of continuing publishing the *Fort Peck Press* at Wheeler ... I am grateful to Mr. Eastly for his kind consideration and cooperation." Thomas announced plans for expansion and new equipment.

A few days before Christmas, after selling ads in the boomtowns, Thomas was driving back to Glasgow when his Model A skidded on ice and slid over an embankment. He was killed in the accident.

A December 27 notice: "Editor John B. Thomas of Glasgow who leased this newspaper on Dec. 13, had legal possession just one week when he was accidentally killed. Mr. Thomas and his family printed the Christmas edition (which was a good one, don't you think?) and now the family turns the paper back to the owner, Mr. Eastly."

The Press grew with the boomtowns. An ad March 14, 1935, read: "For rent. Half of the *Fort Peck Press* printing office building as we have a new and enlarged building moved up from the Government Town giving us more Main Street frontage than present needs...."

Earnest McKeagle, the new *Press* reporter/managing editor, rented the space for his General Real Estate business.

In April the *Press* honored a McCone City "papergirl," and a Wheeler boy who delivered 200 papers every morning before school.

In May the newspaper's new building was moved off its skids and set on a foundation. As the press was lifted into place, it tipped over, spilling its type and forms. News of the accident brought visitors to see what an antique Washington Hand Press looked like.

The Press grew, but with pains. In May, Eastly stated his recently hired editor was no longer *in no-wise connected with the newspaper*.

An ad June 27, 1935, read, "*Fort Peck Press* for sale. The editor and present owner (Eastly), wants to go out of the newspaper business and into the printing of religious tracts. One provision ... you agree to print a Bible verse (a different one) in every newspaper while you own it...in failure, the paper reverts to its present and original owner."

In September, on Friday the 13th, Eastly, in his 70s, took his first airplane ride. He was amazed at the view and said "I prayed a lot."

By 1936, due to Eastly's health, the *Press* was losing steam. The contents had become mostly ads and poor quality ready print.

Competition came with the new *Fort Peck Independent* (Wheeler) in February 1936. Jerry Reinertson, a former *Press* employee was publisher and Harry Sankey editor/manager. The paper resembled the *Press* except the *Independent's* dentist denture ad was missing its teeth. Subscriptions were $1.50 a year or 6 months at 90 cents.

Fire destroyed the Gamble Store, February 20, 1936, in sub-zero cold and damaged the *Fort Peck Press* building next door. The *Independent* reported "Editor M.D. Eastly froze his hands trying to help put out the blaze and remove equipment from his office. He was treated by Dr. Lull in Wheeler and taken to the hospital in Glasgow."

Eastly's injury was doubly painful as he often played the guitar during the Nazarene church services held in the Eastly Apartments.

During February 1936 the *Glasgow Courier* announced Verne T. Hovey of the Culbertson newspaper had leased the *Fort Peck Press.* In the March 5 issue, Hovey, listed as "editor, manager, publisher, proprietor" wrote, "the paper will continue in its endeavor to promote what we believe to be the best interest of Wheeler and the Fort Peck project.... We are now in a position to give our undivided attention to your printing needs ... phone 241-R-5 or write your news."

Hovey added, "M.D. Eastly, former editor and publisher/founder of the *Fort Peck Press,* is slowly recovering from freezing both hands (during the fire) in the attempt of saving his printing equipment."

The *Press* ran local news and ads, a syndicate serial, and national whiskey ads. By late March, ready print, Eastly's Bible verses, local columns, cartoons, and Corps progress reports were gone. And the *Press* was now printing its competitor the *Fort Peck Independent.*

April 1936. The Fort Peck Press goes under new management. Verne T. Hovey ... has terminated his lease.... Harry W. Sankey ... will serve as editor, and Jerry R. Reinertson ... publisher."

The *Independent* was incorporated into the *Press.* The masthead read: *The Fort Peck Press,* a continuation of the *Hogeland Herald, Turner Big Flat News, Chinook News,* and *Fort Peck Independent.*

Theater ads were printed on the front page. A humor column "Project Stroller," was added, and some news and ads returned.

May 28, 1936, Reinertson wrote "The *Press* is always glad to receive your news... however if it isn't printed, don't 'blow up.' You may have forgotten to sign your name, etc. 'Yes' a lady says, 'but my article was omitted ...' Now listen there! Ladies always present problems. Anyway, here's the answer. Very often newspapers get two accounts of important things.... So, the mystery is solved. Give us a pipe, we want a smoke."

By this issue the newspaper had become a shopper with local ads and columns. In June, Reinertson announced he had a second job as a Diesel Institute representative. See him at the *Press* office.

October 15, 1936, the *Fort Peck Press* printed a copy of Ernie Pyle's colorful column about Wheeler.

November 23, Reinertson, Justice of the Peace Frank Breznik, and Wilson townsite owner Walt Wilson appeared in a *Life* magazine photo by Margaret Bourke-White. The "Law Totes A Gun" shot was posed in front of the Moose Market.

In November, Reinertson wrote a lengthy editorial: "The problem of unemployment becomes more acute ... an organization has been formed. All unemployed men are to register at the *Press*...."

His well intentioned plan was to gather the unemployed in a group and through government agencies find employment or relief. He wrote "Being that this organization is built around this newspaper, it is necessary each individual ... have the newspaper ... each individual registering is expected to enter one dollar for a year subscription...."

December: "The Fort Peck Press ... changes. H.J. Hubert is ... manager, James Howell ... handling the printing, Jimmie Wilson ... bookkeeper. Publisher Jerry Reinertson is now working on the local unemployment situation and reports excellent progress...."

On December 10, the *Press* noted an "element of opposition" to the organization. No further note of it or the subscriptions was made.

February 2, 1937, Hubert, Howell, and Wilson became the new co-publishers "proprietors." It was stated Reinertson had moved and was "no longer connected with this paper in any way, shape or form, and he wishes it so stated."

The *Press* was promoted as "The only newspaper published on the FP damsite." Local and national ads replaced local news. Howell and Hubert were listed as publishers. The April 15, 1937, issue was the last full size page edition. Only Hubert was listed as publisher.

April 29, 1937: "In order to better disseminate news, expedite production, ... the short-lived Shoppers Guide is combined with and continued in this tabloid production of the *Fort Peck Press*."

The *Press* continued to run local and national ads, and church notices. A large ad, May 6, listed the remaining Wheeler businesses; "Buy in Wheeler. The metropolis of the Fort Peck Project."

Publisher Hubert ran a "Last word on F.P.P. Publishers."

M.D. Eastly, former *Fort Peck Press* publisher, was seen in Glasgow distributing tracts. V.H. ... has repaired to the Rocky Mountains on account of his health, or something. J.R. is working off his obligations at the *Glasgow Times*. J.W. ... is the new adding machine at the Wheeler Auto Co. J.H. ... left for Butte Sunday to work in the mines. Famous words: 'You can't leave Wheeler without getting drunk.' Other former publishers are living a life of seclusion in parts unknown. H.J. Hubert is 'holding the sack' at the old stand. A paper at least four times a month' is a tentative slogan.

P.S. Come in! We'll put your name in the paper.

May 27, 1937, was the last issue of the Fort Peck Press.

Local and Hi-Line Weekly Newspapers
Subscriptions could be paid with produce and barter

The Glasgow Courier was the only newspaper to provide overall coverage of the Fort Peck project from beginning to end and beyond. It printed the Corps of Engineers' weekly progress reports, news stories, features, maps, photos, editorials about the project, and news columns from the boomtowns and Fort Peck townsite.

Publisher T.J. "Joe" Hocking, a seasoned newspaper man, bought the *Valley County Independent* in Glasgow in 1913 and renamed it *Glasgow Courier*. The paper was well established by the 1930s.

The editor, Sam Gilluly, a 1930 University of Montana journalism graduate, joined the *Courier* in 1932. He was the only editor to cover all the project years. He also wrote news for national news wires; and daily newspapers, especially the *Great Falls Tribune*.

Credit for preserving much of the boomtown and town of Fort Peck history goes to the women correspondents who lived there. They faithfully gathered the news, wrote it in longhand, and delivered it to the newspapers; all for free subscriptions and pennies an inch. Without them, many details of project life and work would have been lost. Woven into their news were bits of history found nowhere else.

Glasgow Messenger, edited by J.C. Hallack, was a continuation of the *Nashua Messenger* moved from Nashua to Glasgow in 1939.

Glasgow Times, owned by Gordon Vallandingham, was sold to M.A. Cromwell, publisher of the *Nashua Independent,* in 1933.

*Glasgow Daily News/*shopper, began in October 1934 by John and Ruth Davis, continued a few years after his death in December.

Merger: After jousting with pens and swatting each other with their newspapers over politics and printing, the *Glasgow Courier* bought the *Glasgow Messenger* and the *Times* in January 1941. The *Courier* continued as Glasgow's official paper, and assumed the *Messenger's* contract as the official Valley County newspaper.

The *Nashua Messenger* started publication in 1927 with Burton Davenport as editor/manager. During the 1930s the newspaper carried Corps reports, and several local interest stories, columns, and ads.

In 1935 the *Messenger* was named "official publication for Valley County." J. Clare Hallack joined the staff. In April 1936 Davenport sold his interests to co-managers J.C. and J.W. Hallack.

The *Nashua Messenger/*printing plant moved to Glasgow in 1939, and became the *Glasgow Messenger*. Along with news, it carried

"Short Shorts" from the *Daniels County Free Press, Scobey; Chinook Opinion; Plentywood Herald; Hinsdale Tribune; Judith Basin County Press, Stanford; Saco Independent; Phillips County News, Malta; Shelby Promoter; and Independent-Observer in Conrad.*

The Nashua Independent, published 1925-1942, by Merle Priest and M.A. Cromwell merged early on with the *Glasgow Times.*

Hi-Line Newspapers Published Thursdays. Subscriptions $2 a year.
Dozens of men with and without newspaper experience started newspapers in railroad siding towns in the late 1800s. Most papers thrived in the homestead era, especially those assigned to print land proofs and legal notices along with their local news and information.

By the 1930s the dry years had driven hundreds of homesteaders away. Small town papers were hurting, merging, or folding. Those that hung on, in varying numbers of inches, included project news.

Hinsdale Tribune, entered as second class matter May 28, 1912, was published by H.F.Tuttle. It carried considerable news about the project, especially in 1933-1934, and stories of the rock quarries in Phillips County. In 1934 Tuttle helped launch the *Nashua Messenger.*

Saco Independent, formerly *Saco Observer,* was edited by Ben E. Luebke until 1936 when W.D. Miller became editor. The paper included the *Cole Independent* community news sheet during the rock quarry days. It later merged with the *Hinsdale Tribune.*

Phillips County News, Malta, originally the *Malta Enterprise* established in 1898, was sold and renamed in 1924. Russell Larcombe took over in 1928. He focused on Malta, with notes on the project.

Harlem News started as *The Milk River Valley News* in 1906. Rumor had it the editor was "run out of town." The *Harlem News* began in 1908. George H. Tout owned and edited the newspaper from 1920 through the project years. It focused mainly on Harlem.

Wolf Point Herald-News, a merger of the early 1900s *Wolf Point Herald* and *Roosevelt County News* owned by Mr. and Mrs. Joe Dolin, printed local news, but carried some project notes.

The McCone County Sentinel published in Circle 1931-1937 by Artley D. Cullum, carried very little project news. News of McCone City was printed in the Fort Peck, Glasgow, and Nashua newspapers.

Newspapers in Helena, Billings, Missoula, Great Falls, Bozeman, Havre, and other cities printed features about the project construction.

Part 6

Women's Work

Hundreds of women worked for the government. Hundreds more owned businesses and held jobs while caring for their families and homes in Fort Peck and the boomtowns.

In hopes of finding desperately needed work in the government offices at the Fort Peck project, a number of northeastern Montana women filled out applications at local reemployment centers. They took typing and shorthand tests then anxiously awaited a letter, phone call, or telegram saying they had a job.

Many of the applicants were recent high school graduates who had taken stenography, bookkeeping, dictation, office procedures, typing, and business classes. A few had attended college or business school.

Some women took Civil Service exams, but according to the 11th United States Civil Service District, Civil Service status would not be required for steno-typist jobs "in connection with the dam" because the jobs were financed by the Public Works Administration (PWA) and carried on as an emergency measure to relieve unemployment. However, Civil Service status was a benefit in promotions and pay.

The first few women on the project payroll were hired in the fall of 1933 to type reports, file papers, and answer telephones in the Corps' temporary office in Glasgow. In late summer 1934 more were hired to work in government offices in the Smith Clinic basement and in other buildings being completed in the town of Fort Peck.

By September most of the offices in the Administration Building were ready. Truck loads of typewriters, mimeograph machines, desks, file cabinets, and other equipment, and furniture were hauled in. The average office was set up with three or four desks, file drawers, and storage shelves for all the necessary onion skin paper and supplies.

Soon dozens of women were at work as receptionists, telephone operators, file clerks, typists, secretaries, stenographers, bookkeepers, and librarians. They held a variety of jobs in the various departments. Among other tasks they investigated accidents for the safety section, did clerical work in the executive and legal offices, cleared property titles for government land acquisitions, and typed the payroll.

Periodically there were temporary jobs in the "steno-pool" and clerical division set up for private contractors. However, most of the contractors hired male bookkeepers who traveled with the crews.

Women worked daytime hours with Sundays off. Overtime was paid or covered with comp time. Wages were based on ability and experience. All stenographers started at $14.40 a week with raises to $16.60 for a senior "steno" position. Experienced workers under Civil Service could earn up to $120 a month.

Most single women sent their paychecks, after the rent and meal deductions, home to their parents. They were aware of the hardships their families faced, and said "that's just what you do."

Many of the younger women were away from home for the first time. They traveled alone to Fort Peck by bus or train from their farms and small towns. In later years some of them told of being "terribly homesick" and having "worried parents" during the time it took them to get acquainted with co-workers and their jobs.

It helped that Valley County women were hired first and some had been classmates. They soon made friends at work, and through dances and activities at the Recreation Hall, and in their churches.

Most of the married women lived with their families in Fort Peck, if homes were available to them, or in the boomtowns. Women from Glasgow and Nashua usually carpooled to work and lived at home.

Most single women lived in the west wing dorm rooms in the Employees Hotel or roomed in one of the two women's dormitories on its south side. The rooms were small and roommates assigned. Some enjoyed the luxury of larger, higher rent hotel rooms where the dining room had tablecloths, and a menu instead of mess hall fare.

Other jobs: Women teachers were employed in the Fort Peck School. Nurses worked in the Fort Peck Hospital or in the Smith Clinic. Others worked as nurses aides, or in the hospital kitchen and housekeeping departments; or as maids in the Employee's Hotel.

A few women worked in the town of Fort Peck as cooks, maids, and baby-sitters for the families of Corps officers. Others found jobs as waitresses at the Green Hut and clerks in the stores. Some jobs were available at the Fort Peck Theatre and Recreation Hall where women arranged events, sold tickets, and ran concessions.

Commissary, mess hall, and barracks food services were bid out to contractors. There were very few jobs for women in them.

Government Laundry: The majority of jobs available to women were in the huge government laundry. The 282x50 feet, steel-frame, insulated building housed eight large washers, three extractors, two mangles, eight shirt machines, sewing machines, sock forms, rows of ironing boards and irons, and mending stations. Laundry came in from the workers, and the collection and delivery services available to residents of the town of Fort Peck and the Employee's Hotel.

Men operated the washers and repaired the large equipment, but it was mostly women who handled the thousands of heavy mesh bags full of dirty work clothes, towels, tablecloths, sheets and pillowcases.

Women worked in pairs ironing sheets and other flat items on the mangles, and individually on the clothes "folders" and "sleevers."

Laundry work was hard, hot, and often dangerous. Women helped each other keep the rigorous pace. They covered for and assisted ill and frail co-workers. They were thankful to have jobs, but said, "it was the kind of work you wouldn't do unless you had to."

Boomtown jobs

Boomtown schools employed a number of women teachers during the project years. Jobs were also available for lady musicians who played the piano and organ in theaters, and performed solo or with bands in bars and clubs. A few women were school music supervisors or band directors; some gave private lessons in music and dance.

Nurses and midwives operated maternity homes or were employed assisting doctors' in their birthing facilities or offices.

Many women owned or managed cafes, restaurants, bake shops, clothing stores, hotels, rooming houses, and small laundries. Others were clerks, cashiers, bakers, cooks, waitresses, dishwashers, and bar maids. Some had part time jobs painting and wallpapering homes.

Several women with small children, ran home based businesses that offered sewing, mending, laundry, and baby-sitting services.

Through their jobs, volunteer work, and home management the project women contributed greatly to the well-being of their towns.

Taxi Dancers

In the 1930s ballrooms hired women, and men, to dance with the instructors or patrons. They were called taxi dancers since they, like taxis, were hired for a short time with no further commitment. The name was also used for women who danced with patrons for a fee.

Dancing was hugely popular throughout the nation, and an every Saturday night event in Montana. People kept on dancing at the dam.

The first government workers at the project were married men and veterans from the farms and small towns of Valley County. Many were relatives and neighbors. Some of their wives, sisters, and friends were the first taxi dancers. With one or more of their husbands as a chaperone, the women met at a club and were happy to earn a dime to dance with the workers, many of whom they knew. In the beginning a few senior high school girls were allowed to work as taxi dancers.

As the area population mushroomed, dancers from everywhere moved in. Some were described as "nice young ladies" or "misguided girls" in need of money. Others were dubbed "party gals" or "rip-tearers." The wives chose not to work with them or to dance with the new workers, tourists, and others in town, so they retired.

Many of the new taxi dancers were trouble. Three North Dakota women followed a 70-year-old man and beat and robbed him of $20. They were arrested and ordered out of town. They were arrested again, for vagrancy. In court they begged poverty, saying they "had been paid five or ten cents a beer until the law said no more taxi dancing." Then the bar owner offered them $1 per night. "We haven't been getting no dollar a night, for three weeks."

A few taxi dancers were underage run-aways. Two men, ages 18 and 21, were each sentenced to two-year prison terms for associating with a 14-year-old. She was sent to the vocational school for girls.

A 16-year-old girl who hitch-hiked from Texas to find work as a taxi dancer was sent to the vocational school in Boulder. She claimed "no living relatives."

Most of the taxi dancers and their partners simply danced for the fun of dancing. It was a way for women to earn money, and a release from a hard day's work and loneliness for the men. Trouble started when alcohol, watered down drinks, and improper conduct entered in.

In January 1935 the Woman's Christian Temperance Union and the Council of Church Women met with Valley County officials to request regulation of beer parlors and dance halls to "eliminate such objectionable features as taxi dancing, nude dancing, and enclosed booths." Scores of complaints had been registered by men and women in the boomtowns and in Glasgow.

Taxi dancing became illegal. A few dancers and bar owners tried to ignored the rule, were arrested and fined. Some bars were shut down. There *was* discussion about the legality, but the order held.

Over time the tales of taxi dancing took on more color with every telling. But had it not been for the five, ten, or fifteen cents women earned, when there were no other jobs, dancers may have been few.

Most taxi dancers were not prostitutes.
Most prostitutes were not taxi dancers.

Prostitution

She's more to be pitied than censured ... more to be helped than despised.... On life's stormy path, ill-advised.... (Song by William Gray)

Prostitution was not legal in Montana in the 1930s, but it existed, and was, in parts of the state, tolerated or simply ignored. Prostitutes and camp followers from around the country moved into the project.

There were few, if any, "painted ladies," and no fancy movie style "parlors," but there were several small "houses" with madams and "girls." Some women worked alone, entertaining men in their homes or cars or wherever accommodations were available.

Not all the women made money. A restaurant/bar owner said she gave many women jobs washing dishes so they could survive.

Prostitution was not always a trade of choice. With no job skills and no jobs, some women earned money however they could. Others were forced into it by a leeching, unemployed male.

In 1935 a man ran ads in Montana newspapers: "Good ambitious girls, popular and willing to make $5-20 a day for a few minutes spare time. Must be well acquainted and ambitious. Work easy."

County Attorney Thomas Dignan stated, "We intend to stop the transportation of women here as taxi dancers or for similar purposes."

In 1939 seven young women testified in Wheeler justice court against a Midwest man who ran ads to hire beer parlor waitresses for $20 a week. He drove them to Wheeler then demanded $5 for the ride and $4 job finder's fee. He offered "easy payment terms." His bail was set at $5,000 for "procuring women for immoral purposes."

Many of the prostitutes had health issues. It was known "the girls" could receive check-ups at the Fort Peck Hospital, but most had no medical care at all. The venereal and other diseases they suffered and passed on, their pregnancies, back-street abortions, alcohol and drug problems, beatings, suicides, and deaths were often unreported or considered the fate of a common prostitute. What compassion there was for them often came from women outside the lifestyle.

Happy Hollow

Over the hill in a treeless coulee north of Wheeler sat the infamous Happy Hollow, dubbed the "center of prostitution." Photos from its heyday show about a half-dozen shacks with suggestive and mostly unprintable names, and a dirt trail with entrances and exits.

The Hollow's bad reputation was sensationalized by writers, and, like other places, it had its day, but embellished hearsay abounds.

91

In a 1936 *Associated Press* year-end story, *Glasgow Courier* editor Sam Gilluly, wrote: "Happy Hollow, where a few shacks and larger buildings house the girls.... Buy a drink and listen to the tinny accompaniment of a mechanical piano."

Some locals and tourists drove the dusty trail to Happy Hollow to gawk, giggle, or visit. Some adolescent boys found it daring to pedal past on their bicycles.

Hollow news rarely appeared, but one story made headlines. In 1936 a Miss. H.M., who had told police she operated "the house of prostitution at Happy Hollow," was the driver in a high speed wreck that killed a female passenger. She was charged with manslaughter.

She swore in court she had not been drinking, although the doctors who treated the three female accident victims testified otherwise.

H.M. testified she and her friends had a *sealed* bottle of whiskey. The surviving passenger, a "maid at Happy Hollow," said she opened the bottle, poured whiskey down the throats of H.M. and the dead girl, spilling it on all of them. A Havre jury found H.M. "not guilty."

Wheel-er-Inn, Ruby Smith Prop.
When looking for real romance, And the snappiest place to dance,
Come to Wheel-er-Inn and see, How Jolly and Happy you can be.

Ruby Smith (alias for Mrs. L.H.S. of Miles City, Montana, and the Klondike), and a partner opened the Riverside Inn three miles south of Glasgow in the spring of 1934. It was the first resort built in that area. Smith sold the Inn shortly after it opened. It changed hands several times and closed in 1936 after the owner lost his license. The building was destroyed by fire in September 1937.

Smith, and Gus Knutsen "of Dawson City-Yukon Territory fame," built the Wheel-er-Inn, most often called Ruby's Place, in 1934. The hyphens in the name were dropped and it became the Wheeler Inn.

Ruby and the Inn gained instant celebrity after her photo appeared in *Life* magazine in 1936. People from all over came by or wrote to ask for her autograph, photograph, souvenirs, and money. After Ruby was arrested and fined for gambling in 1935, and taken to court for writing a bad check in 1937, she said her "rich lady" image was false.

In January 1937 the Wheeler Inn was divided into three parts and moved to Wheeler's North Main Street. It closed early in 1940. The building was razed and the lumber hauled to a ranch near Wiota.

Many stories, true and false, were told about gambling, alcohol, fights, and more at Ruby's. But rarely told were the stories of her generosity shown to people who never asked, and least expected it.

Part 7

The Boomtowns
(Mushroom towns)

Like weeds and wildflowers they sprang up and lived their short lives near the construction sites of the biggest earth dam in the world.

They had no roots and they had no future. Within their limits lived thousands of men, women, and children who called them "home."

The boomtowns were unlike any other towns. They were not one of the many 1930s "Hoovervilles" or one of the Montana "cowtowns" to which they have been compared.

Most Hoovervilles grew up outside of large cities, without plans or organization. Homes were rude shelters pieced together from scraps. Residents came from all over; once proud, self-reliant people, now jobless and homeless, searching for any kind of work they could find.

In comparison, most boomtowns were built on privately owned farms. Their housing was humble but adequate. Each one had some form of government. Most of the residents had been hired through a reemployment office and went to work at the project on arrival. The majority were northeastern and other Montanans, many from large extended families who all lived in the towns and worked at the dam.

The cowtowns that catered to cowboys and early ranchers were few by the 1930s. They had been tamed and were outnumbered by homesteader towns with a family flavor. Boomtowns resembled them.

The boomtown residents were mainly government laborers, small business owners, contractor employees, and their families. They were first or second generation homesteaders, dryland farmers, ranchers, and residents of small towns. They were a mixture of native and transplanted Montanans with a variety of backgrounds, skills, crafts, interests, and educations. Some were immigrants, or the children of immigrants, from several European countries. Many of them had first settled in the Midwest. They were the ones who hung on after others lost hope that Montana could provide a living and left.

They believed in right and wrong, self reliance, and in family and community. Most had a strong work ethic and sense of responsibility.

They fixed what was broken, mended what was torn, darned their own socks, half-soled their own shoes, and played their own dance music. For most of them it was a disgrace to be "on the dole" or to accept charity. They were thankful for jobs and did them well, as was often noted by the Corps of Engineers in their reports and promotions.

They were the boomtown majority.

The First Boomtown–Fort Peck Down By The Dam

There were no houses when the first government workers arrived.

"Workers are allowed to build temporary shacks this winter near the dam, several ... constructed." *Glasgow Courier 11/10/1933.*

"Permission to construct a lodging house near the dam site granted to William Miller, Glasgow.... Permission also granted to workmen on the dam to build temporary shacks." *Hinsdale Tribune, 11/16/1933*

Alvord's Grocery

During November 1933-34 the first workers slept in their vehicles or in tents while they built or brought in shacks. Their homes lined the east side of the graded road south of the boatyard toward the future dam. Within a few months several wives had arrived to join their husbands.

A dozen small frame stores were built or hauled in. The first store built was a branch of F.D. Alvord's Grocery in Glasgow. It opened February 1, 1934; followed by the Dam Barber Shop, "haircuts and shower baths 24-hours a day"; the Fort Peck Coffee House, "lunches, candies, fruit, ice-cream, and soft drinks"; the Hi-Way Bar; Friedl's Men's Clothing; the Eat Shop; Kearney Confectionery/General Store; a movie house with "the talkies"; Northwest Service Store; Polly's Pie Shop, "excellent lunches with a friendly smile for working men and campers"; Reide's Restaurant; Scherrer Confectionery, "plus notions, patent medicines"; Joe's Cafe; and a hardware store with work gloves, tools, and other supplies.

During the town's ten months of life, construction sites grew up around it and the project workforce jumped to 6,000. As planned, the Corps reclaimed the site in July 1934. In a "mass exodus," homes and stores were loaded on trucks and hauled up the road to boomtowns springing up north and west of the dam site.

That *first* boomtown had many residents, but its peak population is unknown. And, if it ever had a given name, it was never officially recorded. The town was referred to as "Fort Peck," "Shantytown," or the "town down by the dam." It was a welcome home for grateful workers during a winter of many hardships.

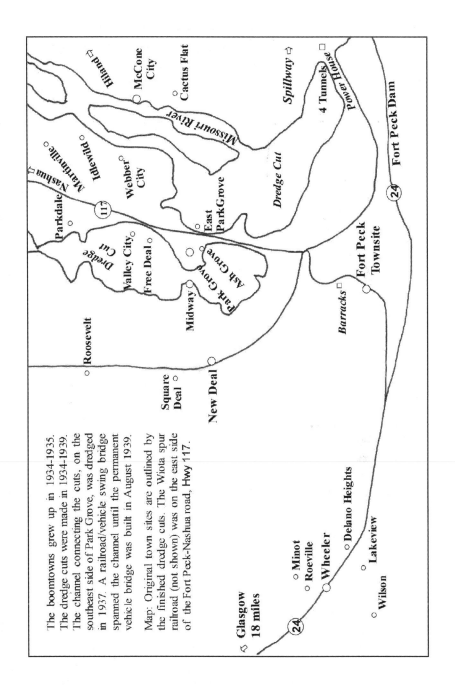

Before the First Boomtown had been cleared away in July 1934,
to make room for construction, eighteen more were in the making.

Early New Deal   Courtesy Army Corps of Engineers

Wheeler   Donated to Fort Peck Interpretive Center by Heidi Olson

Park Grove   Donated to Fort Peck Interpretive Center by Mary Moylan

Ash Grove

"A home-baking shop opened in Ash Grove." *8/16/1934 Fort Peck Press.* Ash Grove was located on the southeast corner of Sam Nissen's homestead, a mile northwest of the dam site. A filling station opened along the Nashua road in early 1934. In August the *Press* reported visitors arriving in Ash Grove. By 1935 the budding community had been swallowed up by Park Grove and its name forgotten.

Cactus Hill/Cactus Flat

Cactus Hill. Few people there. Valley County Census May 1935.
Cactus Hill, also called Cactus Flat, sat on a scrap of government land southeast of McCone City alongside the railroad spur to the spillway. Rumors were the *"few"* living there were women of ill repute. Albeit, the settlement was respectable enough for inclusion in the census. It soon became spillway construction site access.

Delano Heights

Delano Heights swelled with pride the day President Franklin Delano Roosevelt's motorcade drove into town in August 1934.

"Delano" was platted one-half mile southeast of Wheeler in the winter 1933-34 by H.O. Morgan. It was among the first boomtowns named in honor of the president and his New Deal.

A grocery store, and an apartment house "with nice warm rooms," opened in February. By the end of April there was a second apartment house, two service stations, a drug store, two more grocery stores, a clothing store, filling station, tourist camp with ten cabins and a light plant, a grease pit/wash rack, steam laundry, vegetable stand, and three cafes offering "all the coffee you can drink with meals."

Work began on a camp ground. Many houses were moved in and several "attractive cottages" were built behind Bill's Service Station.

Although often referred to as a suburb of Wheeler, Delano Heights flourished through 1936 as a town in its own right. It faded away in the late 1930s. The rolling hills site returned to prairie grass.

Free Deal and Valley City

A new townsite, Free Deal ... free residence lots for two years ... business and residences 50x150 ... a half mile north of Park Grove. Fort Peck Press 12/27/1934.

Free Deal grew up on government land destined to be a dredge cut. Conveniences were few, but struggling workers found the rent was right and the location was within walking distance of their jobs.

In April 1935 the *Press* reported: "Free Deal is growing rapidly. Brownie Gallimore just finished his new restaurant. The theater is being moved from Midway."

A half dozen more stores opened, including G.N. Hardware "also stocking men's clothes"; a meat market; oil station; and pool hall. Most grocery stores were shared with Valley City, its east-side twin.

In early 1936 Free Deal residents moved out and the dredges moved in. Most homes and stores were trucked over to Valley City.

Hiland

C. Nelson the cabin builder from Nashua has platted the new town of Hiland and has some buildings up on the main road four miles from the (Missouri River) bridge, 1/2 mile west of Wunderlich's camp on the spillway. Residence lots ... $2 a month, business lots $5-10 ... a general store is assured, also a filling station, hotel, cafe, garage, drug and hardware store. Fort Peck Press 3/18/1935.

Hiland was located "high and dry" on the McCone County ranch of Sam and Lena Ellsworth, a few miles northeast of McCone City near the north end of the spillway. The Ellsworths lived in Glasgow. "Candy Sam" owned a confectionery and Lena was a dressmaker.

Hiland's residents were spillway workers and their families. It was a busy town for more than three years. When the spillway was completed and the workers left in December 1938, Hiland went too.

Idlewild

Idlewild is a rather new settlement near the river. There are about 15 residents .... It is situated among the trees and has a very 'camp like' appearance. Due to the pleasant surrounding there is a good chance for growth. Fort Peck Press 4/14/1935.

The little settlement was started late in 1934 on government land along the west bank of the Missouri River, a stone's throw north of Webber City and the government boatyard. The population grew by one when a baby was born there November 22, 1934.

Idlewild was abandoned early in 1936 to make way for the dredges. The name lives on in a housing development, Idlewild Park, located near the original boomtown site.

Lakeview

Newbury and Baracher, from Poplar, have platted the new townsite of Lakeview ... the back end of their lots will front on the lake when it is filled. They already have over a dozen buildings built. Fort Peck Press 8/23/1934.

Lakeview sprang up about a mile southeast of Wheeler and rapidly spread over the prairie and hills. W.E. Wilson, owner of the Lakeview Filling Station and Wilson townsite, owned most of the land.

When the first families arrived in August 1934, streets were still being graded, and a Billings firm was completing a $1,000, 110 volt electric light plant. More than twenty-five businesses opened during 1934 and 1935. Among them was the Lakeview Cafe owned by the Bilden Brothers of Malta. It was noted they were the first big firm to pay cash for advertising in the new *Fort Peck Press* in Wheeler.

At its peak, Lakeview had a confectionery, three restaurants, a lunch counter, soft drink parlor, two grocery stores, a meat market, large general store, garage, two service stations, two taverns (one with a new 20x40-foot dance floor), pool hall, barber shop, beauty parlor, chiropractic office, a house moving business, construction company, the Lakeview Dairy milk wagon, and more.

"Lakeview ... clean, healthy location, fine view of the project and countryside, hospitable folks." *Fort Peck Press 6/27/1935.*

No census recorded Lakeview's peak population. A 1938-39 WPA Survey, taken when the town was in great decline, counted 75 residents (probably a fourth or less of what it was in 1936). A few families stayed in the Lakeview area into the 1940s.

Martinville

Martinville is located on the Robert Rawe farm, three miles north of the dam site on the Nashua road. Although this little town has been recently named, it has been here for several months and boasts about 20 residents.... Our town is well laid out with lots for more cabins. So please come see our town. Fort Peck Press ad(s) fall 1934.

The farm was originally homesteaded by Amelia Rawe (Rowe), a Russian immigrant widow with six children. She moved to Nashua from North Dakota in 1917 and homesteaded 156 acres on the river bottom. She married William Martin, a Harlem rancher, and patented her homestead in 1923 as Amelia Martin.

"William Martin has started a dairy and truck garden on his wife's homestead.... He calls his town Martinville ... Mr. Martin has coal, milk and 'spuds' grown on his farm in Harlem to sell, and he makes deliveries to the townsites every ten days. Martinville has plenty of the finest water in the world, and shade. He will rent you a lot at regular prices for business or residence." *Fort Peck Press 8/30/1934.*

Most Martinville residents had farm backgrounds. They brought their homes with them. One family added extra space on their 8x10 feet house to hold sixteen batteries which would provided electricity for a washing machine and electric lights, luxuries few people had.

The struggling young families remembered living like "one big family," thanks to "Grandma Martin," and boasted, "We may be small but we have great musicians and singers."

A school opened with eleven students in September 1934. By 1935 Martinville had a post office, grocery, general store, and gas station.

"Welcome to Martinville, 1/4-mile from the Nashua highway. Sixteen families now here, more coming. Terms on house moving.... River front, three miles from the dam, residence lots and garden spot to lease, plenty of good water and shade. No floods. Far enough apart so if one house burns it won't burn them all: $2.50 a month. Garden plowed free." *Fort Peck Press ad(s) 1935.*

Martinville grew through 1936. By 1940, the homestead, with its river front property reshaped by the dredges, had returned to farming.

Midway

Midway and Parkdale have lots to lease. Good location, good water, shade trees. Business lots 150x150 ... homes 50x117. See Mr. & Mrs. V.G. Archambeault. Fort Peck Press ads 1934/1935.

Midway was platted in the spring of 1934 by Victor and Mable Archambeault. It was located between New Deal and Park Grove on the 160-acre homestead of Mable's grandfather Louis Hoffman, and passed on to Mable's mother Mary Ann (Hoffman) Johnson. While planning Midway, the Archambeaults were also platting Parkdale on their land farther north. Their ads promoted both townsites.

Archambeault originally homesteaded near Willow Creek in 1914, in "sagebrush and cactus." He worked for other ranchers including his wife's parents. Collectively the family amassed hundreds of acres, much of it in what was to become the project area.

Midway was conveniently located between New Deal and Park Grove, the three "towns on the flats." It soon filled with families who set up homes in the townsite and in the shade trees on the north side.

The first business was Phelps Grocery, moved up from the "boomtown down by the dam" in July 1934. Storm's Meat Market ran a "market on wheels" while building their store. The Watterud Sisters

Boarding House and Cafe was built in Midway and moved to Park Grove in September.

The Midway Mercantile, built by a Lustre man, was purchased by Mark and Millie Kotkin from England, in late 1934. They owned the M&M, a moving company, and other businesses. Kids remembered them for the candy they gave away. Parents remembered the Kotkins extended credit during the hardest of times, and that they took in pets that had to be left behind when families moved away.

By December, Midway had more than 20 businesses, including a cafe, two restaurants, two grocery stores, four general stores, a candy and cosmetics store, a confectionery, hardware store, two gas stations, a dance hall, a bar, and a theater which later moved to Square Deal. The Midway coal/wood/ice company delivered in all the towns.

A maternity home opened to welcome new residents. The Gospel Tabernacle, built in August 1934, doubled as a schoolhouse. In 1935 a few homes had to move out of the dredge's path, but families were staying as long as possible. Many of them dug cellars and added porches on their homes.

In July 1935 several homes were damaged in two windstorms and a flood. Most homeowners rebuilt. Some moved up to higher ground, while families from other flooded towns moved to Midway.

In August the dusty trail connecting New Deal, Midway, and Park Grove to the Nashua highway was graded. Spring of 1936 found families planting gardens. Some businesses changed hands and new ones opened. A parsonage was moved near the Tabernacle.

Over at the Midway gas station Art Brown's pet monkey "furnished considerable amusement for grown-ups and kids."

Windstorms full of gritty dust from the busy road connecting the towns, plagued Midway. A storm in June destroyed several small buildings and filled homes with a thick layer of dust and dirt.

"Many new families have located in Midway." Midway news *Glasgow Courier, 9/2/1936*. Families came, knowing the dredges were already digging into the sides of the townsite.

More than half the residents and businesses left in the fall of 1937. But the ice company continued deliveries to project towns, and the Roundup Cafe reopened for tourists in 1938.

In June 1938 several of the remaining homes were destroyed in a flood. Eighteen more were hauled away to make room for the dredges. More families moved after the slide at the dam in September. The few homes left in Midway were cut off from Park Grove by the west side dredge cut. Most of the site was covered by water.

Minot – Country Club Estates

Free rental on residence lots in Country Club addition to Wheeler until April. Helmer Roe, Glasgow. Fort Peck Press 11/22/1934.

Country Club Estates, a half mile north of Wheeler, was named and settled in 1934. A notice in the *Fort Peck Press 5/30/1935*, stated, "The Country Club Estates has changed their name to Minot. There will be signs out designating the new town."

"Let us haul your cinders and gravel. Clean up your premises for the 4th of July.... See me at the Phillips 66 station in Minot (Country Club) Roy LaBar. *Fort Peck Press 7/1935.*

The town's few businesses included an auto wrecking company, a Cash Store, and a bar that was sold in 1935. Wheeler grew out to meet Minot, and Minot soon became another pea in the Wheeler pod.

New Deal
(almost Paradise Valley)

New Deal ... started April 16, 1934. Residences and business places at a rate of four each day ever since. Population more than 500 and growing ... has about 125 residences and tents ...and more than 180 lots leased. Fort Peck Press 6/1/1934.

New Deal was settled near the mouth of Galpin Coulee, two miles northwest of the dam site, on the Charles and Arabelle Whisennand farm. At its peak during 1936, New Deal had fifty businesses and approximately 3,000 residents. It was one of the first "mushroom" towns, believed to be the third largest, and was one of the best known.

Whisennand had not planned, nor did he want, a town on his farm and sheep ranch. When workers asked permission to build houses there in early 1934, he said no; but his family convinced him a town was a good idea. With the help of a Glasgow realtor he platted several lots 200x100-feet, and hired Rudolph Ewy, later a Glasgow jailer, to work for five years as his business agent.

The Whisennands and their four small children had moved to Montana from Oklahoma in 1920 in their Model T touring car. They bought a homestead west of Old Fort Peck and lived there until 1927 when they sold it for $150 and a bay mare and left for Canada with a team and wagon. Five miles into their trip they were stranded by rain at the deserted Eva Stump house near Galpin Coulee. Charles left his family there and went to buy food. He came back owning the farm.

Due to the drought, the buyer of the Fort Peck farm had to turn it back to the Whisennands. They later sold it to the government at $10 an acre. It lies beneath the Fort Peck reservoir.

By 1934 project workers were renting $2 lots before Charles and his sons could finish clearing thistles. They set up tents and shacks. Many of the men were boatyard carpenters who built their own homes and helped their neighbors build theirs.

Whisennand built a filling station for his sons to operate. Soon there were grocery stores, two restaurants, a drug store, bakery, two newsstand/confectioneries, a dress shop, a general store with men's work clothes, laundry, hardware store, garage, barber shop, moving picture theater, a boarding house, junk yard, and a pool hall built from an old barn near Avondale. Residents held a dance in the butcher shop to celebrate its grand opening.

Townsite management regulated the number of businesses in New Deal to prevent over-building. Whisennand would not allow a bar in his town, but enterprising others built bars as close as possible.

New Deal had an excellent artesian well with platforms around it. Water from a second well was pumped through town. Drinking and laundry water were also sold from a water truck.

Charles and his son Herman were among the first workers hired at the project. After a year Charles left to run the town. It had rapidly grown into a neighborly community with an active business district, several organizations, a VFW Post, and churches.

Monthly meetings were held by residents, business owners, and town management. Some voted to name the town "Paradise Valley," but the Whisennands preferred "New Deal" as a tribute to the New Deal offered by the president. It was the first boomtown so-named.

In June 1934 a newspaper correspondent wrote, "New Deal ... administration cooperative and folks like it. Folks ... are running their own town. Those who don't bend to the rules are asked to move."

But the town's rapid growth, plus thousands of tourists passing through, made enforcing the rules difficult. Whisennand had to ask the county for a part time deputy in New Deal.

In August 1934 a light plant was installed. Wires were strung to the many new businesses. The roads in the back streets of New Deal were graded and many improvements made. An airport was staked out near the town. It was operated by a flying service offering flying lessons and flights over the project for tourists and news media.

In October, New Deal was spotlighted on KGCX Radio in Wolf Point and photographed for the Glasgow newspaper. In six months it had shot up to 2,000 population and was still growing.

"A beautiful view of the lights at the government townsite may be had by climbing the hill north of New Deal." *Press* correspondent.

The Whisennands built a home on the hill west of town. They opened a post office in 1935. Businesses grew. The town outgrew the farm and spread onto adjoining land in the Archambeault Addition.

In July 1935 New Deal was heavily damaged by two windstorms, and a cloudburst that sent a five to six foot wall of water down Galpin Coulee, through town and over the flats. Corps officials and workers from the Federal Emergency Relief Administration (FERA) rushed in. Residents had already arranged for typhoid vaccinations and were cleaning up the area with disinfectants paid for by businesses.

Some sensationalized national newspaper accounts of the storms stated: "New Deal has been wiped from the face of the map." Not so.

New Deal continued to grow. In 1936 residents dug basements, remodeled their homes, and planted gardens. Businesses redecorated and painted their exteriors, ready for the influx of summer workers.

By 1937 many phases of the project had been completed. Families were leaving the towns. The dredges were moving through the flats, and the New Deal to Park Grove road would soon be under water.

In June 1938 a cloudburst sent a "huge volume" of water rushing down Galpin Coulee, over the Archambeault dam, and through New Deal. The flood was worse than the one in 1935. Residents again ran for the hills. Later, after seeing their homes, several moved away.

More residents moved after the slide at the dam September 22, 1938. Fearing the dam *could* break, they ran up on the hills. Most returned home until their jobs were done, but some left that day and never came back. New Deal's population was 600 at the end of 1938.

The project ended in 1940. Most New Deal residents had moved. William "Bill" Whisennand, son of Charles and Arabelle, said a few people left their homes, "They felt they got their good out of them."

Some houses were moved to Saco, Hinsdale, and other towns. The school was moved and used as a home. In 1951, Bill and his wife Wanda remodeled the post office and moved it onto their farm for a church. In 1999 they bought the hillside house the Whisennand family built in 1934 and lived in it at its new location in Glasgow.

By 1950 New Deal's population was only three. A few weathered boards, rusted auto bodies, and cellar holes marked the spot of the once thriving boomtown that served so many so well.

Parkdale (Park Dale)

Parkdale ... lots for lease, good water, shade trees, 50x117 foot lots along oiled highway. See Mr. & Mrs. V.G. Archambeault. Fort Peck Press ads 1934/1935.

Parkdale was located a mile and a half north of Park Grove on the west side of the Fort Peck to Nashua highway. It was settled on the homestead of Mary Ann Johnson, mother of Mabel Archambeault. Mrs. Johnson homesteaded the 160 acres, patented in 1913. Her log house and barn were still there. The family platted lots early in 1934 while surveying home and business lots in their town of Midway.

The first business, Parkdale Grocery and Meats, opened in August 1934 selling groceries, men's clothing, shoes, hardware, and notions. The General Store, Battleson's Grocery, Tessman's Dress Shop, and several other businesses opened soon after. Parkdale grew into an active community with civic clubs, churches, and a school for thirty children. News of the town appeared weekly in local newspapers.

Parkdale's population grew through July 1936, then dwindled as residents and businesses moved to larger towns. By April 1938, the town was reclaiming its roots. The local columnist wrote "Quite a number of sheep wandered into Parkdale last week after the storm."

Families enjoyed their friendly little town near the worksites and river. Friends and neighbors gathered for their last annual community get-together in June 1938. By 1939 about all that remained was the old log house and barn, some cellar holes, car bodies, and boards.

Park Grove (Camp) and East Park Grove

Park Grove boasts of its little village of about 350 families. It already has 14 business houses with lots already leased for 5 new buildings. Fort Peck Press 9/27/1934.

Park Grove was settled on the Missouri River Valley homestead of Soren Nissen early in 1934. It was a short mile north and a little west of the boatyard on a tree covered flat west of the Fort Peck-Nashua road. It was named by residents who "parked" near a "grove" of trees.

The town's owner, known as "Sam" or "Rambling Sam," was born in Denmark in 1864. He grew up there and served eight years in the Navy before homesteading in Valley County in 1907. He operated the first ferry across the Milk River while he farmed and bought more land. In 1933 Sam learned the Fort Peck dam would be built just south of his properties; he sold some of the land to the government and began platting a town on his homestead.

Park Grove experienced phenomenal growth in 1934. With the help of his brother's family, Sam turned his "Sam's Corner" on the southeast side of town into a main street with a filling station and grocery store. By August a second grocery, a meat market, sandwich stand, confectionery, cafe, shoe shop, jewelry store, barber shop, oil station, garage, and repair shop had opened. Other new businesses included a roller skating rink, theater, and a house moving service.

In November, Dr. and Mrs. N.A. Currie moved their office from Nashua into the Park Grove Drug building. A dentist, Dr. E.V. Bethel, saw his patients there on weekdays. Park Grove had several active organizations, churches, and a school by the fall of 1934.

By January 1935 heavy traffic problems on the old Fort Peck to Nashua road, and in the town, prompted Nissen to ask Valley County commissioners for a special deputy and a speed limit in Park Grove.

Telephones were available, for residents who could afford them, in April 1935. A public pay phone was installed in Park Grove Drug. The May census showed a growing population of 400 workers and their families, "including seventeen families named Peterson."

In June the Highway Department announced construction would begin on the highway from the dam to Nashua. Most buildings at Sam's Corner had to be moved to make way.

One of the buildings was the homestead log house Sam had built and called home for some thirty years. It sat squarely in the middle of the planned highway. Sam adamantly refused to move it. The highway workers routed traffic around the cabin for a time, then gave Sam the option of moving it or having the road run right through it.

Photo courtesy of Sam's niece Doris (Moon) Reichelt

Sam Nissen's old log cabin was torn down Monday to make room for the highway.
Glasgow Courier 6/20/1935.

(Sam bought a Midway store and moved it to Park Grove for his home)

The wider, graveled road from Park Grove through Midway over to New Deal opened in August, linking the three towns on the flats.

Park Grove merchants and management formed a Commercial Club in June 1935 to discuss fire and police protection, and town policy. They wanted Park Grove to be a "clean and thriving city."

The town attracted residents of all kinds. In the spring the local columnist noted that a bird couple had moved in, and following the trend in make-do housing, set up nestkeeping in a clothespin bag.

The fierce windstorm on July 7, 1935, destroyed eight homes and injured several Park Grove residents. The next night Galpin Coulee flooded and damaged several more homes. Residents cleaned up the mess and rebuilt their houses and stores.

By October 24, 1935, the ten-mile Nashua highway had been graded and graveled, and the finishing touches put on the last half-mile stretch south connecting Park Grove and Fort Peck townsite.

Park Grove residents wired their homes and stores, anticipating electricity by the winter of 1935. But a fire in November destroyed the dynamo and storage building. Nissen searched for "an AC 2,300, or larger, lighting plant" and an operator. But with the exception of a few people with private plants, residents were without electricity.

Project layoffs the winter of 1935-36 created major hardships for the unemployed. In January, Nissen opened an office in his home to register families needing assistance until the men were back at work.

From 1934 through 1936 Park Grove grew to nearly 3,000 population. It had more than fifty businesses, several of them built on the east side of town along the Nashua highway where they attracted thousands of workers and visitors.

County crews improved the Park Grove-Midway-New Deal road the summer of 1936. Businessmen paid to have crude oil spread on the streets. Delegations from the "towns on the flats" asked Valley County commissioners to do something about the choking, blinding dust from the increased traffic, and for oil on the Nashua road.

Park Grove maintained its population for a time after the project's peak employment in July 1936. New residents moved in when the dredges dug up their towns. But now the dredges were moving in on three sides of Park Grove. The residents moved away as dredges continued turning the flats into lake-like cuts and Park Grove into a peninsula in 1937-38. A WPA census showed 1,200 population.

After the dredging was done in August 1939 the vehicle and train swing bridge on the south side of Park Grove was replaced with a permanent bridge for vehicles. In 1940 the GN Railroad dug up the Wiota Spur rails. By 1941-42 nearly all of the families, except those who stayed to make Park Grove their permanent home, were gone.

Sam, in his late 70s, converted his grocery store, once robbed by gypsies, into a home. Nearly blind, he purchased a driver's license for his niece and had her drive him around to collect late rent.

Sam's second home became the Park Grove Bar and Grill. Today the Grill and a few newer businesses along the highway cater to local residents and a growing number of fishermen and tourists.

Park Grove is the only boomtown to survive. It has about seventy-five residents who enjoy their river view, tree filled peninsula, and the picturesque dredge cuts to the south, west, and north.

East Park Grove

East Park Grove was settled in 1934 east of Sam's Corner, north of the boatyard. Small houses and stores moved onto the west bank of the Missouri River near where Fort Galpin was built in 1862.

At the peak of its short life East Park Grove had more than twenty homes, Battelson's Grocery, and a half dozen more stores During the summer of 1936 a power line was strung to the town for lights.

Noise from the boatyard and dam echoed night and day, blended with the hum of traffic on the Nashua road and the rumble of trains on the Wiota Spur. But, workers appreciated their short commute to work and a view of non-stop activity at the dam site and on the river.

Buildings were moved before the swing bridge was built across the channel in August 1937. The dredges pared the river bank to within a few blocks of the highway. The town site became dam fill.

Roeville

We are selling residence lots in Roeville, where it is high and dry. We also allow $3 toward moving expenses for each house and will either rent or sell lots outright. Price of residence lots $15, or $1.50 month rent. Business lots $2.50 a month, not for sale. See Roy L. Fisk at The Cash Grocery at Roeville, 1/4 mile north of Wheeler. Fort Peck Press ad 3/19/1936.

Roeville was growing fast by the spring of 1935. July winds wiped out most of its few stores and homes. In October the largest building, a grocery store, was purchased by the Pentecostal Church and moved to Wheeler. An advertising campaign to revive Roeville ran in 1936, but with limited, short-term success.

Roosevelt

Bacon & Hendrickson are the promoters of the new townsite of Roosevelt, 3 miles from the dam on the old Glasgow Highway. They will rent 1/4 acre lots at $1 per month for residence lots, and business lots will be given free of rent. Fort Peck Press 8/23/1934.

"4 wheel trailer and trailer house, ask at Roosevelt Filling Station" *Fort Peck Press ad 8/16/1934.*

Roosevelt was settled in 1934. Whether it was named in honor of President Roosevelt or the four Roosevelts who homesteaded there, is unknown. Land was patented to George (1913), James and Theodore (1914), and Charles (1915). Little is known about the town. There was mention of a man moving to Roosevelt in October 1934; and a news item in the *Fort Peck Press,* "F.O. Bacon of Roosevelt townsite was a Wheeler visitor. His town is growing by leaps and bounds."

A *Press* note in January 1935 said F.O. Bacon stopped with news his town had been snowbound for a couple weeks, residents were glad to get out. Within a year there was no further mention of Roosevelt.

Square Deal

Square Deal is one mile north of New Deal on the old Glasgow-Fort Peck road three miles from the dam. Many new shacks and tents are appearing. Glasgow Courier, Square Deal column 6/1934.

Square Deal was settled on the hilltop above and north of New Deal, far enough from the project noise for the residents to hear the meadowlarks sing. It was named in honor of President Roosevelt's New Deal in hopes of a *square deal* for everyone in tough times.

The town was started by project workers and their families in the summer of 1934. Residents lived in tents while building their tar paper shacks and stores. Many of the families were relatives and friends.

About a dozen business places opened in August 1934. The first was Thorkelson's store whose ads read "shop on the old Glasgow-Fort Peck road 3 miles from the dam."

Square Deal Grocery was opened by the Stevenson family. The Tunnison's Cafe, operated by Mrs. Rocksey, featured a counter and a few tables. A filling station, garage, grocery, and hardware store came to town. Other businesses included the Square Deal Boarding House, a milk delivery service, and a second filling station.

Four bars opened in the area: Dutch's Tavern, The Fort Peck Club, Square Deal Bar, and Tork's Beer Parlor. In March 1935 the Square Deal Bar moved to Wheeler and Tork's to Park Grove.

According to the local columnist; "Square Deal can boast of five good wells.... Snappy times are being had ... due to the free dances given by the local beer parlors. Good music and fine times for all."

By September 1934 the town was booming. A census counted 42 school-aged children of non-government workers in need of a school. Arrangements were made for them to attend other boomtown schools until a building could be found and a teacher hired.

Church services were held in homes or outdoors. Summer Revivals with Rev. Nels Norby were held in a tent with tree stump seats.

A small cyclone blew through Square Deal in September 1934. Tents were torn down and small homes damaged. Families rebuilt.

Several businesses were sold or closed in the fall of 1936 after the peak employment at the project. Square Deal's population was not officially recorded until a WPA Census in 1938 counted 175, two years after the peak population. There were still enough school children in 1939 to hold the traditional Christmas program.

A few Square Deal residents stayed a while after the project. In the 1940s the buildings they left were hauled to nearby farms. The open prairie, meadowlarks, and view of the valley are all that remain.

Trubell Grove

Trubell Grove is a settlement three miles northwest of Wheeler. Fort Peck Press 7/1935.

Peter Trubell (Truebel) was an Austrian immigrant who settled in the Old Fort Peck trading post area in the late 1800s. In 1909 he and his German wife Augusta homesteaded 160 acres near Second Point on the Missouri River. They later moved to a farm a few miles north.

In 1935 the Trubells rented rooms to single project workers and home lots to families. They shared their water, wood, and garden space, and helped their renters in whatever way they could.

A destructive windstorm in July 1935 wrecked several houses in Trubell Grove. Most were rebuilt, and workers stayed until their jobs at the project ended. The Trubells lived on their farm until the 1940s when they retired and moved to California.

Valley City and Free Deal

Valley Town Site ... good water, free rent for two years, no obligations. A.C. Light and Power-Current. Picture show, grocery store, meat market, hardware, drugstore, dentist, pool hall, beer parlor, two restaurants, apartments and houses for rent, garages, filling stations. We have everything to make a town. Come help us make it. Streets are wide and houses numbered. New business opportunities. Fort Peck Press 12/1934.

Valley City, like Free Deal, was settled on government land destined to become a dredge cut. It was located three-quarters of a mile north of Park Grove. The first residents arrived in the fall, 1934.

By 1935 there was a "lively commercial club," and new businesses that included one of four Battleson groceries built in the boomtowns, Economy Grocery, Stutler Meat Market and Grocery, and some of the stores moved from Free Deal. The Valley Drug Store carried drugs, cosmetics, candy, ice cream, and tobacco; and had one of the few public telephone pay stations in the area.

There were two bars; one was shut down shortly after opening for serving minors, and hiring women of "immoral character" as barmaids.

"Valley" residents held a community auction in April 1935 to enable new families to buy, sell, and trade household furnishings.

Park Grove residents held a Basket Social in August to help Valley City get a much needed road through town and out on to the highway. The August 5, 1935, *Fort Peck Press* reported, "Sufficient funds were raised. Valley now boasts a good road."

The peak population of the short-lived little town was not recorded. In April 1938 Park Grove's local news columnist noted, "Most of the untenanted houses of Valley were burned to the ground by government workers to make way for the dredge."

The free rent in Free Deal and Valley City attracted a diverse group of inhabitants. For a short time a hobo jungle with both hard core trouble-makers and jobless men looking for work, settled nearby. The majority of the residents were dam workers and their families.

Webber City

In 1934 ... little towns had sprung up everywhere ... there was ... Parkdale, then you crossed the tracks to Webber City. Thelma Bondy, Montana Historical Society Oral Histories.

Webber City was a riverside settlement on government land just north of the boatyard on the east side of the railroad spur to Wiota. Its residents worked at construction sites nearby. They and their families set up tents and shacks among the trees where the shade, river view, and walking distance to work made up for the noise, dust, and insects.

News of Webber City families appeared in local columns from 1934 to 1936, but without details as to how many there were or how the settlement got its name. The little boomlet was short-lived, and abandoned as dredges churned up the river bank.

Wilson "The Friendly Village By The Lake"

Wilson Townsite, own your own home, clean desirable lots and acreage for sale. Beautiful location 1/2 mile south of Wheeler and 1/2 mile west of Lakeview. Some lake frontage. See W.E. Wilson, Sternhagen Agency, Glasgow. Fort Peck Press ad(s) 5/1935.

Wilson was platted in the spring of 1935 by Walter E. Wilson and named for his family. Streets were named after the first residents. At its peak the town covered more than sixteen blocks.

Wilson homesteaded his first 40 acres at the site in 1913. He filed on 280 acres more in 1917 before he was called into World War I with Glasgow's National Guard Company G. He made final proof in 1919. He filed on a second 320 acre homestead which he patented in 1925.

In 1935 he sold 460 acres of his river front property to the government for the future Fort Peck Lake. He platted his land nearby into a townsite which he promoted as "The Friendly Village By The Lake," envisioning it a permanent resort town and recreation area. Therefore, he initially offered lots and acreage for sale instead of rent.

The first of several families purchased a $15 lot in May 1935. Soon nine lots were bought by I.J. Iverson and one by the Mann's Confectionery for their businesses.

In June the *Fort Peck Press* reported Wilson townsite had well platted lots, booster people, and business opportunities. More than a dozen families moved in the first week of June, and in one day "more than 100 lots and many acreage tracts were sold."

High winds and rain swept through the project area on July 8, 1935. Most of the homes and businesses in Wilson were still under construction, and buildings recently moved in were still up on skids. Boards were ripped off and houses thrown against each other. Several people were injured by flying debris. When the storm was over, Wilsonites picked up the pieces and rebuilt their town.

The Wilson Townsite Association organized in 1935 to plan a school and discuss an agenda. Fire and police protection were left to the residents, with a little help from the county. Fresh water was plentiful, but two additional wells were drilled to accommodate the growth. A few residents dug their own wells.

Wilson's business district included an office building, the Cave Market, Nielson Grocery, Evans Restaurant, Dodson's filling station, and the Hollywood Inn. More stores were moving in. A new church, The Glad Tidings Mission, was opened.

During the cold winter of 1935-36 Wilsonites helped each other shovel snow and haul wood. In April, in celebration of spring at last, the Wilson family served 75 of their residents a buffet supper in their home, with dancing until dawn to a three piece orchestra.

Ads: "Come to Wilson. Lots, houses, beautiful location, clean and sanitary, good roads, new school, water." *Fort Peck Press 1936.*

By summer, families were arriving in large numbers. Wilson offered lots in exchange for labor at his townsite and at his filling station over in Lakeview. Workers appreciated the easy access to everywhere from Wilson. The Fort Peck highway ran nearby, project shuttles picked up workers in town, and for a time a community bus made six runs a day from Cave's Market to the dam.

In February 1937, a worker's house burned down. Wilson had fared well through three winters under its original fire safety plan, but after the fire decided on improvements, and organized volunteers.

In April, Wilson ran a *Fort Peck Press* notice: *To all VFW members who are unemployed: Free lot rent in Wilson Townsite.*

His other ads read: "Come to Wilson 'The Friendly Village by the Lake' houses and lots for sale or rent, easy terms, clear title, beautiful location, good school, well drained, sanitary."

Wilson was still a busy town in 1938 as the project wound down. The Wilson family dug a basement for their new home, and residents added rooms and porches on to their houses.

Everything changed in May when Walter Wilson was involved in an automobile accident in which he suffered "severe head injuries."

By 1940 most of Wilson's residents and businesses were gone and so was the dream of "The Friendly Village By The Lake."

Today, Wilson's vision of a recreation area has partially come to pass. There are several permanent homes, fishing, and recreational sites along Fort Peck Lake, at or near where Wilson used to be.

Valley View Farm

The William Malunat family farm was located in the Whately-Center Community between Glasgow and Nashua. It was one of the several farmyard boomlets on the outskirts of the project.

In 1934 the family began preparing meals at 50 cents each for the Montana Power lineman and telephone installers in their area. They rented their yard to workers for their tents. For additional income they raised and sold chickens in the boomtowns. Like many other dryland farmers, their resourcefulness got them through the Great Depression.

The Almosters

Rumor is there is going to be a new town between Wheeler and New Deal, to be called Fair Deal. Fort Peck Press 2/7/1935.

Fair Deal never got past its planning. Nor did Pleasantville, Spring Valley, Riverside, and others. It may have been the timing, location, a faster growing neighbor, or simply a change in plans.

Wheeler

Wheeler, Best Dam Town By a Dam Site. Wheeler Queen of the Boomtowns. Wheeler population 17, four Roys and one old sorehead.

In 1933, with the Fort Peck Project a sure thing, business friends of Glasgow barber Joe Frazier and his wife Bertha, encouraged them to plat their homestead into a town. Their land lay two miles west of the dam site on prairie and knobby hills, the new Fort Peck to Glasgow highway would run right through it, there was a good artesian well, and room to grow in every direction.

In early 1934 the Fraziers hired surveyors to stake out main streets on both sides of the new highway, and to plat business and residential lots behind them. Streets were numbered, and avenues named by the first residents: Johnson, Frazier, Snell, Flint, and Miller for starters.

The Frazier's assistant planners called the townsite *Frazier Place* but they named it *Wheeler* in honor of Senator Burton K. Wheeler.

Frank and Rosetta Beachler rented the first business lot and moved in their 20x40 feet Moose Market. Ruby Smith was building the Wheel-Er-Inn, the first business built on-site. Both opened in June 1934, followed by a branch of Markles Hardware in Glasgow.

The business district grew in July when some stores from the First Boomtown moved in: Alvord's Grocery, Fort Peck Coffee House, Polly Pie Shop, Joe's Eat Shop, Friedle's Clothing, Northwest Service Store, Reide's, the Dam Barber Shop, and the moving picture house.

Wheeler grew daily as project workers began hauling in their farm homes. At the same time, contractor Bill Miller and Pioneer Lumber Company in Glasgow were bringing in pre-built 8x10 and 10x12 feet houses for sale. Miller moved several rental cabins to Wheeler, to which he added stucco and multi-colored shingle roofs.

Two six-unit apartment houses and a large log house were trucked from Opheim. Several other apartment buildings and rooming houses, 20x96 and 20x48 feet were built on site. Two construction companies erected 54 two-family houses. Movers hauled in dozens of buildings from farms and other towns for sale and rent.

Two sawmills set up south and east of Wheeler. Stores in town sold doors, millwork, hardware, wall coverings, linoleum, and paint.

The Fort Peck Press opened on the north side of main street in August 1934. A new theater was about to open when one of the two partners, a "flashy dresser" and experienced con man, was jailed and his unsuspecting partner was left holding the show.

Dr. C.C. Lull saw patients at the Tourist Camp in 1934 until his Main Street office and maternity home/hospital cottages were ready. Dentist E.V. Bethel opened his office in the Taylor Boarding House.

Wheeler's 30 stores grew to 64 during August and September. A Commercial Club made up of businessmen organized to assist them.

The Frazier's opened a land office in their Wheeler Garage and showed lots around the clock. In the rush, Mrs. Frazier lost her "nose glasses" and ran ads in the *Fort Peck Press* to find them.

Several Wheeler stores originally had "Fort Peck" in their names. Most changed to avoid confusion with Fort Peck townsite businesses.

East Wheeler: By August 1934 Wheeler had filled twenty blocks and was spilling over into East Wheeler where an additional 23 houses were under construction in the Miller Addition.

West Wheeler: The *Fort Peck Press* reported, "Joe Frazier platting new townsite on the heights ..., has leased an 80-acre airport to an aviator and is leasing choice ... lots 150x200 feet at $2 per month."

Wheeler had two claims to fame: fastest growing city in the USA; and the widest main street, 300 feet (Highway 24), in any country.

In August 1934 Wheeler Power & Light set poles and announced "lights" by December. In 1935 a 75KW generator was installed.

In November, Mountain States Telephone strung its lines, switched through Fort Peck, and installed 100 party-line phones in businesses and a few homes. A public phone was placed in Hall's Drug.

Notice: "Business houses and residences must remove all garbage cans and ashes ... a dump ground has been provided 1/2 mile west of town, beyond the gravel pit ... by order of the state Board of Health." Frazier, *Fort Peck Press 11/29/1934.*

A Police Station-Bus Depot opened beside the highway in January 1935 with space between for fire fighting equipment and the sheriff's car. A jail was built in November. The facility was funded by the bus company, and stores who paid $5 a year for ads on the depot wall.

By July 1935, Wheeler had 2,000 residents and a waiting list for homes. More apartment and boarding houses were under construction.

Workers and thousands of tourists filled hotels Wheeler, Valley, Boline, Tassa, Baugatz, Jacobson's, and Luckman's Rooms. Day and monthly rentals at the Honeymoon Cabins and the Fort Peck Tourist Camp across from the Wheeler Inn were full.

More stores opened, existing businesses added on and built board sidewalks. Weary merchants discussed Sunday closing but three shifts of workers and a steady stream of visitors wanted them open.

Soon the "excellent pure water" from Frazier's well ran low. The spring water delivered by truck doubled from 1 to 2 cents per gallon. Residents watched for "water thieves" who brought barrels and drained the well. In March 1935 a second artesian well was drilled. The $1,500 cost was paid by the Frazier Company and businessmen.

The boomtowns asked the government for post offices in 1934. The shared Wheeler, Delano Heights, and Lakeview fourth-class post office opened in Wheeler in July 1935. By December the facility needed a Third Class rating and a raise for postmaster Albert Hole.

Wheeler Heights: "A close-in addition south of the ice-house, all grassland ... 250 lots platted ... beautiful location on the hill ... a fine dam in a coulee with lots of soft water." *Fort Peck Press 6/20/1935.*

In addition to the Heights, land to the east owned by E.J. Lander Company, was platted. Two dozen more houses were built south of the highway. Frazier-Davis Company foremen set up their own homes, and several families moved from apartments into houses.

The Fraziers ran ads promoting their town. "The Best Dam Town: Hi-way, Post Office, 24-hour electric service, bus line, phones. Free wash water at our dam; 2 theaters, airport, ice, coal. Many modern stores.... Spring water daily (5 tanks), 3 months lot rent $2; thereafter $2 per month for flood and wind sufferers."

Wheeler homes were damaged by wind in June 1935. On July 7, a tornado touched down. Two people were killed and fifty injured. Several homes were destroyed. Residents rebuilt.

A move to incorporate Wheeler began with a few town leaders in May 1935. The owners objected, saying incorporation, among other disadvantages, would nearly double the taxes.

Joe Frazier wrote a *Fort Peck Press* notice stating the Fraziers were doing their "utmost" to make their town the best place to live. "Your welfare is ours.... No windbag from North Dakota or political leeches will ever have any power in the management of Wheeler."

He said nearly all the money the family made in Wheeler went back into it, and added, "We believe it will be a permanent town."

Incorporation was dropped.

By July 1936 Wheeler reached its peak population of 3,500. Ads read: "Move to Wheeler, south side of highway lots may be bought for $6 per month. On north side $9 per month.... One year to pay, no taxes or interest until 1937. We pay $3 of the moving expenses ...." *Frazier, Fort Peck Press 3/5/1936.*

Wheeler's decline began after many phases of the project were finished in 1936. Half of the workers were gone by December. Some families from dying towns moved into Wheeler while its government workers were moving into vacated houses in Fort Peck.

Dozens of businesses closed. In June 1937 the Beachlers sold the Moose Market and moved to California. Twenty-one stores, "The Last Frontier," remained. Over at the Warnecke Drug their pet magpie "Blackie" still greeted visitors with "Oh boy" and "Hello Sweet."

Bill Miller hauled most of his cabins and seventeen government buildings to Polson. Paul Mann moved his houses to Malta for a tourist camp. Many other buildings were razed and rebuilt elsewhere.

Frazier's crew was busy filling cellars and grading streets while he continued to promote sale of his lots: "When your work is through here ... close your house ... no lot rent will be charged unless used, or we will sell it or rent it for you. When the lake is filled, we have more than one-mile of shoreline ... three-fourths of a mile from Wheeler.... buy one lot ... $10. These most desirable lots may be worth $50 or $100.... Move to Wheeler The Permanent Town."

In 1938 owners of the Hotel Wheeler bought the stucco cabins next door for a tourist camp. Businesses from smaller dying towns were moving in. Store owners painted their buildings and signs. The Wheeler power company replaced poles and power lines.

Wheeler's population was 2,500 in December 1938. Tourists were still coming; an estimated 12,000 stopped by in July.

Dozens of project workers left the area in the fall of 1939. More left after a major layoff in July 1940. Houses were moved away. The Moen family razed the Valley Hotel and rebuilt it in Sidney.

A fire May 22, 1941, started in Keefe's Dress Shop and spread to the Moose Market, Markles Transfer, and the Post Office. Wheeler's volunteer firefighters and the Fort Peck Fire Department could not save them. The town's main stores were suddenly gone.

Courtesy of the Fort Peck Interpretive Center

More families left Wheeler when school let out in May. Yuly's Market was moved to Glasgow. The Silver Dollar, Boline, and Tassa hotels, and other buildings were razed.

Decline continued through 1943. But the Tuesday Evening Bridge Club, the Stitch and Chatter Club, and Bible School still met. In May 1942, some 1,149 residents registered for war time sugar rationing. School opened in September with 30 students.

The "permanent town" was not to be. The last major landmark, the Hotel Wheeler (1934-1943) was razed and hauled to Chinook in 1944. The Fraziers moved to Oregon in the late 1940s.

Wheeler's population was 24 in 1951, down to five in 1977. About all that remained was the rebuilt Buckhorn Club (Bar), opened in 1934 as a poolroom by two men from Opheim, its colorful past a composite of fact and fiction woven into a worker's memories of dancing the Waltz Quadrille on the hardwood floor.

Wheeler. As wild as it was, the wildest thing about it was its reputation. A lot of good and gentle people called it "home."

McCone City Camp

McCone City Camp was settled on the east side of the Missouri River just north of the future dam site in the winter of 1933.

On October 30, the McCone County Reemployment Office called its first 100 workers to cut brush along the east side of the Missouri River. "The men were notified that they should bring their own bedding and cooking utensils, and they were expected to furnish or obtain their own lodging." *McCone Sentinel 11/2/1933.*

Thankful for their jobs, the workers brought axes, saws, and other small tools for work; and cots, pots, and pans for their temporary shelters. They gathered on the McCone County side of the river just north of the bridge and dam sites and set up their tents and shacks.

Some wives came to join their husbands. They cooked over camp fires and small gas stoves, and washed clothes in water they carried from the river. They earned money preparing meals and doing laundry for the workers whose wives were still on the farms.

R. H. Benson of Malta hauled a building to the camp and opened a grocery and supply store. Other stores soon followed.

By the end of March 1934 the project work force was 1,531. The Corps reclaimed the McCone City Camp site for the project. All residents and stores moved north to the Frank McPherson ranch. The Camp provided a place to call home during that first harsh winter.

McCone City

McCone City, in northwest McCone County, was one of the first project towns. With its peak population of 3,600 it was the largest.

"In the spring of 1934 McCone City Camp was moved onto the Frank McPherson ranch two and a half miles below (north of) the bridge." *Fort Peck Press McCone City history review 3/15/1935.*

The ranch was located on the east bank of the Missouri River in an ideal location for a town serving both spillway and dam workers. It had a good well, room to grow, and was a short commute to both work sites. Three project families were already living there along the river among the cottonwood and willow trees.

Frank McPherson and his wife Frances were among the area's "old families." They trailed cattle from Texas to Galpin Coulee in 1900 where they traded cows for the homestead of Bert and Bessie Perry, three miles northeast of Old Fort Peck, and began ranching. Along with running the ranch, Frank was a two-term deputy in Nashua.

As the drought deepened in 1934 the McPhersons and their seven children were holding on to their ranch by running a drayline, and an ice and coal business on the side.

With McCone City Camp residents waiting to move in, the McPhersons and their son Tom hastily platted a town with home lots for rent at $2 a month and business lots for $15. They were still clearing brush and grading roads when Camp families and hundreds of others began setting up their tents and shacks among the trees.

Gidley Grocery & Service Station was the first business, followed by Feeder's Drug Store from Circle and Lawson's Barber Shop. Tom McPherson opened a bar in one of the family's two log houses, and added a dance hall with live music and taxi dancers. A boarding house was built beside the railroad where workers caught the train.

Within a month McCone City had 400 residents. Frank purchased a neighboring farm to accommodate the growth.

A private school opened the fall of 1934. The teacher held classes in her home until the new schoolhouse was ready for the growing number of students. Women started sewing clubs, school support groups, and helping hand clubs. Church services were held in homes until the schoolhouse opened. A Sunday School, the project's 14th, was started by the American Sunday School Union.

In September work began on the six mile McCone County side extension of the railroad to the spillway. The town was filled with the noise and dust from hundreds of trucks and heavy equipment.

The river froze over in December. A steady stream of trucks began hauling houses, stores, building materials, merchandise and supplies from Glasgow and the railroad across the ice to McCone City.

McCone City was one-year-old in March 1935. It had 600 residents and more on the way. Many new stores opened, including three groceries, a meat market, three restaurants, a cafe, beer parlor, drug store, men's store,  a family clothing store, two ladies-ready-to-wear shops, a shoe shop, two laundries, a second filling station, welding shop, dance pavilion, and ice house. The new theater opened with more than 350 people in attendance for the show. An optometrist and a dentist opened offices.

McCone City had its own full time deputy and a jail.

The McPhersons dug a second well and tested for more. They filled coulees, installed culverts, cut down trees, and graded roads.

The city held its first semi-annual clean-up week in April. Brush was cleared, and ash piles and debris hauled away. Residents planted gardens and set about making their town "a place to be proud of."

The Missouri River separated McCone City from the boomtowns and work sites in Valley County. The first workers crossed the river using a pulley and cable system, and a small boat. At the end of April 1935 the Nashua ferry was rebuilt and launched at McCone City, giving residents access to the Nashua road, US 2, and the other towns.

More workers arrived in May 1935 and built homes. Several of the families living in the dozen or so Addison Miller Apartment buildings moved into houses to make room for the incoming crews.

Visitors came in May, the county commissioners and assessor, the county and state health departments, and a deputy appointed to collect taxes door to door "for the convenience of the residents."

During the summer, McCone City residents organized baseball teams and planned recreation for all ages. They watched from their side of the river as boats traveled to and from the boatyards on the west side. They cheered when the John Ordway came in sight, and again when men at the ferry landing caught a runaway barge.

In June 1935, Mountain States Telephone and Telegraph completed their lines and installed a public-use telephone in Feeder's Drug Store. Electric power was provided by a generator operated by diesel engines owned by Moody & Bennett of Mason & Walsh Construction. The Addison Miller Company built a water filtration plant and bathhouse for its homes. The post office, with its 192 metal boxes and general delivery mail, opened in August in Feeder's Drug Store.

McCone City was again pushing the limits of the McPherson's land. Another farm was purchased and land leased for expansion.

An airport was built nearby and the flying service of Mr. and Mrs. George Hight of New Deal provided tourist flights over the project.

The new three-room school opened in September with seats for 79 students. By October there were 163 school aged children of non-government employees. The population was 1,300 and growing.

In October the *Fort Peck Press* reported "Many homes in McCone City are being remodeled ... enclosing a back porch, new siding, entry-ways ... and additions."

McCone City had something other boomtowns did not have. Several thousand feet of 28-inch pipe ran through the town carrying slurry from the dredges to the dam. The pipeline rested on wooden rails that stretched out through the trees. It was a must-see for visitors.

The cold winter of 1935-36 and the layoff of 2,100 workers at the project devastated all the boomtowns. McCone City fared better than most since the majority of its residents worked at the spillway, but it was a hard winter for all the unemployed. People helped each other get by. They were all thankful in the spring when the *Fort Peck Press* headlines declared, "Unemployment has ceased considerably."

In February the *Nashua Messenger* reported a "power struggle" in McCone City. Residents met with operators of the McCone City Light Plant at the Beer Parlor to discuss installation of meters for the electric appliances not allowed in the $3 monthly rate.

June 1, 1936, the *Glasgow Courier* reported ... *the old log ranch home of Mr. and Mrs. Frank McPherson, a landmark in this section for more than 30 years, was destroyed by fire.*

The McPhersons were out in the yard when their kitchen gas cookstove exploded. Instantly the flames engulfed their log home. Volunteers rushed in with a truck and barrels of water, but could not save it. The Fort Peck firetruck arrived in time to keep the fire from spreading to the Tom and Leila McPherson home next door.

During 1936 McCone City's population skyrocketed to 3,600 and more as project employment rose to 10,546. The city was awake day and night with three shifts of workers, business people, and residents coming and going. Supply trains, trucks and other vehicles ran by the town at all hours, dredges, barges, and tugboats moved up and down the river. Many visitors added to the activity and noise, traveling through in large numbers to see the spillway under construction.

In less than two years McCone City had become the largest of the project boomtowns, and the biggest city ever in McCone County.

Decline began in March 1937. The Keck family, some of the first business owners, moved ten of their rental cabins to a Chain of Lakes project near Havre. The light plant, burned out in May, was sold at a sheriff's sale. In November the *Fort Peck Press* reported that Howard Lawson, the city's first barber and biggest booster, "sold his business buildings and donated his dance pavilion to raise school funds."

By June 1938 the Addison Miller and Fielding & Shepley companies had completed their spillway contract. They discharged the last of the workers and began dismantling their concrete mixing plant.

McCone City's population decreased significantly in 1938. There was a small increase in 1939, then a drop to 140 by the 1940 census. The post office closed in 1941. Homes and business buildings were moved or razed for lumber. Scraps and left-overs were burned.

Frank and Frances McPherson sold their ranch in the 1940s and moved to Nashua. Time turned the townsite back to nature, leaving only traces that the biggest boomtown of all had ever been there.

McCone County, Montana

McCone County was sparsely populated, and devastated by drought in the 1930s. Many early 1900 homesteaders moved away, followed by some families who came on the Northern Pacific Railroad in 1928.

Circle, the county seat, had been settled in 1905 and named for the Circle Ranch brand. It prospered before the dry years came and left its nearly 600 residents and the county people barely hanging on.

Hundreds of the unemployed workers from McCone County found jobs at the Fort Peck project. A few businessmen moved their stores there. The taxes paid by the workers and contractors operating in the county were a boost to the economy. But Circle, 90 miles from the dam on a narrow dirt road, was too far away for much direct benefit.

McCone County can always claim the biggest boomtown at the project, and it will forever be the home of the Fort Peck Spillway.

The Incorporated towns—Glasgow and Nashua

Glasgow began as Great Northern Railroad Siding 45 in 1887 (the GN was then called the St. Paul, Minneapolis & Manitoba. Numbers began in Minot). The siding was north of the Milk River, 20 miles northwest of Old Fort Peck. It was staked out by Charles Hall and ready for settlement before the railroad arrived. Its first businesses were tent saloons, a restaurant, general store, and a post office.

Residents wanted a name instead of a number, so a Great Northern clerk in St. Paul spun a globe and Siding 45 became *Glasgow.*

Glasgow was named the Valley County seat when the county was formed in 1893. It had several stores, banks, bars, schools, churches, and a newspaper when it incorporated in 1902. It served as a business center for the railroad workers, cattle and sheep ranchers, and new homesteaders. Its population was 2,059 in 1920.

By the 1930s Glasgow residents had survived cold winters, hot summers, floods, fires, smallpox, diphtheria, typhoid, and influenza. They had hosted a Carrie Nation attack on "John Barleycorn" in 1910. And they sadly watched their sons go off to World War I in 1917.

Glasgow was 45 years old, with 2,200 residents, when rumors of a Fort Peck project began circulating in 1932. It had electricity, running water, telephones, "the talkies," several large businesses, and medical facilities. City government was strong. The people were struggling, but fighting back as the Great Depression tightened its grip.

A year later when project rumors became reality, the October 6, 1933, *Glasgow Courier* reported, "Glasgow jubilant." Celebrations went on for hours. Speculation was 3,000 men would be employed.

Glasgow welcomed the first Corps surveyors in the spring of 1934. Engineers came and opened their office in the First National Bank. A soil testing lab and miniature model of the dam was set up in the Pattison Implement building. Corps families, including the family of district engineer Major T.B. Larkin, moved to Glasgow temporarily while Fort Peck town was being built.

A severe housing crunch developed as hundreds of workers and their families, transients, and others arrived. Residents divided their homes into apartments and turned their basements, attics, garages and sheds into rentals. Builders erected apartment houses and a men's dorm. Former mayor Dr. G. H. Klein built a replica of a log fort for a service station and added cabins for rent.

The old two-story red school, boarded up in 1928, was turned into apartments and rented until it was demolished in 1939 by the WPA.

The Hurd Livery Barn and other old buildings became homes. More were needed. In August 1934 farmers were asked to list empty buildings that could be moved to Glasgow or the boomtowns for homes. The Chamber of Commerce stated that an average of ten to fifteen families a day came looking for a place to live.

Everything was happening at once! New and used car sales shot up. Businesses grew. The schools, hospitals, post office, jail, and the police and fire departments were over extended and out of space.

All the while, city officials and the state and local chambers of commerce were promoting tourism in the area. A *Courier* editorial noted that *one good crop was needed and tourism might be it.*

During the 1930s, while Glasgow dealt with the growing pains and later the decline of the project, WPA workers graveled streets, built a $120,000 underpass, a Civic Center, pool, courthouse annex, and courtrooms in the new federal building.

After the Fort Peck project ended, and most of the project people had gone, the 1940 census numbered Glasgow's population at 3,799.

Nashua - Gate City to the Fort Peck Dam

Nashua was settled in 1887 by Charles Sargent, twelve miles northeast of Old Fort Peck, west of the confluence of Big Porcupine Creek and Milk River. Its Indian name means *Meeting of the Water.*

Sargent, a Civil War veteran, had ridden with Gen. George Custer. He was delivering a message during the Little Big Horn massacre. He had been an Indian agent, and railroad worker before homesteading 160 acres near the Milk River where the new railroad would be built.

He and his Indian wife opened a mercantile store and saloon along the railroad track. The settlement soon grew to include a school, bank, post office, hotel, grocery/dry goods store, a dray line, lumberyard, hardware store, blacksmith shop, grain elevator, laundry, restaurant, bakery, dairy, oil station, power plant, and doctor and dentist offices.

The town was incorporated in 1920 with a population of 272, up to 351 by 1930. It had a mayor and council, city clerk, city attorney, and a marshal to handle traffic and law enforcement.

In December 1933 the Chamber of Commerce ran an ad in the *Nashua Messenger,* sponsored by 23 businesses, inviting new project workers to their "established town with progressive merchants." They offered a few free lots. The population had already grown to 600.

More and longer trains were rolling through town day and night with supplies for the project. In spite of the drought the four grain elevators were operating again, adding more cars to the train traffic.

Tourists were turning off Highway US 2 north of Nashua to visit the project. Their vehicles joined the big supply trucks traveling down the main street, and could be seen along the sidewalks at all hours.

Nashua's population peaked at more than 1,200 in late summer 1935. In 1936 Chamber officials and mayor Alfred Lee reported an increase in business and predicted brisk growth for the year ahead.

A wild fire, June 28, 1936, wiped out an entire block of Nashua's biggest businesses. Fire started in the Saveway and spread to the West Side Store, Buttrey's, Eddy's Barber Shop, Gateway Hotel, Orpheum Theater, Mayme Taylor's Beauty Shop, and the Nashua Hotel, Cafe and Beer Parlor. Flames raced through the old First National Bank building, the post office, jail, several small buildings, and two homes.

Volunteers controlled the fire until the water ran out and flames, fanned by high winds, jumped from building to building. The Fort Peck Fire Department came and saved what was left of the town. The cause of the $70,000 fire was believed to be faulty wiring.

Business owners considered rebuilding, but peak employment at the project would be over before they could reopen.

In September 1936 officials advertised *the largest land sale in the history of Valley County* to sell deserted property with five or more years back taxes. Ninety lots were appraised and sold in Nashua.

By fall Nashua was recovering. The depot was open 24 hours. A two-cell jail was built. WPA workers were building new sidewalks. A funeral director and a dentist opened their offices. In October, Nashua received a $16,364 government grant for a new water system.

By summer 1937 the new post office had opened, and the railroad skidoo was hauling mail. A theater, Cash and Carry, Farmers Union store, and a clothing emporium were all in business. In September a huge crowd attended the Labor Day dance in the community hall.

Nashua received word in 1938 the WPA would beautify its school, and build on tennis courts, and track and football fields.

Nashau was devastated by two back-to-back floods in 1939. The first came when the Milk River overflowed during the spring thaw, and the second when a dam broke and a wall of water rushed down Porcupine Creek. The floods destroyed the Nashua Community Hall and damaged or destroyed many homes and businesses.

Nashua had two fires in 1939. The former blacksmith shop burned in April, and the Hardware Store in August.

In spite of trials by fire and water, Nashua survived and entered the 1940s with a population of 943. It is still a busy little town today.

Part 8

Living in the Boomtowns

Hundreds of workers and their families arrived at the Fort Peck project during the early spring and summer of 1934. They traveled in whatever vehicle they had that would carry them and their belongings. They moved into the townsites before the owners could finish clearing the lots. In some of the smaller towns they had to cut brush and dig latrines before setting up their homes. Many strangers became friends while helping each other get a roof over their head.

Some farm families hauled in their houses and sheds to live in. Others brought small houses on wheels (trailerhouses). A few, where hillsides were available, had dugouts. Several set up tents. Many of the workers were carpenters who built their homes and helped others with theirs. Hammers echoed day and night. A new family and the neighbors could turn a pile of boards into a home in a few short hours.

Construction companies in Glasgow and Nashua started building small houses for sale during the winter of 1933-34. The Pioneer Lumber Company in Glasgow ran newspaper ads picturing a 10 by 12 feet frame home with side windows and a door for $59. The house could be set up in a townsite on 24 hours notice.

Movers brought in hundreds of houses for rent. Contractors built apartment buildings, duplexes, and rooming houses. There was a long waiting list for rentals and a quick turn over of houses for sale.

Trailerhouses, usually built with 2x4s and quarter-inch plywood, were slid off their wheels or set next to a house for an extra room. A few workers built garages which doubled as storage areas.

Home exteriors were covered with plaster, stucco, tarpaper, or green asphalt sheet siding. Interior walls were painted, calcimined, whitewashed, or wallpapered. Floors were covered with linoleum, or home hooked rugs over plywood. Windows were trimmed with flour sack curtains or curtains brought from a farm or bought in a store.

In the beginning, the walls of some of the houses were papered with newspapers or magazine pages to keep out wind, dust, and the cold. Windows, door frames, and the cracks between the boards were "chinked" with newspaper and rags or worn out socks. Families used whatever materials they had to make their homes comfortable.

Most families took pride in their homes no matter how humble or temporary. As time passed, paychecks made it possible for them to make improvements and build additions and porches.

Tents were furnished with small tables, and wooden boxes or logs for chairs. Cupboards were made from crates or apple boxes. Room dividers were fashioned from clothesline and blankets. Beds were cots, bedrolls, and feather ticks. Large tents had roll-up sides that stretched out into awnings. Some families had two tents, one to sleep in and the other for a kitchen and dining area.

For Sale: Beds, chairs, mattresses, rugs, stoves, linoleum, lamps, tinware, and more.

New and used home furnishings were sold in boomtown stores, and through exchanges and newspaper ads. Most farm families brought furniture from their farm. Others built tables and benches. Some people used wooden apple boxes for dressers, chairs, bench ends, and storage. Drop-leaf tables and folding beds conserved space. Wall hooks, nails, and home-made closets held clothes. Large trunks were used for storage and doubled as seats. Wooden crates were set outside the door for extra storage.

Kerosene lamps were used to light most homes without electricity. Wood and coal stoves, some with reservoirs for hot water, were used for cooking and winter heat. A few people had oil burners. During the summer a small gas stove was set on the "range" top to provide cool cooking. Families with farms, or with relatives on nearby farms, often did their weekly baking, canning, and laundry there.

Most homes had an icebox to keep milk and food cool. Ice was delivered by a truck; chunks were chipped off in the requested size. Kids gathered around the truck to catch the flying ice chips.

A few families had batteries to power their washing machines and lights. A very few had pianos, rocking chairs, or radios.

Most women did the family laundry on scrub boards (washboards) and hung their "wash" outside on clotheslines to dry. In winter time additional lines were strung inside. The ironing was done with heavy "flat irons" heated on the stove. Gas irons were available but many women were afraid the irons would blow up and didn't use them.

Washtubs used for laundry and bathing were stored in a crate near the doorstep. In winter, wood was stacked in the yard then carried inside to the woodbox to warm and dry before it was burned.

Some homeowners dug cellars under their houses to store potatoes and vegetables canned in glass jars. The cellars also served as a refuge during windstorms, and sleeping quarters for men working graveyard shifts during the hot summer.

Cellars were often used as the family bank where savings were hidden in cans or jars in preparation for the future after the dam.

Hovels: Not every homeowner or renter took pride in their home. With the constant movement of people with few means, and others with little regard for regulations, hovels happened.

Landowners were accountable to county and state boards of health for the sanitation violations of the renters. When their renters ignored the warnings to "clean up," townsite owners evicted them.

If residents were unable to maintain their homes because of illness or troubles, friends and neighbors pitched in to help them.

As the project wound down from its peak in July 1936, houses were listed for sale: "Cheap. Well built bungalow type house. Can be moved." "2-room house, frame building, lined floor, $25 on terms, $20 cash." "8x12, built of drop siding, good floor. For quick sale, $50." "7x12 celotex house, double walls, bed, stove, table and chairs $65." Several owners offered terms.

When workers left the project, most of them took their houses back home. Some were sold and moved by the new owner. Others were used for tourist cabins or torn down for lumber. After all usable structures were moved or razed, most of what was left was burned.

Managing the Boomtowns

During the winter 1933-34 some farmers with land in the project area began platting towns. A few hired real estate agents to assist with planning and management. Others staked their own sites and ran their towns as a family business.

Commercial clubs were a popular form of government in the larger boomtowns. The land owner or manager, the business owners, and residents elected officers and held regularly scheduled meetings to discuss community issues. In smaller towns the owner, with input from businessmen and residents, made the rules.

Water for most towns came from community wells. A few land owners allowed residents to dig wells. Water wagons and ice trucks owned by the towns or private businesses ran regular routes.

Mail was delivered to a temporary post office opened in a boatyard barracks early in 1934. It provided general delivery service for contractors, workers, families, and businesses. As the population increased, 2,500 boomtowners signed petitions asking the government for post offices in their towns, stating the Fort Peck facility "could not adequately serve them" and Glasgow and Nashua were too far away.

Patrons were frustrated by long lines and mixups for people with the same name. Also, con-artists were perpetrating a variety of scams that took advantage of the general delivery mail system.

Three post offices were approved during the summer of 1935: the first serving Wheeler, Delano Heights, and Lakeview; the second went to the New Deal and Square Deal communities; and the third opened for patrons in the Midway, Park Grove, and Valley City areas.

Electricity for lights and small appliances became available for a few boomtowns during 1935. Not everyone could afford wiring and fees, and continued using kerosene lamps, egg beaters, and battery operated radios. Most of the smaller towns did not have electric power in spite of efforts to maintain generators and power plants.

Electricity in the home, office, or manufacturing establishment is not a fad ... to be discarded as a passing whim. Montana Power & Light Company ad 1934.

Phones. In late 1934 Mountain States Phone Service assigned 100 telephones to Wheeler, switched through Fort Peck town. Park Grove, McCone City, and other larger boomtowns had similar service. Public pay phones were installed in drug stores. The majority of residents did not have a phone, but neither did the people they wanted to call.

Nashua received the "most modern automatic phone exchange in Montana" in 1936. Patrons could dial "O" for emergencies. "Toll phones" for long distance and non-subscriber calls were available.

Noise from the project construction, combined with the sounds of the towns, echoed day and night. Residents got used to hearing it but visitors asked, "How can you stand it?"

Dust from the work sites rode every wind. It swirled in clouds behind vehicles on dry dirt roads and filtered through the tightest of doors and windows. It was the scent and taste of summer.

Sanitation in the boomtowns was a problem during the early days due to hundreds of people arriving at the same time. In March 1935 Dr. W.F. Cogswell, director of the Montana Board of Health, met with Valley County officials, boomtown owners and managers, and Corps representatives to discuss the pick-up and disposal of garbage, ash piles, and refuse. Spring cleaning was already happening.

A Spring Clean-Up got underway in the eight "mushroom towns": Wheeler, New Deal, Midway, Park Dale, Park Grove, Valley, Delano Heights, and Lakeview. In April the state Board of Health approved the first year-around garbage truck routes at 25 cents a month for residences and $150 for businesses. In May, Valley County health officials drafted a county wide sanitation policy:

Privies must be fly-tight; have ventilators from below the seat out through the roof and screen; and be disinfected with lime or other substances that will kill odor, not less than once a week. Pits have to be three or more feet deep. Seats have to have covers that close when the person rises.

Garbage must be stored in fly-tight containers and buried or burned once a week.

Notices similar to a composite of Wheeler's were posted in all the towns*: Business houses and residences: Garbage cans must be used and premises kept clean ... to prevent epidemics and flies. Do not dump refuse on the roadside ... all garbage, refuse and slops must be kept in covered water tight, metal containers ... and hauled, burned or buried regularly. These services will be done by the owner of the land at the expense of the tenant, unless taken care of satisfactorily by the tenant. By order of the State Board of Health, routine inspections will be held, and violations dealt with accordingly.*

Garbage truck routes were started by private businesses or town owners. Several dumps opened throughout the project area. Spring and fall clean-up weeks were held in all the towns.

Residents of McCone City and others in the trees also cleared brush from around their homes to prevent fire.

Most residents were already used to dealing with garbage disposal, outhouse maintenance, and ash and "clinker" piles from wood and coal burning stoves.

The state and county regularly monitored compliance with health regulations. The Corps encouraged sanitation. Residents wanted clean towns for their families. Land owners wanted their farm land cared for; many of them rewarded hometown pride with picnics and parties. Most sanitation problems arose during times of high population turnover or extreme weather conditions.

Law and order in the boomtowns were mostly kept by the owners. The county sheriff's department sent deputies to keep the peace and direct traffic when needed. Fire calls were answered by neighbors and volunteers, with back-up from the Fort Peck Fire Department.

In many ways, living in the boomtowns was much like living in any other little eastern Montana town in the 1930s, except the streets were not rolled up at dusk and they had a lot more rowdy visitors.

Business In The Boomtowns
You could buy most anything you needed in the boomtowns.

The first project area stores opened down by the dam site during the winter of 1933-1934. Hundreds more opened soon after.

Most businesses had one owner, others changed hands up to four times during their three days to five years in business. Buildings were usually one-story, 20x40 feet wood frame structures with false fronts, moved in or built on site. Merchandise was stocked up front, and often times the owner or manager lived in the back.

Business men and women worked long hours in high risk ventures, serving a constantly changing base of regular customers and visitors. They contributed much to community projects and gave generously to schools. They were often asked to extend credit. Some were robbed.

The majority of boomtown businesses were owned and operated by northeastern Montanans who moved their stores from other towns. Approximately one-third were Glasgow branches run by managers. A few had first time owners or were opened by entrepreneurs who made their living by moving from one booming area to another.

Businesses on wheels sold water by the gallon, ice blocks for ice boxes, and milk in glass bottles with sealed paper disks. At least one meat market sold beef and poultry from a truck. Ads for their delivery service in the boomtowns ran weekly in the *Fort Peck Press*.

Home based businesses were operated by women who did sewing, baking, and laundry while caring for their children. And by men who did auto and small tool repair. Both men and women hired out to paint and wallpaper homes and businesses.

Farm produce routes were established by farmers delivering "roasting ears," "dressed chickens," "grain fed" beef, and milk and eggs. Ads such as "2,000 bushels of spuds to sell, deliveries every 10 days," appeared in the local newspapers.

Coal delivery was offered by farmers with mines. Northeastern Montana ranchers ran ads that read: "Culbertson Lignite Coal, burns clean and leaves no clinkers, delivered anywhere on the project for $5 a ton or 30 cents per hundred weight." They also sold seasoned slab or body wood for $7 per cord. Signs appeared near the highway.

Business routes. Several large town businesses had boomtown routes, such as the Havre steam laundry, Scoby bakery, Wolf Point creamery, and a motor company "48 miles east of the dam."

Traveling men. Hundreds of honest and dishonest traveling salesmen came and went. In 1935 the Nashua Chamber of Commerce heard complaints their town was being overrun with house to house peddlers, most without licenses, "robbing merchants of thousands of dollars annually." Other towns shared their problem.

"High Pressure Boys" swept through the towns selling ads on maps and placemats printed in other states. Businesses were warned of "the folly of cheap advertising."

It paid to advertise. Most stores ran ads in the *Fort Peck Press* in Wheeler, and some in the *Nashua Messenger.* "Sell, buy, rent, loan or borrow." "Due to past credit loses, we add 10 percent to all accounts carried past payday." "We now have a new electric sign for nites."

Ads From the *Fort Peck Press*

Apartments: Nice warm rooms.

Autos: Buy a Terraplane, America's only bodies all of steel...88-100 hp, $585, with optional electric hand. 1936 Chev coach, sell or trade. For sale: Model 12 Hup sedan.

Barber and Beauty Shops: Licensed barber. Shower baths 35 cents, haircut 50 cents, shave 25 cents. Water waves and permanents.

Clothes: Pick of the pelt fur coat sale: $35 to $225 for seal, mole, raccoon, and squirrel. Children's underwear 60 to 95 cents, anklets 15 cents. Easter hats.

Coal (poetry sells): Order your coal...you'll cast aside those BVDs: *When it's Coal Time in Wheeler, And the skies have lost their blue, It's time that we were wheeling a load of Coal to you.*

Dentist: Boxed ad featuring a drawing of upper dentures: 15 years experience, Guaranteed work, Reasonable prices. Park Grove.

Dray Services: Light-heavy hauling, order at Flint's Beer Parlor.

Drug Stores: Drugs, stationery, cosmetics, candy, ice-cream. Pops, magazines, sun glasses, tobaccos, drugs, goggles, and respirators. Drugs, souvenirs. Registered pharmacist. Special: buy two 25 cents tubes Dr. West's tooth paste 33 cents; Squib tooth powder 33 cents. "Ask about our vacation."

Electrical Work: We specialize in all forms of auto repair & electric work; light lathe work.

Furniture/appliances: New ice boxes. Beds, chairs, mattresses, rugs, stoves, linoleum, lamps, tinware.

Groceries: Corn Flakes 25 cents, cabbage 3, pigs feet 25, tall milk seven cans for 50 cents, sardines 5. Home bakery, lunches, tobacco, candy, soft drinks, papers and periodicals. Smoked meats, fresh fruits & vegetables, men's clothing and shoes, kitchen, hardware, dishes, and notions. Bringing a load of hogs. Radios. Bulk kraut 10 cents.

Our beef, pork, veal and fresh-killed poultry are noted for their tenderness and sweet flavor. Maybe a cent higher but worth it.

Garages: 18-hour service, valve refacing & reseating. I guarantee my work. We do our best to please. Accessories, Grease Rack, Tires, Tubes. "Service Mit A Happy Grin." Gas, oil, tires, radiators, more.

Garbage: Pick-up year 'round under the State Board of Health: 25 cents for residence and $150-200 month for business.

Gasoline: White Eagle gasoline, Mobil oil, heavy hardware, tools. Jobbers stocks, Goodrich tires, Alemite fittings, guns, welder's supplies and equipment.

Hotel: New management, completely remodeled and redecorated. Efficient care and thorough cleanliness is our policy. Quiet, peaceful location. Rates $5 a week and up." "Nice clean beds 50 cents and up."

Jeweler: Watch repair, 47 years experience.

Maternity Home: Reasonable prices and excellent care.

Meat Markets: Fresh meat daily from Glasgow. Chuck pot roast for 12 1/2 cents per pound.

Meat Market/Grocery receipt: "The world is coming to an end. Pay your bill so I don't have to look all over Hell for you."

Night Club: Free shrimp Friday nights; refreshments, sandwiches.

Recreation: Pool games, candy, tobacco, soft drinks.

Shoe Repair: Limp in, walk out. Shoe Hospital: "It's the 'soles' of the people I keep in view, For I am a doctor of Boot and Shoe."

Restaurants: All the coffee you can drink with your meals. Homecooked meals served family style. Great steak, chicken on Sunday 40 cents. Hamburgers 5&10 cents. "Take 'em home and save the wife." If you want good home cooked, sanitary food, call on us. Excellent lunches for working men and campers. We serve Dutch lunches to patrons providing their own refreshments.

Theaters: Weekly 7 p.m., matinee at 2:30 p.m: *Riders of Destiny,* John Wayne as Singing Sandy. *The Show Off* with Spencer Tracy. *Borderland* featuring Hopalong Cassidy, a bang up Western. Also, March of Time, News & Shorts.

Water: "Let me haul your spring water this winter."

National Ad: Lady was wasting away! Gets new strength with Army doctor's formula.

Classifieds:

For Sale: Cash register $10. Desks. Favorite wood and coal range. Trailers, hitches, plywood house 8x24. Green enamel wood and coal range with regulator oven, reservoir; preserving kettle. Electric fan,

Coleman gas iron, icebox, Mason jars. Skyrover radio, sanitary cot, Singer Sewing Machine. Ties, reptile slippers, 6-tube radio, Western Electric washing machine $10, two milk cows. Terms. Speed Queen washer, Carbide light plant, $10. Banjo and phonograph records.

Swap Column: Will trade baby buggy for shoes or chairs; radio for couch. Want to teach band/orchestra music for furnished room.

Wanted: Articles bought and sold; tents, shacks, stoves, all makes of autos. A kerosene cookstove.

Help Wanted: Young man or boy of good habit to learn the printing trade at this office (*Fort Peck Press*) for his board.

Help Wanted: Middle aged lady to cook for four men. Mill Apts., in East Wheeler."

Work wanted: Dish washing, general restaurant work, dancehall waitress, or light housework. Wanted plain sewing. Piano tuning.

Lost: Black and white Boston bulldog, near reservoir. Reward.

Questionable advertising

Boomtown Bar: "If your girl quits you, What's the difference? You can have fun, frolic with 14 luscious, scintillating honeys as hostesses.... $10 given every Tuesday entirely free. Boy, what a night that will be!"

Shortly after the ad ran, the bar was shut down. It reopened under new management: "Bring your family party to this newly modernized club, cool ventilation, and requests by your favorite orchestras."

Yes we have Tarantulas

A tarantula was discovered on bananas at Buttrey's barracks store in Fort Peck in May 1937. Due to its rarity in Montana it was put on display at the Fort Peck Theatre.

A second tarantula was found on bananas at the Moose Market in June. It was preserved in a glass jar at the store for public viewing.

Boomtown Fires and Fire Departments

It was a common but dangerous practice to jump-start fires in wood and coal stoves by adding a little dash of kerosene, gas, or the cheaper but highly volatile distillate fuel oil.

A dozen adults and nine children died in their boomtown homes from 1935 through 1939 in explosions and flash fires accidentally set off by someone using a fuel to ignite damp wood or coal. The fires destroyed an estimated two dozen homes and twenty businesses, and damaged many others. Several people were injured but delivered from death by quick thinking neighbors.

Bucket brigades were the first responders to every fire. With their precious little water and few tools they saved many homes and lives.

Brigaders, mostly neighbors, administered first aid to burn victims and rushed them to medical facilities. After a fire, they got together to "raise a purse" and help the family rebuild their home.

Volunteer fire departments were organized by the residents in all of the boomtowns in 1935. Businesses made generous donations and fundraisers helped pay for equipment. Meetings were held to promote safety and review county fire laws for unincorporated towns.

Fire departments

Wheeler had its first fire in August 1934, when a man accidentally set off a kerosene explosion and fire that destroyed his tent. The new Commercial Club worked out a fire fighting plan.

By April 1935 they had appointed a fire chief, installed a fire alarm on the bus depot wall, and raised funds for a water tank on a car chassis to pull to fires. The alarm was tested and called a "pip." As incentive for a quick response to it, a $5 bill was given to the first man to "hook on to the water."

In March 1936 the Commercial Club arranged for the Fort Peck firechief to train Wheeler volunteers. They bought a truck and reserve water tanks. Their equipment was tested the next week when a home and four two-room apartments were destroyed by overheated stoves.

The Park Grove Commercial Club organized its volunteer fire department in June 1935, with donated equipment. Residents held fund-raisers to purchase an auto chassis, water barrels, and sand.

McCone City organized its fire protection force with all donated equipment in July 1935, as did all the larger boomtowns. Smaller towns relied on their bucket brigades and donated equipment.

The Fort Peck Fire Department, stationed in the town of Fort Peck, was organized in 1934 to protect the government town and the project buildings. It answered some calls from the boomtowns.

Injuries and death

Three people were severely burned, in separate accidents, while lighting cookstove fires with distillate in the winter of 1935-1936. Two teenage sisters were burned when gas they were using to clean clothes ignited. A young woman was burned and her home destroyed when gas she was using to clean clothes ignited. A neighbor man crawled through a window and saved her baby. A couple in Nashua suffered burns when their gas stove exploded. They saved their cabin by throwing dirt on the flames until volunteer firemen arrived.

Three men died, in separate fires, while filling or lighting stoves with distillate. An 8-year-old girl died of burns after she accidentally used gas instead of kerosene to start a cookstove fire. A young woman, her baby, and her mother died when a can of distillate she was using to start a fire, exploded.

A McCone City truck driver was burned when distillate he was using to light a fire, exploded. Neighbors caught him as he ran toward the river. They smothered the flames and rushed him to the hospital where he died on his 38th birthday.

In 1938 two little girls, ages three years and eighteen months, died when their home was destroyed by a fire of undetermined origin.

Home fires. In December 1934, a New Deal home burned when a gas heater exploded. A Wheeler man lost his home in a fire that also burned his brother's house next door. A bucket brigade and the Fort Peck Fire Department kept the flames from spreading.

In November 1936, a house and all its contents, except the wood box, were burned. A Wheeler cabin, in which a fire had been left to dry wallpaper, burned. A Wilson trailerhome caught fire when a leaky distillate burner ignited.

Businesses. In November 1934, a vehicle fire burned the Choffie Garage in Park Grove, then spread to the Torkelson Beer Parlor next door. The fire destroyed an electric dynamo stored in the garage to furnish electricity to Park Grove. A bucket brigade fought the flames until the Park Grove fire engine arrived with chemicals. The Fort Peck Fire Department came, but too late.

Neither business had any insurance because "insurance companies refused to write policies on buildings close to the railroad tracks."

In April 1935, a movie machine, film, and furnishings valued at $2,600, burned at the Wheeler Theater. The bucket brigade and their two trucks, and the local water wagon responded. The Fort Peck Fire Department kept the fire from spreading.

A gas stove explosion in Finch's Bakery ignited a flash fire. Mr. Finch smothered the flames with a sack of flour.

A "terrific explosion" in the G&N Store cellar in McCone City blew off the store front and severely injured the owner. Some thirty gallons of gas had leaked from a pump and ignited. A barber and his patrons gave the G&N owner first aid and took him to the hospital.

During the severe cold in February 1936, the Wheeler Gamble Store was destroyed when an overheated stove caught fire. The *Fort Peck Press* newspaper office next door was extensively damaged. The Fort Peck Fire Department kept the fire from spreading.

The McCone City Westley/Christenson & Howe Truck Company garage partially burned after a bucket of transmission oil left by the stove caught fire. Five men shoveled snow on seventeen trucks and nearby buildings until the Fort Peck Fire Department arrived.

During the below zero temperatures, overheated stoves burned the Hansen Apartments in Lakeview, damaged the Eastly apartments in Wheeler, and burned a building behind the Wheeler Inn. A stovepipe fire destroyed the roof of the Cozy Cafe.

Fire Prevention. Boomtown owners encouraged residents to purchase fire extinguishers to lessen damage and save homes, but few people could afford to buy them.

In October 1935, the *Nashua Messenger* printed tips on proper use of gasoline, kerosene, distillate, and crude oil, "all deadly explosives when vapors ignite."

Fort Peck town fire officials posted notices: "When firemen tour the city for inspection of chimneys and fire hazards, please treat them with respect and courtesy. It may be your home that will need their services next." Boomtowns posted similar notices.

In October 1936 a huge crowd from the project area attended the Fort Peck Fire Department demonstrations on safety and fire control, in observance of Fire Prevention Week.

Vandalism and arson. An empty store in Wheeler burned after boys tossed firecrackers through a broken window. Children playing with matches started a fire in dry grass in Park Grove, and another under the stage at Wheeler's Majestic Theater.

About a half dozen homes burned of "unknown causes" while owners were away.

A small fire at the Casino Club in June 1938 was investigated as an arson after the Fort Peck Fire Department found gas had been poured on the ground and ignited. Vandals broke into the Hudson-Terraplane garage in Wheeler and burned a 1936 uninsured sedan.

Part 9

Marriage and Family
Valley County marriage licenses sold: 1932 (91); 1933 (72); 1934 (269); 1935(382); 1936 (320). Numbers declined 1937-1940.

Couples cut short their engagements and were married soon after the government announced married men would be hired first at the project. But then, as if love and marriage didn't face enough obstacles during the Great Depression, the 1935 Montana Legislature added one more, the *Gin Marriage Law.*

The well intended law was to discourage "quickie marriages" and those entered into under the influence of "the cup that flows well but not wisely." It decreed that no license would be issued by the county clerk until both parties had submitted recent health certificates, with a Wasserman test, to show that they were free of venereal disease, infectious stage tuberculosis, or other diseases that could "lead to congenital diseases in offspring." Applicants had to be certified "of sound mind" and "legal age" to marry. Certificates had to be issued by a licensed physician practicing medicine and surgery in the state, and living in the county of application.

The estimated cost was a whopping $30.

The clerk of court was empowered to refuse licenses to minors, applicants without medical certificates, and any person appearing to be incompetent or under the influence of alcohol or drugs.

Gin's July 1, 1935, deadline sent a record eighty-eight couples to the county clerk's office in June. After Gin, only two licenses were sold in July and August; twenty-two couples entered into contract marriages, and several were married in other states.

Petitions were signed by citizens and the clergy, and supported by physicians and newspapers. In September Secretary of State Sam W. Mitchell announced the law was "inoperative pending its submission to the voters." Voters didn't like it either.

Showers, weddings, honeymoons, and chivaries
"Justice Frank Breznik read the rites." *Fort Peck Press.*

Bridal showers were happy events given by the family and friends of the bride-to-be. The guests played word games. The guest of honor opened gifts of embroidered pillowcases, handmade quilts, crocheted doilies, and kitchen ware. Lunch was served on tables decorated with ribbons and flowers in season. Details appeared in the local paper.

Only one groom's shower was mentioned. In 1937 the *Glasgow Courier* reported that fifty men had gathered at the Fire Hall for a "surprise kitchen shower" for the Chamber of Commerce (male) secretary. "He received many beautiful and useful gifts," including a sack of potatoes and a quart of vinegar. Ladies were not invited but sent a loving cup presented by the Chamber president. Guests played cards and enjoyed a Dutch lunch.

Weddings took place in the couple's church or the bride's home, followed by a dinner served by her mother and family. Wedding dances were usually held in the school house or community hall.

Some weddings were officiated in the homes of local pastors or the home of a justice of the peace or a judge, witnessed by their family. A few weddings were held at the courthouse, or outdoors in scenic settings. One couple was married in the Casino.

Boomtown brides ranged in age from 16 years old (average 24) up to 56; grooms 18 (average 28) to 56. Law required women to be 18 years of age and men 21 to marry without parental consent.

The bride's wedding dress and bouquet were described in detail in the newspaper announcement of the nuptials: The bride wore "a dress of soft white silk crepe with a long lace veil, she carried a bouquet of rosebuds." "The bride wore a powder blue suit with gray accessories and held a gardenia corsage." "The bride and groom dressed in brown, her bouquet was petunias and snapdragons."

The groom's attire rarely made the society column. Tradition dictated he wear a suit, if he had or could borrow one, or his best dark pants, white shirt and tie. One groom wore "a suit of Oxford gray."

A summer wedding was described thus: "Mosquitoes played the *Wedding March*. The couple drove to Saco for the Reverend, then had to cross back into Valley County where they bought their marriage license. They were married in their car at the county line with the minister reading the ceremonies from the front seat."

Most newlyweds postponed their honeymoon until financially better times. Only a few could afford to "motor to the World's Fair" in Chicago or visit Yellowstone Park. There was no pressure to keep up with the Jones, they didn't have a honeymoon either.

Chivaries (shivarees) were "surprise" events held shortly after the wedding. Friends descended on the couple with noise makers, music, food, and gifts. When one boomtown couple tried to keep their wedding a secret, their friends brought a wheelbarrow and cheered while the groom pushed his bride down the main street of their town.

Divorce: *Marital troubles formed the greater part of the legal business in Valley County District Court last week (nine divorces). Court report October 1935.*

Divorces in the 1930s were printed on the front page of the local newspaper along with the couple's names and grounds for divorce. The most common grounds were desertion, non-support, joblessness, violence, and alcohol. Many divorcing couples were from other states.

A divorce was granted to a man who accused his wife of cruelty and associating with other men, several of whom he named. She claimed he deserted her and made false charges against her chastity.

A divorce was granted to a man claiming desertion and that his wife nagged him and called him names. An "absolute divorce" was granted to a woman beaten and deserted after her wedding in Arizona.

Officials were called to investigate complaints made by parents seeking annulments for under-age daughters wed without consent.

The clerk of District Court reported although 1935 was a record high year for divorces, there were five times as many marriages.

Project babies, children, and teens

Births annually have increased about 500 since the start of the dam. Glasgow registrar, 1936.

Hundreds of babies were born in the project towns, brought into the world by a doctor, nurse, midwife, family member, or a neighbor. The majority arrived in boomtown maternity homes or in the home of their parents. Only a few were born in hospitals.

Babies slept in their padded wooden applebox beds or handmade cradles. They wore cloth diapers, flannel kimonos, and knit booties and caps from layettes made by their moms and ladies sewing circles.

They received immunizations at the schoolhouses along with the students. They suffered from measles and chicken pox brought home by older brothers and sisters. A few babies, although in numbers no larger than the state average, died from heart ailments, "liver strictures," and other causes. Pneumonia claimed the most.

In 1934 boomtown and Fort Peck town babies were part of the statewide "Register Your Baby" campaign sponsored by the Montana State Board of Health "to insure proper registration for every baby born in the last 12 months." They contributed to Valley County having the highest birth rate of any Montana county in July 1935, and the highest number of births (604) for the year. Another 739 births were recorded by the Glasgow registrar in 1936.

Several babies were born in McCone City in McCone County.

Project babies whose parents lived in Glasgow were included in a Fingerprint Day for children on June 20, 1936, sponsored by the Glasgow Junior Chamber of Commerce. The day was part of a nation wide movement to fingerprint all children, prompted by the kidnap and murder of the Charles Lindbergh baby in 1932.

Parents and children lined up at the Lewis-Wedum store as Mayor Leo Coleman led civic leaders through the line first, to demonstrate the procedure. The JCs reported "2,200 fingerprints ... mostly women and children were taken." Families were still lined up at closing.

Children pre-teen
My dad worked on the spillway and my mom took in sewing.

Most school children whose fathers were government workers or whose families owned businesses, came from farms, ranches, or small towns in northeastern and central Montana. They had lived in close knit communities where the school was the center of community life.

The children of project contractors and Corps personnel came from all over the county, mainly the Midwest and Kansas. Many of them had moved to new locations several times.

Children, especially in the boomtowns, were aware their families were going through tough times, but being "kids" they didn't realize just how bad things were because "everyone was the same." Most remembered their childhoods as being happy and focused on their family, friends, and school activities.

Few farm children had gone hungry. Their mothers supplemented poor gardens with whatever wild plants and berries they could find, and served both venison and prairie chicken in and out of season. The children drank skim milk separated from the cream which was sold, and ate whatever eggs weren't traded for groceries. They had more to eat when they lived on their farm than in the boomtowns where the food had to be bought in stores or raised in small gardens.

Toys were few, but some children, especially older boys, owned or shared bicycles and wagons. Children played marbles, softball, kick-the-can, and other group games. They had fun making and walking on stilts, and jumping rope. The older children swam in Corps designated areas of the dredge cuts in the summer. In the winter they built snow caves and turned out in large numbers for sledding and ice skating.

Boomtown children whose families had electricity for the first time recalled the thrill of turning on their one light bulb. They remembered buying penny candy; and taking turns playing on the playground swings, slides, teeter totters, and monkey bars at school.

Hundreds of project children were members of boys and girls clubs and Sunday Schools. They had daily chores at home, and a few earned money from odd jobs and saved for their wanted items. They collected bottles, cans, and egg cartons to exchange for movie matinee tickets. In the summer farm children returned home with their mothers to help with haying and whatever field work there was.

In later years, the children recalled there *were* some difficult days; the death of a family member, the hard times when their fathers lost their jobs, illnesses, changing schools, and saying goodbye to friends. But for the most part they remembered "wonderful childhoods."

As the project population dwindled, some government workers from the boomtowns moved to Fort Peck. Their children delighted in their "mansions" with electricity, indoor plumbing, and running water.

As adults most children remembered the dam construction, but were too busy with their friends to pay attention to details. It took years before they realized they had been part of something big.

Teens. *Many of them learned to drive on the project roads.*

Teenagers were aware they were part of their parents' struggle to survive the Depression. Some had seen their family farms auctioned off, older brothers go to Civilian Conservation Corps (CCC) camps, and their fathers desperate to find jobs. Most believed it was their responsibility and a privilege to help their family however they could.

Boomtown teens, whose parents owned businesses, worked for them after school. Others took any of the few jobs available. Farm teens spent vacations working on their family farm or for neighbors.

High schoolers rode a bus to school in Glasgow or Nashua or lived there and worked for their room and board. Teens who were eligible, attended the government high school in Fort Peck during the few years the higher grades were offered there.

Teenagers shared many good times with their friends. They went to dances and movies, and had bonfires and marshmallow roasts after skating and sledding. Many of them were involved in school and community clubs, music programs, and church organizations. Both boys and girls were involved in organized, and pick-up sports.

Most teens, especially the boys, watched the dam construction with interest and took bus tours of the project sponsored by the Corps.

Teenagers made lifelong friends while living at the project. Many of them met their future mate there.

In the early 1940s hundreds of them stepped forward to enlist and serve their country during World War II.

As adults project children paid tribute to the perseverance of their parents. They remembered them as fearless, hard working protectors. Children from large families recalled how their mothers somehow managed to clothe and feed everyone. They considered their parent's love and sacrifices worth more than any amount of money.

Years later many of the boomtown children traveled back to the project area to try to find their roots and the vaguely recalled pieces of their childhood. There were no hometowns waiting, no familiar streets or playgrounds, and few people they used to know. The unfamiliar open spaces raised the question of whether the towns and people had really ever been there at all.

Children less fortunate

Not all the area children of working or transient parents had loving homes. Some suffered neglect, abuse, or abandonment. Homelessness, unemployment, alcohol, and divorce made horrific lives for children without the safety net of at least one strong parent or grandparent.

Montana counties had few resources with which to help them. Officials working with limited public welfare programs, welcomed the Child Welfare Provisions of the Social Security Act in 1935.

A Nashua judge and a Bureau of Child Protection Agency deputy investigated one family they called a "pitiful" case. A woman had abandoned her husband and "several" young children living in a shelter of tin and gunny sacks. The men reported, "The children seemed healthy in spite of their destitution and lack of care."

In July 1936 the Bureau of Child Protection hired a special worker for Valley and Daniels counties to assist the district deputy with the growing number of delinquent children, especially in Valley County. Most cases involved the children of transient families, and run-away teens, who came to the area in hopes of finding jobs.

Reports of neglected children and family troubles tapered off as the project ended in 1940, and rain brought better times.

The Neighbors

Guy Family Home

Bergstrom Home

Culver Home

Funk Family 2-story Home

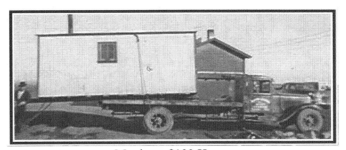

Moving a $100 House

Photos courtesy of Doris Hansen, Lois Damstrom,
Earl Culver, Elizabeth (Funk) Brandt, Paul McFarland.

144

Little Miss Violet

Culver Family

Cowboy Movie Fans

Worley Kids

The Cornhuskers

Photos courtesy of Ethel Tanner, Earl Culver
Chuck Worley, Alvin Fisher

Project Schools

All children whose parents are working for the government, Mason and Walsh, or Frazier (Frazier-Davis Construction Co.) must attend the school at Fort Peck. They can not attend schools of Wheeler, Park Grove, New Deal or any boomtown.
Department of the Interior, Washington, D.C. Fall 1934.

"The War Department has provided at Fort Peck for all children of workers on the project. It would be a duplication of relief to pay for their education at any of the new towns. The federal government is not responsible for the congregation of children other than those of workers and supervisors ... it will be up to the districts to ... provide education for all children who are not eligible to attend Fort Peck School. Teacher's salaries and other funds will have to come from other sources. State Superintendent Elizabeth Ireland, states that the state may be able to give some assistance from the Equalization Fund." *Valley County Superintendent A. Jerome Wall.*

The mass migration of families from northern Valley County to the project meant some schools there would have to close while new ones opened in the boomtowns. And, arrangements would have to be made for the increased enrollments in Glasgow and Nashua.

In July 1934 Superintendent Wall organized a Committee On Schools with three representatives each from Wheeler, Park Grove, New Deal, Parkdale, and Midway. A census was taken to determine the number of students eligible to attend the government grade school in Fort Peck, the number returning home with their mothers to community schools, the number being homeschooled, and how many needed boomtown schools.

Wheeler already had 100 students in need of a school, with more expected by fall. A similar situation existed in all the new towns.

The Wheeler Commercial Club, business owners, and the parents donated $1,000 to build a school. Twenty carpenters had it ready for a Grand Opening Ball on October 8. A fire, possibly caused by a "carelessly thrown cigarette," flared up after the crowd left a fund raising dance and burned all but $100 worth of furnishings.

Parents scrambled to raise money to rebuild. School opened on schedule with 130 students. Funds raised: $405.33 in five schoolhouse dances and $1,056.50 in donations for lumber, nails, windows, tables, benches, coal, stove and chimney, blackboard paint, dance music and guard, tin cups, gas for lamps, tar paper, and $10 for outdoor toilets.

1934-1935 school term (September through May)

Square Deal School 1935 Photo Courtesy of Lois Damstrom

Through the combined efforts of parents, business people, and school officials, classes started on time in nearly all the schools.

Lakeview and Delano Heights students rode the bus to Wheeler in 1934 and 1935 while their school was being planned.

Midway parents and businesses bought lumber and remodeled the Gospel Tabernacle into classrooms they shared with **Park Grove** and *New Deal* until their schools opened. Classes began with 135 students.

A thief stole some boards during a Midway fund raising dance. He was chastised with a poem "Meanie Man," in the *Fort Peck Press.*

Martinville school was accepted by the Antler School District. It opened in September 1934 with 11 students.

Wilson residents built their school with donated lumber and land. It opened with 26 students, soon 33, in eight grades with one teacher.

Square Deal parents appealed to Senator Burton K. Wheeler for help in obtaining a building and teacher for their 42 students.

In November Superintendent Wall, Senator Wheeler, and Lt. Ewart Plank accepted the War Department's offer of five government buildings for schools. They were sold to Wall, then to the district for $1 each for Parkdale, Midway, New Deal, Wheeler, and Park Grove.

Parkdale remodeled its 12x28 feet building in time to open in November with 30 students and one teacher.

Park Grove filled its 40x50 feet school, and by March 1935 had 90 students, grades 1-8, in one room with a divider. A room was added.

High School students rode a bus to Glasgow or lived there paying room and board. Students living in Nashua attended school there.

Most parents wanted their children to attend their town schools. In January 1935 the *Fort Peck Press* noted, "The state superintendent is checking up on the Wheeler school and sending several children to the Fort Peck site ... their fathers are employed by the government."

Another School Fire. April 1, 1935, Wheeler's new school, its furnishings, a piano, and $700 worth of books burned in a flash fire during a dance. The possible cause was another "carelessly thrown cigarette or match," an "overturned gas lamp," or a "fruit jar of gas stored in a corner." More than 200 dancers fled through windows and doors. The Fort Peck Fire Department saved the barracks classrooms next door. A $2,000 insurance policy could not replace the loss.

Wheeler parents and businesses again dug deep in their pockets for funds. They borrowed one building, added another, and cleaned the barracks classrooms. Classes were in session within two weeks.

Benefit dances and card parties were held almost every Saturday night in response to the plea "We need more money for our schools!"

The Fort Peck Press printed school news written by students. They promoted their *Och Hone* operetta with its grand cast of 140. They announced that a Fort Peck girl and a New Deal boy had won the American Legion Flag Contest to represent Valley County in the Regional Meet. And they wrote about their concerts, plays, the Buttrey's Spelling Contest, May Pole Dances, and their Christmas programs. Special note was made of Eighth Grade Commencement, and the last day of school picnic with sack races and games.

1935-1936 (September through May)

Enrollment increased dramatically. Park Grove had 200 students. Another 26x40 feet building was added. First graders attended half days. Square Deal, New Deal, and Midway had similar plans. Wheeler had five teachers for 235 students, and more coming.

Wheeler parents were still struggling to replace their burned school when *Fate* stepped in: The Hollywood Inn, allegedly owned by a Chicago gangster, suddenly became available. Rumor had it that his wife had an auto accident in North Dakota and a suitcase full of money fell out of her car. Valley County authorities investigated then auctioned the dance hall to the school board at $1 for tax deed. It was moved to Wheeler, hastily remodeled, and opened with 255 students, more than 60 in some rooms. Voters approved a new building.

The January 1936 school census counted 384 students in the Wheeler district (West Galpin) including Lakeview and Wilson; the New Deal area (South Galpin) including Square Deal, Park Grove, and Midway enrolled 804. Glasgow registered 1,838 and Nashua 452.

The Park Grove School burned down February 17, 1936, after a heater in which a fire had been left low during the extreme cold, caught fire. The $1,000 loss was covered by insurance. A new school was built and ready for students by the end of March.

Midway opened its new school for grades 1-6 in March, with room in the former tabernacle classrooms for 7th graders.

Although the 1935-36 winter was one of Montana's coldest, the schools were in session almost every day. Children were bundled in warm coats, scarves, mittens, and overshoes and sent off to classes. Teachers helped them "wrap up" again before they left for home.

In March 1936 trustees from school districts 6 and 21 requested emergency funds. So far only liberal allowances from the Equalization Fund and the county and state apportionments had made it possible to operate. Most schools exceeded pupil-to-teacher recommendations: District 21 had 11 teachers with a student increase from 273 to 553. District 6 had nine teachers with enrollment up from 181 to 336.

The Glasgow school divided its lunch room into classrooms. It had up to 60 students in rooms designed for 30. Enrollment at 1,246 was 158 more than 1934. Nashua's overcrowding was relieved a bit by the opening of its new WPA-built school.

Project teachers improvised and made-do. Parents held fund raisers and did whatever work at the school needed to be done.

Students took everything in stride; they performed well with their harmonica-rhythm bands in the First Valley County Music Festival. They participated in Grade School Achievement Day. They entered and won pencils in the Christmas Seal Essay Contest. In May the 8th graders took their state exams and were advised they "rated high."

1936-1937 (September through May)

Boomtown schools reported "heavy enrollment." Lakeview opened their new school with 19 students. Wheeler registered 335, more than in the two years they included Lakeview and Wilson. Classrooms were added but still averaged more than 40 pupils each. Glasgow and Nashua schools were overcrowded, and dorms had a long waiting list.

In the spring, teachers were notified of the new Department of Instruction requirement which meant some of them would have to attend college summer school and take certification exams.

1937-1938 (September through May)

Fall enrollment decreased ten percent in the boomtown schools. Fourteen Valley County school districts, including Wheeler, Nashua, and New Deal had budget cuts. Bus services were curtailed. Midway and Park Grove consolidated, with grades 1-6 at Park Grove and 7-8 in Midway. Glasgow's enrollment decreased 177, due to the four-year high school opened in Fort Peck. Nashua enrolled 359.

One day in September the 35 students in the Park Grove/Midway school discovered their school was missing! During the night, project workers had moved it to Park Grove to make way for the dredges.

Wheeler students printed their *Wheeler High Lights* and "*No-So-We-Ea*" (north, south, west, east) annual "for posterity a pictorial and written record of a unique school in a unique community."

The December 1937 Valley County school census noted a decrease of 1,000 students, mostly in the Glasgow, Wheeler, Nashua, and New Deal districts. Even fewer students enrolled in January 1938. Wheeler dropped to 115 students with seven teachers. Drastic budget cuts were made. The Glasgow/Fort Peck school bus was discontinued, leaving 31 project high schoolers to use public transportation or live in Glasgow.

In May, Glasgow students organized a "picture taking club." Their school hosted 87 graduates at the 31st 8th Grade Graduation.

Enrollment 1939-1940 increased slightly in Glasgow and Nashua. Schools were still open in Park Grove/Midway, New Deal, Wheeler, and Square Deal. The 1940-41 school term began with 290 pupils. The Wilson/Lakeview bus was discontinued. Most schools closed in the next few years. Square Deal-New Deal was one of the last.

Fort Peck *"The government school"*

School opened in Fort Peck in October 1934 in temporary quarters, with 213 students in grades 1-8, up to 300 before November. Buses picked up the children of government workers in the boomtowns.

The new school, under construction northwest of the Employees Hotel, near the town's temporary residences, was ready by second semester. It featured large modern classrooms and a fully equipped playground. It was overcrowded and growing when it opened.

In addition to the required curriculum, teachers started a Safety Patrol, physical education classes, achievement programs, and several extra curricular activities, including selected *moving pictures.*

In September 1935, due to heavy enrollment, four barracks were moved beside the school for additional classrooms. Enrollment had reached 329 students for 11 teachers. Grades 9 and 10 were added.

In August 1936, Principal L.O. Fjerstad registered 362 students. Enrollment increased for the 1937-1938 term. Grades 11-12 were added. By January there were 503 students.

Fjerstad, who helped start the school in 1934, reported enrollment and facilities had been equal through "phenomenal growth."

Workers began leaving the project and enrollment dropped to 475 by May 30, 1938. The 1939-1940 school term began with a peak enrollment of 512. Several families left in December. Enrollment was 132 in 1941-1942 after workers and most Corps personnel were gone.

Each year in May, 8th graders received diplomas and all grades exhibited their work. Closing day was celebrated with a picnic and games. At the May 1939 commencement 27 seniors presented a three-act pageant covering Fort Peck "50 million years ago" to the project. Hundreds attended the musical narrative and called it "outstanding."

Christmas Programs at Fort Peck School

The Fort Peck School was just two months old in December 1934, but students were rehearsed and ready for the first annual Community Christmas Program. The event was held in the Recreation Hall and drew huge crowds. Everyone sang Christmas carols. A jolly Santa handed out candy and fruit to all the children in attendance.

The *Nashua Messenger* editor wrote, "The Community Christmas Program presented at the Rec Hall by the Fort Peck School was inspiring ... and broke all attendance records. Families came from miles around to hear choral singing, see the beautiful tableaux, and welcome Santa."

The programs were an annual community event; 1,000 people attended in 1937 to hear the school's new orchestra, and see the high school presentation of *The Holy City* with scenes of the Nativity.

Christmas Programs in the Boomtown Schools

Schools were open for only a few months in 1934 before the first Christmas programs. School buildings were warmed by crackling fires in pot bellied stoves. Evergreen trees decorated with popcorn, paper ornaments, and a star or angel stood in a front corner. Bed-sheet curtains were hung on wire strung across the room to create a stage.

Excited students, dressed in their best, stood tall and recited their "pieces," then donned homemade costumes for the plays. Parents and family members stood, for the lack of seats, and applauded. Everyone sang *Jingle Bells, Silent Night,* and all the old Christmas carols.

Cued by sleigh bells, Santa Claus arrived with "Merry Christmas!" to give treat bags with an apple, orange, and candy to every child. The PTA served coffee and cookies. Hard times were forgotten.

McCone City School, McCone County

A private school opened in the home of teacher Mrs. Lila Watson in September 1934 for the growing number of McCone City students.

Parents formed a Parent Teacher Association (PTA) and bought a government building for $1 from the Corps, for a school. Businesses helped pay for remodeling, desks, books, playground equipment, and a fence. The school was accepted in McCone County District #2, and opened in January 1935 with 40 students.

The 1935-1936 term began in September with two teachers and 94 students, soon up to 200. Three classrooms and teachers were added. Enrollment grew to upward of 300 before it peaked. Several students moved away in December; the school year ended with 185.

Parents held dances to purchase books and school supplies. They bought a piano with proceeds from a Chop Suey dinner, and baseball bats, balls, gloves, and other equipment with card party funds.

McCone City students were invited to submit their news to the *Fort Peck Press* school column. They reported: *The First Grade is working on The Three Bears. Many kids (2-3 graders) are absent with measles and pneumonia. The entertainment committee told jokes and sang songs. A declamation was given. The 4th Grade is making health posters. Fifth Grade was given an entertainment for language. The Citizenship Court, 7th & 8th Graders, have been holding court every Friday. They gave some unpleasant punishments. The teacher is in the hospital in Glasgow.*

School visitors included county superintendent Edith Mahlstadt, county officials, their health officer Dr. C.C. Lull, and parents.

The students held concerts and programs. They all participated in the annual Spelling Bee and Track Meet. Their eighth grade exams were held in Circle with graduation in McCone City in May.

Christmas was celebrated with a program, plays, and carols for student's families and their community. Hard times could not curb the excitement, and funds were always raised for the special treat bags.

A parade, picnic, and games for everyone marked the last day of school in May, and goodbye to many new friends.

Enrollment dropped in 1937-1938. The school closed early in the 1940s when the project ended and families moved away.

Project Parents placed high priority on their children's education. They worked hard to help the district provide good schools. Children adapted to overcrowding and biscuit lunches in lard pails.

Teachers met the challenges of teaching, and the expectations that they be professional, dress modestly, and set a good example. Most were high school graduates with two years or less of "normal school. Experienced teachers made $95 a month in 1937-1938.

Wish Lists for schools included maps, encyclopedias, blackboards and chalk, text books, *Community Sing* songbooks, phonographs, globes, pencils, paper, and sweeping compound.

School furniture included a teacher's desk, and desks or tables and benches for students. Water was carried in, and kept in a crock jar with a spigot or dipper, on a back wall shelf above the wash basin.

Hooks were placed on the back wall for "wraps" (coats and hats). A pot bellied heater, poker, coal bucket, ash shovel, and broom stood near the middle of the room so the teacher could tend the fire.

Outhouses, one for boys and one for girls, stood behind the school near the woodshed. The older boys shoveled the paths in the winter.

Parents helped clean and repair school buildings. Students "dusted erasers" outside, clapping two together until the chalk dust flew.

On a typical school day the teacher rang her handbell at 9 a.m. with "take your seats." Inspection (mainly for clean hands) followed. Students marched outside to raise the flag ("salute the flag") and say the *Pledge of Allegiance.* They returned to their seats for the singing of four songs, including *America* and a hymn.

Class registers for 1934-1939 showed the 5th grade curriculum: Spelling, arithmetic, history, geography, language, penmanship, phonics, word drill, and hygiene.

Fridays included an art project or a "radio show." There were 15-minute recesses morning and afternoon, and an hour "intermission" at noon. Dismissal was promptly at 3:30 p.m.

Health Care at the Project

Mrs. J., in spite of her illness, is quite cheerful.

In the spring of 1934, although warned not to come, hundreds of unemployed adults from around the nation traveled to Valley County in search of jobs. Many had small children. Their health care needs were added to those of a growing number of local residents without funds for medical treatment. In December county officials reported an "extreme emergency" in the County Poor Fund.

County commissioners appointed Dr. A.N. Smith, whose practice included treatment of jail inmates and the poor, as county physician until December 1935 when Dr. C.B. Larson was named to the office.

Dr. C.C. Lull, of Wheeler, was appointed McCone City health officer in 1935, to care for school children and families there.

In August 1935 the new Social Security Act authorized a number of public and child welfare programs. The County Public Welfare Department, under the supervision of county commissioners and the state, provided services the *Act* did not cover. The new programs were welcomed by local authorities, churches, and organizations trying to cope with the overwhelming needs in their counties.

Social Security programs paid doctors to examine school children for diseased tonsils and adenoid, and to test their eyes, ears, teeth, heart, lungs, weight, and orthopedic conditions.

County health nurse Kathryn Worrell checked for skin diseases, lice, and impetigo; and taught hygiene. She also held Baby Weighing Days for pre-schoolers to determine if they were "normal," and she arranged immunizations and visits to families with health problems.

Parents in the smaller boomtowns, assisted by health officials, held child development meetings and pre-school clinics in their homes. In 1938 the Fort Peck Health Center, through the Montana Board of Health, held a series of baby conferences in Wheeler, New Deal, McCone City, Park Grove, and the town of Fort Peck.

Medical information was available from state and county health departments. Newspapers ran syndicated and local health columns. National foundation speakers spoke in schools about tuberculosis, cancer, heart disease, infantile paralysis, and the danger of cigarettes.

In March 1936 commissioners appointed Glasgow doctor M.D. Hoyt health officer for Valley County. The state Board of Health approved a sanitation inspector for the project area. Most of the new programs and appointments were paid for by Social Security.

Dr. C.C. Lull, a Kansas medical school graduate and World War I medical officer, opened his practice in Wheeler early in 1934. He was named the Veterans Administration physician in the Fort Peck area in October 1935. In February 1936, he left to fill a medical vacancy at an Idaho CCC Camp. Dr. Lull returned to his office in Wheeler in December to work until his retirement to Kansas in the fall of 1937.

Dr. N.A. Currie moved to Nashua in 1920. He was a World War I veteran, medically discharged with tuberculosis. During his recovery he and his wife lived in a tent in the California desert. They opened an office in the Park Grove Drug Store in 1935. Along with his office practice, Dr. Currie and nurse Lois (Bissell) McCoy delivered dozens of babies in project homes and in the Nashua maternity home.

Dentist E.V. Bethel moved to Wheeler in March 1934 and set up his foot-operated dental machine in a tent. He soon opened offices in Park Grove and Wheeler, and stayed on until the project ended.

A few other doctors and dentists practiced briefly in the towns.

There were several doctors, nurses, and dentists at the Fort Peck Hospital and clinic, and the Smith Clinic, for the town and workers.

Hospitals and Maternity Homes

The Fort Peck Hospital treated Corps personnel, and government workers and families in need of emergency care.

Glasgow Deaconess Hospital was incorporated in 1914 and had long served patients in Glasgow and Valley County. Project people were treated there, as were workers in need of extended care.

The new, fully equipped, three-story, 60-bed hospital opened in 1936 with a full staff, generous benefactors, and volunteers. Some hospital supplies were provided by a government loan and grant.

Valley County Hospital 1917-1942. "General Hospital" had 20 beds in 12 rooms for low income and indigent patients, people with communicable diseases, and children with enlarged tonsils/adenoids.

Maternity homes, with two to four beds, where midwives, nurses, and sometimes doctors, delivered babies were established in the larger boomtowns. Among them were the Miller Maternity Home in New Deal and the Doebler Maternity Home in Midway.

Communicable diseases

The numbers of communicable diseases in the boomtowns were comparable to those state wide.

Highly contagious childhood diseases spread through the project area schools almost every year. Outbreaks were expected. Teachers and parents recognized the symptoms and treated the children with TLC and the home remedies used in their own childhoods.

Children recuperated at home where large bright red or green "Quarantined" signs were posted on their door.

Chicken pox with itchy pox all over the body, usually broke out in the spring. Park Grove schools were hit hard in April 1934.

Diphtheria was rare.

Measles with a headache, fever, and red spots, were common. In December 1934 the Wheeler school had a "measles epidemic." In February 1935 it reported 15 cases of "regular" measles, and 35 cases of red measles. Square Deal School averaged 20, as did other schools.

Mumps were accompanied by fever and painfully swollen neck glands. In December 1935, McCone City School had several cases.

Scarlet Fever with its bright red rash was uncommon. Medical officials reported only a few cases.

Small Pox, a severe outbreak of pox that left scars, and often caused death, was mostly under control by the 1930s. A few cases were reported in December 1935 in New Deal and McCone City. Dr. Lull vaccinated 300 children in McCone City to prevent an outbreak.

In January 1936 small pox was diagnosed in Valley County. The school district provided vaccinations for Glasgow children, and 230 children without vaccinations in the project towns. The 1935-36 Montana Board of Health reported that Valley County had most of the 34 cases of smallpox in the twelve state locations reporting.

Whooping Cough spread through schools nearly every winter, but no epidemics were reported. Children were examined for pneumonia.

Polio (infantile paralysis) was a dreaded disease in the 1930s, some 25 years before the Salk and Sabin vaccines. Victims such as President F. D. Roosevelt were crippled, and many died. Most parents banned swimming and took other precautions during the summer "polio season." Few new cases were reported in the project area.

Tuberculosis (TB) Montana had an aggressive prevention program with screening, chest x-rays and skin tests. The Valley County health officials routinely inspected cafes, soda fountains, hotels, and dairies.

Typhoid was a deadly infectious disease, spread from person to person, or by unsanitary conditions. A number of cases were reported in Montana in September 1934. To prevent its spread to the new boomtowns, the health inspector called for an anti-typhoid screening.

Notice: Typhoid vaccinations: Complete immunization for every-one in project towns..50 cents, the cost of the vaccine. Dr. A. Veitch, of Fort Peck, deputy county health officer, and O. Morgan, health inspector with the State Board of Health, will conduct vaccinations.

Influenza and pneumonia: During January and February 1935 a number of schoolchildren, teachers, and area residents were ill with flu and pneumonia. A few were hospitalized.

In January 1936 an influenza epidemic spread through Montana. State health officials reported new cases suddenly increased from "a few hundred to 2,796." Many boomtown residents of all ages were hospitalized and several died within a few days of becoming ill.

In January 1937 Dr. Lull reported only 50 cases in the project area.

Health Regulations. Most people complied with health regulations and quarantine and vaccination orders. In one case a couple failed to appear in court for not reporting the wife's scarlet fever. They refused the health officer entry to their home, then disappeared.

The number of cases of communicable diseases among transients is unknown because most were not diagnosed or reported.

Immunization clinics were held in all project schools. Students, pre-schoolers, and adults lined up for their shots.

In March 1935 the county nurse reported nearly 900 children had received a series of three typhoid shots "with more to do." Pre-schoolers were vaccinated for diphtheria and smallpox during a special conference in Wheeler. Dr. Lull inoculated students in McCone City and reported, "the children were all in good condition."

Notice for adults: "Vaccination necessary if you have no scar."

Deaths and accidents of babies and children 1934-1937

Approximately fifty babies to three-year-old children died in the boomtowns during the project years. Pneumonia was the most common cause. Other causes included various heart ailments, "liver strictures," and spinal meningitis. A few babies died at home of "unknown causes." A baby suffocated in a car.

Hospital records show children were admitted for illnesses such as "summer complaint." A large number of them had their tonsils and adenoids removed. Children broke their bones on school playground equipment, bicycles, and skates. Some caught their hands in washing machine wringers. Boys got hurt hooking sleds to cars.

Adult accidents, illness, death: Mr. D. is sick with the prevailing indisposition. Mrs. G. has bronchitis and lost her speech. Mr. N. took a violent heart attack and succumbed. Fort Peck Press news.

Adults suffered grippe, diphtheria, quinsy, pleurisy, bronchitis, and rheumatism. Some had childhood diseases. A few suffered nervous breakdowns. A woman was poisoned by tainted canned food.

A commissary worker died of alcohol poisoning from non-stop drinking after he lost his job. Another died of peritonitis after surgery. A few people died of tuberculosis, heart ailments, and cancer.

Men broke their arms or were "painfully injured" cranking their vehicles. A Park Grove woman was overcome by gas from her stove. A worker chopping wood was hit in the face by a flying chunk. A man installing a meat market cooler fell through the store's roof. A woman was injured when she stepped on a nail.

Boomtown people were generally in good health, even though they could not afford much dental care or medical treatment. They were strong from hard physical labor, and able to manage most illnesses with home remedies. Women, especially those from rural areas, were able to diagnose ailments and give first-aid for broken bones, cuts, and burns, using skills they learned at home from their mothers and grandmothers. Many of the women had delivered babies. Being able to respond to their family's health care was part of who they were.

Abortions were not legal, but were performed by a few "doctors" of questionable credentials, and some women who claimed to "help women and girls," especially "prostitutes in trouble."

In 1933 newspapers reported a "doctor" newly arrived in Nashua was charged with murder after an 18-year-old girl died from an abortion consented to by her boyfriend and mother. In 1935 a 25-year-old married woman died after an abortion performed by the female operator of a Glasgow nursing home.

In 1936, a "drugless doctor" was charged with performing an "illegal operation." He was sent to prison for two and a half years for performing "numerous offenses of that nature" in the boomtowns.

Suicide. Overwhelming despair, loneliness, and loss of hope for a better day resulted in several suicides. Among others who took their lives was a doctor addicted to drugs, a dentist, and a mental patient.

At least three women, despondent over domestic troubles and unable to find jobs attempted to take their lives.

Part 10

Church at the Project

In the 1930s there was at least one church in every Montana town, and several in rural communities. When their members moved to the project they took their religion with them. Church services were held in boomtown homes, theaters, schools, and outside in tents during the summer, due to a shortage of church buildings.

Glasgow churches were the first to invite Corps families to their services in 1933. During the project years residents of Nashua and the rural areas also shared their pastors and churches with project people.

In December 1933, a group of boatyard workers got together to sing Christmas carols at the Deaconess Hospital in Glasgow. In January 1934, about fifty of them formed the Fort Peck Dam Workers Booster Club. As part of their activities they invited Rev. Blythe H. McLean to preach a series of Sunday sermons in their barracks recreation hall. Services continued with pastors from Wolf Point, Malta, Chinook, Richey, Glasgow, Nashua, and around the area coming weekly, in all kinds of weather, to meet with the workers.

Fort Peck townsite churches:
Report by Capt. Ewart G. Plank Fort Peck town manager, 1936.

Church organizations ... were a subject of discussion from the onset of the project ... the Catholic and Lutheran churches indicated definitely that they had sufficient number of communicants to warrant church organizations. The Home Missions Council of Montana, realizing that other denominations would be generally too small to organize individually, proposed the organization of a Community Church. This was done.... The Lutheran congregation secured ample funds to insure the erection of a church building, and ground space in the central portion of town at a charge of $1 was assigned to them.

"To avoid the expense of erecting and maintaining church buildings, the Community Church and the Catholic Church utilize the Recreation Hall, at nominal rentals, holding separate services under schedules agreeable to all. Each church calls and remunerates its own pastor. Needless to say, each of these churches is a positive asset and a great credit to the community."

Fort Peck Community Church. In January 1935, forty-five area pastors and church leaders met at the Fort Peck School to organize the Community Church. Each congregation was given a scheduled time to hold services in the Recreation Hall. Members formed groups and held fundraisers to pay their expenses and conduct charity work.

To better coordinate relief efforts, individual congregations joined to form the Community Church Relief Association. They all collected household goods, clothing, and bedding. The items were displayed and distributed in a donated room in the Recreation Hall.

The Fort Peck Lutheran Church had the largest congregation. Members built a three-room church building across the street from the Fort Peck Theatre. It opened in February 1935, and was dedicated in May. Rev. O.N. Rue served as pastor. His sister came to the project most summers to teach Bible School in Fort Peck and Park Grove.

The church had a choir and active clubs for all ages. The *Fort Peck Press* reported "a goodly number" attended Sunday services.

The Ladies Aid held clothing drives for needy families. They sold homemade candy, had bake sales, made embroidered dishtowels, and held bazaars to raise funds for their church and charities. They were known for their "sumptuous suppers" to support various causes.

Boomtown churches.

Bars were full, so were the churches

In 1934 Rev. Blythe McLean began holding church services where ever there was room in the new towns. By 1935 several more pastors were traveling to the project to preach in tents, churches, theaters, and schoolhouses. They helped their parishioners from home start Sunday Schools, and officiated at their boomtown weddings and baptisms.

The Community Church was the first one in Wheeler. Members met in various places until their 4th Street church was open in 1935.

Trinity Lutheran, Missouri Synod, was Wheeler's second church. Rev. E.G. Kleidon held services in the theater until the 20x30 feet building was ready in November 1935. The church sat on a knoll at the southeast end of Main Street. Its cross could be seen for miles.

The Pentecostal Church purchased an empty store in Roeville and moved it over to East Main Street in October 1935. Members invited everyone to "Come! To Sunday School and Preaching."

The Nazarene Church was organized in 1935. Services were held in the Eastly Apartments behind the *Fort Peck Press* in Wheeler.

The Methodist Church met in homes. In 1936 they were part of a community program for "members in big and small towns."

Other Boomtown Churches

The Midway Gospel Tabernacle was built in September 1934. The Mormon Church of Jesus Christ of Latter Day Saints met in the New Deal School. The Non-denominational Holiness Mission and the Gospel Tabernacle opened in Wheeler. Glad Tiding Gospel Missions and Union Gospel Missions met in New Deal, Park Grove, and Wheeler. The Catholic Bible Study Club, Mission Bible Conference, and Baptist Congregation met in New Deal. There were several small groups due to the lack of large meeting places.

Bible Camps drew dozens of children for their two week Vacation Bible School. In 1936 nearly 300 project children attended camps in Wheeler, New Deal, and Park Grove. The American Sunday School Union enrolled 346 students in its three week Bible School.

Missionaries came from all over the world. A Chinese missionary gave a concert at New Deal; A Russian pastor preached at Park Grove, his wife played hymns on her autoharp, and did violin imitations. An American missionary to Egypt visited Wheeler Glad Tidings Mission.

Evangelists came from all over to give their testimonies. A man traveling through the area sang hymns and played his Hawaiian guitar.

Local evangelists included "The Ruby Evangelists," Misses Ruby Howe and Ruby Nystro. They held a series of services in boomtown schools and in the Midway Gospel Tabernacle.

Congregations ran newspaper invitations and large crowds came to hear their speakers and attend their services.

Newspapers printed weekly service schedules, with special notices on Thanksgiving, Christmas, and Easter featured on their front pages. The *Fort Peck Press* included a Bible verse and selected reading in every issue of the paper. KGCX radio station in Wolf Point broadcast special messages.

Sunday School Union. By February 1934 Rev. Blythe McLean, a northeastern Montanan and member of the non-sectarian American Sunday School Union, had started Bible Classes and Sunday Schools in every one of the large and small boomtowns.

In 1935, Wheeler Sunday School Union members built a 20x32 feet building a block west of the school. It opened with 100 students. Its *Fort Peck Press* ads read: "Wanted: Boys to attend Sunday School in Wheeler. Girls not barred."

McCone City Churches. Residents held Bible study and worship services in their homes, the theater, and the schoolhouse. Reverend McClean helped start an American Sunday School Union class in 1934. Several area pastors preached in McCone City. Some families attended church in Fort Peck and the other towns.

Christmas Services

Special services were held in boomtown churches, schools and theaters on Christmas Eve and Day, with record attendance.

Glasgow Courier editor Sam Gilluly wrote about Christmas in Wheeler, "It is refreshing to note how residents of this busy project town responded to the spirit of Christmas."

He noted the "brightly lighted cross" atop Trinity Lutheran Church that could be seen for miles. "These evidences, in spite of many rumors to the contrary, give us to understand that there are many powers for good at work in the project settlement."

The Christmas service scene was the same in all the boomtowns.

In Fort Peck town, services were held at the Lutheran Church, and in the Recreation Hall for the several individual congregations who made up the Community Church. Glasgow and Nashua churches were filled for Christmas services, concerts, and holiday events.

The holidays were brightened for project patients in the Glasgow and Fort Peck hospitals where volunteers decorated trees and gave patients gifts of flowers, fruit, and tray favors made by school children. Groups came to sing Christmas carols in the hospital halls.

The Christmas spirit drew people together through their faith. Their shared traditions brought peace and hope during difficult times in the short, dark days of December.

Organizations–No Idle Hands
Project people had fun working on worthwhile projects.

Home Demonstration Clubs were launched nationally in 1910 to promote adult education in home economics and community service. By the 1930s every Montana county had at least one. Women who belonged to HD clubs back home started new ones in the boomtowns.

Clubs were organized under the direction of the county agent, who also loaned out the county's can sealer and pressure cooker. Officers were elected. Clubs were named *Sunflowers*, *Square Deal Hilltoppers*, and such. Children and guests were welcome.

Members sewed new and repaired old clothes. They made aprons, potholders, clothespin bags, and toys. They pieced quilts from scraps, made pillowcases from old sheets, and hooked rugs from rags and no longer darnable socks. At least one more life was wrung out of every item. Women learned techniques for reed and willow weaving, and candlewicking. They also sponsored business and financial classes.

State and county extension agents visited the clubs to present programs on health and nutrition. They gave demonstrations on how to garden, can vegetables, bake bread, and serve surplus foods such as cheese, rice, and apples. Sewing demonstrations included making baby layettes and children's clothes.

Women learned to make patterns and dress forms, and how to care for their sewing machines. Many women learned how to unravel old sweaters, dye the yarn, and hook them into colorful rugs.

Some HD clubs held bake sales and organized food displays. The musically inclined formed jolly kitchen bands and provided light hearted entertainment for fund raisers. In December 1936, the Valley County club members learned that, through their combined efforts, they had helped 500 families in 20 communities.

The clubs merged as boomtown numbers decreased, and continued meeting until the last families left.

Sewing circles. *The ladies sewing circle met. A dainty and delicious lunch was served after which the ladies plied their needles. Fort Peck Press community news, 1935.*

Sewing circles were generally informal groups such as the *Stitch and Chatter Club*. They met in each other's homes to embroidery towels and pillow cases; crochet or knit scarfs, mittens, and sweaters; and to tat and crochet lace collars and doilies. They trimmed aprons with rick-rack and appliqué for apron exchanges and sales; and made gifts for brides, babies, and fund raisers.

Homemaker clubs were numerous. They were outgrowths of the 1920s *Tomato Club* which first taught canning, then expanded into family and community projects. Their meetings were similar to those of HD clubs, but with more emphasis on fund raising. The many clubs included *Cozy Home Club* and the *Dam Helping Hand Club.*

Ladies Aid groups were affiliated with the churches. Members had numerous family oriented fund raising projects and drew large crowds to bazaars and suppers. They collected, sewed, and distributed clothes and household items for people in need. Members were frequently called upon to assist families in crisis, and help the county nurse with meetings. Ladies in the boomtowns, Fort Peck, Glasgow, and Nashua often shared events.

Bridge and Whist Clubs were popular with many project women. Clubs included the *Shanty Town Bridge Club* and the *Wheeler North Side Bridge Club.* Fort Peck had the *Jolly Twelve Club, High Five Card Club,* and others. Members met in each others homes. Most clubs were small, for one to four tables of cards. Lunch was served with emphasis on table decorations. Prizes were awarded. Evening card games often included their husbands and a dance. Clubs met for entertainment, but often made donations to community projects.

Others. There were several special interest groups for women who enjoyed reading, art, music, and hobbies. Groups were usually small. They met in each others homes, the hostess planning the program.

Most women enjoyed socializing and club work. But there were some who were isolated by choice, circumstance, constant moves, or their jobs, and kept to themselves. Many women developed lifelong friendships while visiting over the backyard clothesline or playing in the yard with their children. They held coffee klatches, traded baby sitting and shopping time, and helped each other in times of trouble. Their informal get-togethers strengthened boomtown neighborhoods.

Groups for Girls: There were a number of clubs for girls: the *4-H Rinky Dink Club, Busy Bees, Jolly Eight Girls,* and more. The *Kitchen Canaries* learned to cook while the *Nimble Needles* and *Sunshine Sewing Club* learned to sew. Several girls joined Girl Scouts and study groups led by their mothers.

Groups for Boys: Boys had 4-H Clubs, Scouts, and Junior Fire Patrol. They played organized and pick-up baseball and other sports.

Girls and boys both enjoyed summer sports programs planned by the Recreation Association, and the organized events and outings planned by parents. The Corps arranged summer bus tours of the project for students. Churches sponsored numerous youth activities.

Men's clubs. Men had clubs for stamp collecting, fossil hunting, flying, and other special interests. Duos, trios, and groups got together to sing, play musical instruments, and carve willow canes. Readers discussed fiction, drama, psychology, and politics. An Elephant Club was formed, members wore "tropical hats in Frank Buck style."

Married workers with children were usually involved in parent and teacher organizations, and various family oriented activities.

"Several men have formed a literary society to study classical literature to help spend their leisure time to better advantage. The first meeting was held in the tool house." *McCone Sentinel* 1934.

Organizations

"The first meeting of the Veterans of Foreign Wars (VFW) Fort Peck Post #1307...." *Fort Peck Press, 10/11/1934*

The Post and its auxiliary organized in Fort Peck in 1934, assisted by the Glasgow VFW. Members were from the town of Fort Peck and the boomtowns. They promoted patriotism and community projects, and assisted honorably discharged veterans and their families.

Post #1307 joined the American Legion and other organizations in fundraisers for community betterment. Their joint events included the annual Armistice Day dance at the Recreation Hall.

Fort Peck American Legion Post #83 and its Auxiliary organized in October 1934, with 54 charter members from Fort Peck and the boomtowns. Dr. Lull, the first commander, was succeeded in 1935 by Paul Harper. The Auxiliary's many projects included Poppy Day.

Townsend Clubs met in Wheeler and New Deal in 1936. The 100 members were affiliated with the national organization advocating retirement at age 60 with a federally funded $200 a month pension. Their plan to open jobs for younger people was rejected by Congress and died away, but had some influence on Social Security.

There were many active organizations in all the boomtowns and the town of Fort Peck. They provided socializing, help for those who needed it, and opportunities to learn from each other.

Helping Hands. Groups, churches, businesses, and individuals in the boomtowns were generous with what little they had.

Churches, organizations, businesses, and the people of Fort Peck supported numerous local and national causes.

Part 11

Entertainment and Recreation
Movies and baseball were the favorites

While planning the project, the Corps considered the "isolation of the area" and the need for year-round, on-site recreation for workers and families. The district office authorized a non-profit Recreation Association. Its purpose, according to Captain Ewart G. Plank, was to "organize activities and present events which appeal to the bulk of the people employed at the project."

Government employees and the residents of Fort Peck town were automatically members of the association, without dues or fees.

A recreation hall and a theater were built on the west side of the housing area in Fort Peck. Both were owned by the government and rented, staffed, and run by the "Rec" Association.

The Recreation Hall measured 145 feet long by 64 feet wide, with a seating capacity of 1,200. It opened in October 1934, fully equipped for athletic events, and with a stage for "amateur theatricals." Dances, meetings, activities, and special programs were held there.

The first of several dances sponsored by American Legion Post #83 and VFW Post #3107 was held in October. It drew 1,200 dancers. An Armistice Day Dance, billed as "Gigantic, Stupendous, Colossal, Startling," took in $500 for hall projects, "Gents $1, ladies free."

The 1935 New Year's Eve dance drew the largest crowd ever, partially because a car was given away. The Costume Party in 1936 raised funds for the Legion Auxiliary, the Sons of Legionnaires, and Junior Baseball. Dancers were advised, "Costumes don't have to be elaborate – it's more of a Hard Time Dance."

The District VFW Convention dance in 1936 drew record crowds. A Fireman's Charity Ball, and the Reserve Officers Masque Ball raised money for families in need.

Dance music at the Recreation Hall dances was played by the Billy Hamilton Orchestra, The Montanans, and the many other local and touring road bands. Dancers did country steps, jazz, and swing dances under the watchful eye of hall guards.

Other Fort Peck town dances included a High School Booster Club Frolic in 1934; and the Fort Peck Dinner Dance at the Employees Hotel, dubbed "the biggest social event of the season."

The Fort Peck Theatre opened in November 1934, with all 1,209 "comfortable seats" filled for a showing of *The Richest Girl In The World*. The theater remained open 24 hours a day with all the latest movies at 30 or 40 cents for adults, and 10 cents for children.

Periodically, the cameramen from Fox Movietone showed their project newsreel, narrated by Corps officials. Corps photographers showed weekly progress film to capacity crowds from the area.

Theater fare included vaudeville, stage shows, and musicals. Acts included the *Original Southern Hillbillies* with dancing personality girls performing their tap, buck, toe, and hula dances; the *Kentucky Coon Hunters,* heard on 200 radio stations; and *The Great Raymond.*

"The Club" was opened in 1934 by M.J. Dunn of Lewistown. The 40x100 feet recreation center featured pool, billiards, soft drinks, and candy 24 hours a day. Workers went there to socialize and unwind.

Boomtown Entertainment

Most boomtown residents came from rural areas where people danced until dawn, put on home talent plays, played cards, and turned every event into a community get-together. Many of them sang and played musical instruments for entertainment and dances.

Schoolhouse dances were held on Saturday nights to raise funds for supplies. The dances were well attended family events to which women wore their best dresses and men wore white shirts and flatiron creased pants. Couples square-danced to *Golden Slippers*, and two-stepped to *Redwing*. They did the schottische, waltz quadrille, and polka. Musicians, many in family bands, playing a combination of fiddles, guitars, banjos, drums, accordions, and horns provided music.

The schoolhouse floor was slicked with cornmeal. Kids loved to slide around on it during the dance breaks. At midnight a "supper" of sandwiches, pickles, cake, and coffee was sold to raise funds.

Dancers rested and children slept on the benches along the walls. Coats were stacked on the teacher's desk. Songs like *Home Sweet Home* or *Until We Meet Again* were played for the last dance before everyone pitched in to sweep the floor and move the seats in place.

Liquor was not allowed inside the school, but occasionally men "wet their whistles" from bottles out in their cars.

Drunks were rare. If there was one, he was put in his car to sober up. Fights were few. If one broke out it was moved outside away from women and children. Fighters were allowed a couple of punches then made to shake hands. Sometimes guards were hired but male dancers were usually in charge of keeping the peace.

Music from the bars spilled out into the streets. Large clubs hired up to seven piece local or traveling bands. Smaller clubs had a piano and boisterous sing-alongs. The smallest places featured nickelodeons. Couples could dance in most bars, and, during the short time it was legally allowed, taxi dancers danced with men without partners.

Clubs along the Glasgow to Fort Peck highway, and a couple of larger ones in Wheeler and the other boomtowns, were popular with tourists and a few of the workers.

At times alcohol-altered egos clashed. Bartenders were usually able to control their unruly patrons, but more than one had his shirt ripped off or was roughed-up before officers arrived. A few clubs relied on hired bouncers to keep order.

People danced in all kinds of weather. In February 1936 a crowd attended a club dance during 60-below-zero temperatures. When their cars refused to start, they stayed and danced until morning.

Movies were the most popular form of entertainment. Nearly every town had a moving picture house featuring "the talkies" and popcorn. Usherettes with flashlights showed patrons to their chairs. A few theaters had piano players during intermission. The latest newsreels and cartoons were shown before the movie feature.

Moviegoers regularly attended the Kiwanis Club free movie nights in Glasgow. On April 15, 1937, some 4,325 Valley County residents and project people watched movies provided by the Forest Service.

Bank Night and Gift Night were popular theater attractions. Patrons entering the theater dropped their names into a hat for a drawing during the movie. Both nights were deemed a lottery and outlawed by the Valley County attorney in October 1935. Attorneys tweaked the procedure and the special nights resumed in November.

Dish Night drew large crowds. Adults were handed a free dish from a crate as they passed through the ticket line. A different dish was featured each week.

The County Fair with its exhibits and entertainment was fun for everyone. Boomtowners were among the record 6,400 people who visited display booths, cheered horse racers, and enjoyed rides and shows at the Valley County Fair in 1934.

In 1935 more than 500 4-H clubs, including the boomtown clubs, brought projects to be judged. United Shows was on the midway. Crowds appreciated the grandstand improvements made by transients.

Richland, McCone, Phillips, and other Montana counties reported "unusually good turn outs" for Fairs in 1935 and the rest of the 1930s.

The Circus created great excitement among children and adults. Several traveling circuses known as "truck shows" or "mud shows" came through the project area. Among them were the 20th Century Shows in Glasgow, 1934, and the Barnes Circus in 1936. The Schell Brothers Circus came to Wheeler in 1936, and the Siebrand Brothers Great Piccadilly Circus in 1937. Others stopped in the smaller towns.

Most circuses featured two to four rings of elephants, tigers, and other "exotic" animals, along with clowns and daring high wire acts.

Thousands of adults and children watched as the Big Top tent was raised, then lined the streets for the circus parade.

Sideshows at fairs and circuses offered viewing for a dime of "human oddities" and "freaks" such as Siamese twins, bearded ladies, and dog faced boys. Carnival games with prizes; and a variety of soft drink, popcorn, and cotton candy carts lined the midway.

Carnivals featuring small traveling shows, all trying hard to stay in business during the Depression, were held in most of the towns.

Memorial Day was observed on May 30. Businesses closed during the noon hour so everyone could attend the parades and ceremonies to honor the nation's fallen veterans. Dances were held in the evening.

Annual 4th of July events at Wheeler
(1935-1939)

The Wheeler Commercial Club held its first annual 4th of July celebration in 1935. The widely advertised three-day extravaganza featured a circus, carnival, seven shows, eighteen concessions, and sporting events, baseball games, and bar-b-cued buffalo-burgers.

Highlights were an air show, rodeo, and a complete Indian village. Several bands played music for bowery and open air pavilion dancing. The special evening activities were lighted by "several large lamps, with 350,000,000 candle power ... seen 60 miles away."

The town was packed with people enjoying the celebration when a wild windstorm, accompanied by heavy rain, toppled concessions, soaked the celebrants, and turned the streets to sticky gumbo mud. Dampened and damaged the activities resumed after the storm.

Pilots, minus one storm-battered plane, thrilled the crowd with stunt flying and rides. The local press reported, "businesses had a fine trade, and the carnival and picture shows were well attended." The deputies assigned to keep peace reported few arrests.

The traditional 4th of July celebrations included parades, picnics, races, dances, and professionally set fireworks. All events, except for those daring to use forbidden firecrackers, went off without a bang.

Wheeler's second big three-day 4th of July celebration, in 1936, featured an Air Circus, airplane rides, the Siebrand Shows, Piccadilly Circus, street dances, concessions, and political speakers. The rodeo featured Madison Square Garden stars, and $1,100 in prizes. Eastern Montana Shows showed "the largest steer in the world." Wheeler night spots sponsored a State Get-Together board to locate friends.

Proceeds of the event went to the Wheeler Fire Department. Huge crowds attended in spite of the wind, dirt storms, and wilting heat.

A similar 4th of July celebration was held in 1937. It was another huge success, but saddened when circus high wire aerialist Gladys LeTouneau, 25, fell from her trapeze. Shocked spectators mourned when she died eleven days later in Deaconess Hospital in Glasgow.

The 4th of July event in 1938 was scaled back in size. But for the most part it went as planned as hundreds of people celebrated.

The 1939 4th of July event was hit with winds that toppled the Ferris wheel and damaged a tilt-a-whirl owned by Siebrand Brothers Carnival/Circus. Debris littered the midway after the wind storm, but rain-soaked celebrants stayed and had fun.

Radio parties were events where radio owners invited friends, who could not afford the sets, to "come on over." Everyone gathered around the Crosleys and Atwater-Kents, and after the tubes warmed up, listened to Walter Winchell's news, *Charlie McCarthy,* the *Lone Ranger, WLS Barn Dance,* and *Ma Perkins* soaps.

Listeners heard the Hindenburg explosion in 1937 and *The War of the Worlds* in 1938. Everyone gathered around the radio and tuned in to President Roosevelt's *Fireside Chats.*

KGCX, Ed Krebsbach's 1,000 watt radio station in Wolf Point, provided local programming. In 1937 three Wheeler men won first place in the *Amateur Hour* while their barracks buddies listened in.

President Roosevelt's Birthday Balls, the first in 1934, were held in Fort Peck, Glasgow, and Nashua to raise funds for polio research. The balls ushered in the first annual March of Dimes collection in 1938.

Project people worked hard and played hard. Fun and laughter softened hard times. They said, "All was not gloom and doom."

Dinosaur trails and hunts

The Fort Peck Recreation Association reported that 700 to 1,000 "bone hunters" turned out on Sundays between May and October for fossil hunts. Hundreds of pounds of bones were collected.

Project workers, area residents, visitors, professional and amateur paleontologists, college students, families, and individuals took part in the hunts. Carrying lunch bags and water jugs they ventured out in search of bones and fossils. They drove the 20-mile scenic trail that ran south of the dam along the badlands to visit the Hell Creek area in northwestern Garfield County, one of the richest dinosaur bone spots.

Several local expeditions were led by Dr. Barnum Brown, curator of the American Museum of Natural History. He was recognized nationally after discovering his first Tyrannosaurus Rex in 1902, and a second in 1908, at Hell Creek.

In January 1936 plans were underway for a National Park at Fort Peck Fossil Fields. In May the Dinosaur Route opened on the east side of Fort Peck heading south on a badlands road to Jordan. Large signs pointed out sites of interest. One of the most popular was at the base of Buffalo Hill where scientists were excavating a triceratops.

Bone hunters purchased a dinosaur hunting license (a membership in the newly organized Montana Society of Natural History) to help raise funds for existing fossil collections and further the society work.

In August 1936 large crowds watched a motion picture film and slides, *Methods of Excavation and Preservation,* at the Recreation Hall. The presentation from the American Museum of Natural History in New York City was introduced by paleontologist Darwin Harbicht, a member of the excavation party when the movie was made.

In September 1936 approximately a thousand people took part in the last dinosaur bone hunt of the season. During one of the last hunts in October 1937 more than seventy autos full of hunters traveled to the badlands on the Dinosaur Route and noted "outstanding finds."

The chief clerk at the Fort Peck district, Beryl Brooks, found an "unidentified prehistoric reptile, apparently of the turtle family." Its claws resembled those of land mammals near water. Other hunters found a rare, intact, palm tree stump; fossilized cones and dinosaur teeth; and the well preserved head of a large three horned dinosaur.

Fort Peck Theatre display. Thousands of visitors viewed the specimens kept at the Fort Peck Theatre. Two large display cases were added in 1937 for the growing number of fossils, Indian relics, and the collection of Montana agates, quartz, chalcedony and jasper.

Promotional materials noted "bullets dredged up from the river bottom, and a few cannon balls and buffalo skulls plowed up near the dam ...," also "a portion of a duckbill dinosaur jaw with about 100 perfect teeth in place and part of a head found in a fossil field."

Frank LaFournaise. A special showcase displayed the carvings of the project carpenter, mason, and cement finisher whose hobby was carving Montana native wood, especially juniper, cottonwood and cedar, into busts and "figuretes." LaFournaise was respected as a self-taught carver who worked "without a complete set of carving tools."

Jack Sather worked at Buttrey's store in Fort Peck. His hobby was sculpting miniature life-like pre-historic animals from clay.

The May 1937 *Scientific American,* featuring his work, was noted in the *Glasgow Courier,* "a collection comprising nearly every known dinosaur that roamed the earth ... Darwin Harbicht, paleontologist at Fort Peck, is keenly interested ... and has rendered valuable assistance toward the completion of the miniature models."

A newspaper article "Fort Peck Dinosaur Field South of Dam is Valley of Monsters," by paleontologist Darwin Harbicht appeared, with photos, in the November 30, 1937, *Glasgow Courier*. The article reviewed the discoveries of fossils in the area , and commented on the enthusiastic work and contributions of interested project people.

Sports – Recreation
They all turned out for the ball games

Baseball meetings were held in the Recreation Hall each spring to organize teams and tournaments for the workers. Hundreds of them played ball. Project workers living in Glasgow played on teams there, and also took part in Glasgow's horse and donkey baseball games.

Several scrub teams formed to compete with teams in Hi-Line towns and from the quarry sites. Wednesdays at the diamond in 1936 were dubbed "Grandpa's Day." A local sports enthusiast noted, "to loud and long cheers, they got a man out after several weeks of play."

Softball. Notices were posted encouraging project workers to join one of the intramural or kittenball leagues. A dozen or more teams were organized and named for the crews they represented. Glasgow project workers were *The Commuters*. Nashua encouraged workers living there to form a Nashua Softball League and "get in the game."

The Recreation Association organized softball teams for women, and teens in Fort Peck townsite. Several other teams were organized in the boomtowns with a full schedule of games for everyone.

Basketball teams were organized. Scores in 1935: Boatyards beat Barracks, Tunnels defeated Dredging. Construction won 25-22 over Tunnels for the championship. Teams included: Warehouse, Utilities, Laboratories, Concessionaires, and General Engineers.

In January 1935 a record "813 paid" turned out in Glasgow to see the Great Falls Northern Goats play the Harlem Globe Trotters. The Recreation Association hosted the Beavers and the Colored House of David. In 1936 the Fort Peck All Stars "the best players from the four project league teams" challenged the Acme Colored Giants.

Bowling teams and leagues were organized for men, and women. Matches were held throughout the winter in the Recreation Hall.

Tennis and golf. Tennis was played on courts on the north side of the town of Fort Peck. Golfers played on a course near Glasgow.

Boxing. Five Knock Outs in project tournament. Amateur boys throw leather thick and fast in good card. Second round of Golden Gloves Tournament to be held Friday. Glasgow Courier, 10/35.

Workers boxed in numerous matches with other workers and out-of-town opponents. Wheeler promoted a "fight card" as early as August 1934. Glasgow hosted several exhibitions.

Wrestling. Fans of all ages came out in large numbers for matches at Fort Peck, Wheeler, and Glasgow arenas. Promoters offered a variety of "rassle cards" with favorites Mickey McGuire, Rob Roy, "The Eskimo Villain," "The Hollywood Sheik," and their opponents.

"Lady artists" were featured in April 1937. "A section of the bleachers in the Recreation Hall will be reserved for children."

Wrestling promoters promised: "Lady wrestler Betty Bushey, the bone crusher, will attempt to smear Butcher Boy Jorgensen all over the mat." Betty fiercely "bit and pulled hair" and fought to the end, but apparently it was Butcher Boy's turn to win.

Women's gym classes were held in the Recreation Hall. The program included indoor sports. Volleyball was the favorite.

The Fort Peck Riding Club offered lessons, horseback riding, and board for privately owned horses. The club was managed by a former rodeo trick rider who led overnight camping and weekend pack trips.

Gun Clubs included a Skeet Shooting Club, the Fort Peck Pistol Team, and Fort Peck Rifle Club. Men, and a few women, competed in shooting matches at the indoor range. Rifle instruction was available. Turkey Shoots gave prizes for marksmen matches and luck targets.

Swimming. Project residents went swimming ("bathing") in the river and dredge cuts. The Corps posted the safe sites and cautioned swimmers to stay within them. There were several drownings.

*A **Ski Exhibition*** was held near New Deal in March 1935. Expert jumpers from Glasgow, Fort Peck, and North Dakota, demonstrated "leaps" of one-hundred feet and more off a hillside scaffold. Large crowds turned out to enjoy the event.

In February 1937 the first Ski Tournament and Exhibition of the season was held on the new slide at Snake Hill south of Harlem off US Highway 2. The hill was promoted as the "best natural site height" with a 25-foot scaffold "making jumps of 100 to 125 feet possible."

Hockey teams competed in games against each other and against teams in nearby towns. Games drew a good attendance.

Ice skating and sledding. Two areas, one behind the Recreation Hall, were flooded for ice skating in Fort Peck. Warming houses were built and the facilities maintained by the fire department.

Boomtown residents flooded and maintained rinks in their towns.

Sledding ("coasting") was fun for all ages and could be enjoyed free anywhere there was a hill. Coasting parties with hot chocolate and marshmallows were popular with youth groups.

Boating. By August 1937 boating was happening on the thousand or so acre lake created by the dredges in the upstream borrow pit. A number of sailboats, light motor boats, aquaplanes, and others were hauled in on trailers and launched in the relatively calm, up to fifty feet deep, water. Clear water with little current was found in coves.

Fishing. Many boomtown fishermen fished to feed their families or to have fish to trade for groceries. In September 1936 a tool house employee hooked a 25-pound "monster" sturgeon. A Nashua man caught a 22-pound sturgeon in May 1937 near the Milk River bridge.

In September 1937 fishermen were reminded to buy licenses from the Department of Fish and Game. Fishing at the diversion tunnels outlet portals had become popular after the river closure because pike, catfish, and other "kindred species" could not buck the swift current and remained in outlet pools. One fishermen caught 47 fish in one hour, measuring 23 inches and weighing over three-pounds each.

As the supply dwindled, fishermen were limited to 25 fish or 20 pounds of fish per-person, per-day until the fish were all caught.

Hunting. Men, and women, hunted deer and elk below the dam and near the project. The meat, plus ducks and prairie chicken, helped feed many families. The Corps reminded hunters appropriate action would be taken against federal employees violating state game laws.

Sports of all kinds. Among the sports and popular games in the "too numerous to mention" category was ***horseshoe pitching***. It was a long time favorite and the equipment never wore out.

Part 12

Roads and Transportation

Vehicle registration Valley County 1932 (1,890) peak 1936 (7,486). McCone County 1932 (946) peak 1936 (2,082).

Workers began arriving at the project in their worn out Model A, and Model T "Tin Lizzie" Fords, Chevrolets, and other make vehicles in October 1933. Most of their trucks and cars were old and in need of repairs, held together with whatever could keep them running until the owner could afford new parts or at least junk yard replacements.

Drivers considered themselves fortunate if they had a crank, a trusty jack, an inner tube repair kit and patches, a tire pump, and some tools. They carried jugs of water on the running boards to refill leaky, overheated radiators; they blew out clogged gas lines, cleaned spark plugs, and tried to fix broken fan belts and faulty brakes and clutches.

But when, in spite of their best efforts, it all came down to push and park, not even a good cussing helped. A better vehicle was a high priority for workers, especially the young men of courting age.

You've got to have a license. A bill requiring all drivers on Montana public roads to obtain a driver's license was brought before the legislature in 1931. Opponents argued Montana did not need "big city ways," and they did not need another "infringement on their rights." The law passed, but many drivers purposely ignored it, just like they were ignoring the vehicle license plate law passed in 1914.

Permits, issued by the War Department and sold at the Fort Peck Police station, were required. Drivers had to carry them at all times.

In 1934 Montana began cracking down on all license violators. Hundreds of drivers at the Fort Peck project area appeared in court for non-compliance before they finally purchased their fifty-cent driver's license, and a $10 maroon and gold vehicle license plate.

Headlamps and electric hands

"Many accidents on the highway from Fort Peck to Glasgow. Several were caused by vehicles without proper illumination. Only late model cars have a dimmer switch." *Fort Peck Press 11/1934.*

Officers ticketed scores of vehicles for missing headlamps, and for poorly adjusted lights that blinded oncoming drivers.

Few vehicles had an "electric hand" and drivers often failed to use proper hand signals. *Right turn: left arm stuck out of the driver's side window, forearm and hand up, palm forward. Left turn: left arm straight out, palm forward. Stop or slow down: left arm out, forearm and hand down and backward.*

Vehicle accidents and deaths in Montana the first six months of 1934 (148 compared to 90 in 1933) reflected the greatest percentage increase in the United States, according to the Travelers Insurance Company. Alcohol, intersection violations, and speed led the causes.

Deaths and injuries at the project included roll overs; sideswiping during passing; and collisions with other vehicles, animals, and fence posts. Accidents occurred when tires blew out or brakes failed, and when drivers lost control in loose gravel and rolled into the ditch.

Dust, mud, ice, snow, and wind contributed to accidents. Cold weather froze radiators, cracked blocks, and caused brakes and steering mechanisms to malfunction. Hot weather made radiators boil over, often scalding the person removing the cap to add water.

Accidents had many causes. Carelessness resulted in a man with a broken leg falling from an overturned ambulance. A driver ran off the road while tuning his new radio.

Two vehicles struck houses being moved on flatbed trucks. Both drivers, one drunk and one sober, said they had not seen the house they hit. A driver slid into a New Deal cafe during a snow storm. He was unhurt but the cook was injured when a jug of vinegar fell off a shelf and hit her on the knee.

Several drivers broke their arms or wrenched their wrists while cranking vehicles or pushing them when they stalled.

Pedestrians were warned to walk on the left side of the roadways, still accidents were above average, especially on the highway running through Wheeler. Two accidents were the result of drunks wandering into the road in front of vehicles. Children had many close calls.

Road rage on the busy, narrow roads, especially when fueled by alcohol, provoked assaults. Sheriff's officers reported several smashed windows and windshields, and "fistic encounters."

Speeding on the main street highway through Wheeler, and driver involvement in vehicle "leap-frog" drew huge fines. One speeder, fined $50, told the judge he was on his honeymoon and only had $40. The judge suspended his fine and remanded custody to his bride.

Drunk Driving

"We can no longer afford to be lenient to drivers arrested for drunken driving." *Henry Beverly, Glasgow police magistrate, June 1935, commenting on the large number of DUI accidents.*

The Corps issued a Notice on October 10, 1935: *In a determined drive to end drunken driving in the Fort Peck government area, Maj. T.B. Larkin, district engineer, has issued an ultimatum to workers that arrest on this charge will result in immediate discharge and possible federal action. He noted two deaths and property damage ... caused by intoxicated drivers. He announced checking stations at various points and all traffic would be watched.*

Police Chief Lyman E. Moore posted officers at the Fort Peck town gates to spot check driver and vehicle licenses, and to note the "condition of the driver." Drunk drivers included project workers, residents, job seekers, visitors, and tourists. Also a legislator and a former liquor store officer from Butte; they were fined $75 each.

Fines were usually $50 and up. In 1935 a man received his second DUI while driving a car without the owner's consent and was sent to prison, the first such sentence under the new state Highway Patrol law.

The first drunk motorcycle driver arrested was fined $100 and his driver's license revoked for two months. He was stopped for riding his friend's motorcycle and carrying two passengers.

A drunk tourist struck and injured five gravel train crew workers in 1935. A drunk worker wrecked his new coupe trying to jump a 20-foot cutbank while fleeing officers. A drunk was jailed for running Sheriff Ed McPherson, his former classmate, off the road. Another drunk was arrested for speeding, but protested he didn't know it was the sheriff he was "racing."

A visiting teenager lost his arm in a rollover he claimed happened when a stranger jumped in his car and stuck a gun in his ribs. He later admitted he and two friends had been drinking while driving.

Vehicle and train accidents at the busy road and rail crossings in Glasgow, Nashua, and on the railroad spurs resulted in at least three deaths. Foggy, icy windshields; failure to stop; stalling; and stopping on the tracks while inebriated were given as causes.

A man died in a fall from the railroad trestle after his truck became stuck on the Missouri River Bridge. An eleven-year-old Glasgow boy was killed when he crawled between two "stopped" railroad cars. A Great Northern engineer for 38 years, died in a fall from his train.

At least one child was killed and others injured when struck by cars. A "youth" was injured when he fell beneath the wheels while running after the Wheeler Volunteer Fire Department truck.

Auto theft and stripping. Drivers were used to leaving their keys in their vehicles, thereby attracting joyriders and thieves. The vehicles were usually wrecked or run out of gas and abandoned.

A musician's car and his three guitars were stolen by two drunks. The men were apprehended in the barracks trying to play the guitars.

The Glasgow mayor's car was stolen from a service station pump. Several others disappeared from in front of post offices.

Five men were jailed for auto stripping. The owner told officers he couldn't make his monthly payments so his friends, owners of a wrecking yard, were helping him out. A worker's stalled vehicle was pushed over a hill and stripped. Others lost tires, wheels, and gas.

Roads

State Highway 24 Glasgow to Fort Peck

Construction of a hard surface highway between Fort Peck dam and Glasgow was authorized by the Montana Highway Commission in 1933. Land acquisition got underway.

In March 1934 the *Fort Peck Press* reported the state had filed suit against twenty-two individuals/corporations owning or holding liens on land to be "traversed by the highway." In May appraisers reported right-of-way allowances and damages to the land for the 16.6 mile highway totaled $8,643. Seven landowners were contesting the sale.

Heavy equipment was moved in and road construction continued day and night until the highway was finished. It was oiled in time for President Franklin D. Roosevelt's first visit August 6, 1934.

Thousands of autos, buses, and trucks traveled the highway around the clock. Heavy traffic, bad weather, and changing road conditions contributed to numerous accidents and deaths. Highway 24 became known as "the most dangerous road in the state."

Nashua's road to the dam— State Highway 117

Nashua's main street and the GN railroad track ran parallel to each other east-west through town. Vehicles turning off US 2 toward the dam and spillway turned south at Nashua, crossed the railroad track, and drove 12 miles on a narrow, winding, dirt road to the dam.

As of October 1935, in spite of heavy project and tourist traffic, no major improvements had been made. Several meetings were held and frustrations voiced, but work was held up by traffic and funding.

The problem grew in August 1935 when a dirt road from New Deal, passing through Midway and Park Grove, was graded out to intersect with the Nashua-Fort Peck road, creating blinding dust.

The state graded and graveled five miles from the dam past Park Grove toward Nashua in 1935. The Nashua Chamber of Commerce graveled the rest. Traffic soon destroyed the improvements.

A June 1936 traffic count at the Milk River crossing near Nashua showed 1,193 vehicles crossed every 24 hours, making it the "most heavily traveled road in Montana." Nashua pleaded for the road to be placed under state control as an Operational Number 2 route.

In September 1936 the first five miles of the road north from the dam were oiled, with plans to finish in 1937. April 22, 1937, the *Nashua Messenger* editorialized, "That dam road again," urging Governor Roy E. Ayers to follow through on his promise.

In May a man was killed at the railroad crossing. The *Nashua Messenger* again noted the danger of 1,100 cars in 24 hours driving over a nearly blind crossing with no warning device, and one lone flagman for the fast passenger and mail trains.

Valley County road crews tried to keep the road in shape. The town of Nashua and the bordering boomtowns dug into their pockets to pay for labor, gravel, and dust control. They continued to ask the state to consider the road a main line and treat it accordingly.

In August 1937 the Corps built a swing bridge on the south side of Park Grove so dredges could pass through the channel to the west side. The unique bridge drew even more visitors and vehicles.

In 1937 the Highway Department announced work would start soon on the Nashua-Fort Peck highway. In the spring of 1938 county crews graded the stretch to be surfaced by the state and widened the road to eliminate sharp curves. WPA workers surfaced the stretch from the Park Grove bridge through Nashua and onto US Highway 2.

County crews graded Nashua's main street, built railroad crossing and bridge approaches, and eliminated a steep grade to the highway. In August 1939 the swing bridge at Park Grove was replaced with a permanent bridge. The road was oiled in September. The project was winding down, but thousands of vehicles still traveled Highway 117.

McCone City/County roads

Building roads in McCone City called for the removal of trees, installation of culverts, filling coulees, and bypassing the Corps' slurry pipeline that ran through town. The McPhersons used teams of horses and machinery from contractor E. Howe to do the work.

179

Spillway contractors built the roads used by workers and residents leading to the Missouri River bridge, the railroad spur, spillway, and other work sites. They graveled all but a half mile into McCone City.

A City delegation asked McCone County commissioners in Circle for gravel, reminding them that they and the spillway contractors paid a lot of taxes and deserved a "competent road." But the county was without resources to make the improvements.

Bus service to the project became available in February 1934 when Great Falls Coach Lines began making its three round trips daily from Glasgow to Fort Peck. Riders were project residents, high school students, visitors, and some Corps workers who lived in Glasgow. A few tourists left their autos in Glasgow and rode the bus.

In December two double-deck buses were purchased to replace several smaller ones. By February 1935 there were three large buses and a few smaller ones on the road from Glasgow, daily.

Buses traveled between the boomtowns and Fort Peck School for 65 cents a week. Daily ten-cent runs between the Wheeler and Park Grove depots were added in 1936. Buses ran a full schedule until after the peak project employment in 1936 when ridership declined.

There were two major bus accidents. In 1934 one passenger was killed and eight injured when a bus plunged down a thirty-foot bank. In 1935, during a rain and sleet storm, a bus and several cars slid into a ditch. Passengers pushed the bus back on the road and went home.

The Greyhound Bus Company operated a line between Fort Peck and Glasgow in December 1934 for long distance passengers.

Nashua started a morning bus route in February 1935 to pick up workers there, and along the road, for rides to the tunnel portals. By December buses were making three trips a day. Rides were arranged by the Chamber of Commerce, paid for by businessmen. The bus was full during the winter but canceled in the spring due to lack of riders.

Taxi service for trips up to twenty miles away was available in Wheeler and a few other boomtowns during the busiest project years.

Planes over the project
The Corps hired private pilots for survey and inspection tours

The Glasgow Airport was enlarged in the 1930s to accommodate additional air traffic generated by the project. Facilities included three runways from 2,700 to 5,400 feet long. Pilots Frank Wiley, Hub Ames, and Burleigh Putnam operated a flying service that contracted work for the Corps, chartered flights, offered flying lessons, and flew tourists and news photographers over the project.

The boomtowns had a half dozen or so small private airports near Wheeler, New Deal, and Lakeview, along with the grass landing strips on nearby farms. Most of the pilots were World War I flyers turned farmer turned project worker. A few were women. Some were former barnstormers. They used planes to spray crops, hunt coyotes, poison grasshoppers, and drop supplies to snowbound ranchers.

At the project, the pilots gave flying lessons, sightseeing flights, charter services, and a few offered contract work for the Corps.

Air Shows, tamed by federal laws enacted in the daring-do days of barnstorming, drew huge crowds. One of the first shows was held to dedicate the Glasgow Airport. A show in 1934 featured parachute jumpers at Flynn Airport on West Wheeler Hill.

In February 1935 crowds watched two Army Snowbirds on winter tests from Selfridge Field, Michigan, land at Glasgow. In September everyone was invited to see the Tri-motored, 10-ton, 20-person Boeing Air Transport, with two pilots. "Fly in comfort and safety in the world's largest air transport."

In July 1936 pilots, hired by the promoters, flew over the project area dropping leaflets promoting the Louis-Schmeling fight.

Dozens of pilots flew to Glasgow and left their planes while they toured the project, including: ten members of a Canadian Flying Club who arrived in their Waco bi-plane, three Gypsy Moths, and a Puss Moth 3-place cabin plane.

Log books detailed thousands of hours of safe flight, but there were accidents. Two men in their 20s died near Nashua during an upside-down plane maneuver; the pilot crashed after his passenger fell from the plane. A 30-year-old veteran pilot project worker and his 47-year-old rancher passenger died when their plane crashed near the Wheeler Airport. A project worker was killed, east of Glasgow, when he and a co-worker crashed his plane while stalling to shoot a coyote.

An experienced pilot survived a forced landing after his plane flipped over and the propeller flew off. He was making a test flight before taking photographer M.A. Ellis up to shoot photos.

Several pilots were experimenting with airplane radios. By 1936 communications were being made between pilots and the Corps' short wave radio station W7EUO in Fort Peck.

In May 1935 some 40 pilots and students formed a flying club at the Fort Peck Recreation Hall. Later, many of them used their flying skills and experience while serving in World War II.

Part 13

Transients

Notices have been posted throughout the northwest warning workers to stay away from the project. Edna T. Hawley, state director, Federal Transient Service (FTS), June 1934.

When work at the Fort Peck project made national news, hundreds of unemployed men from around the country ignored the warnings that there would be no jobs for them, and headed for northeastern Montana. Desperate for work, they walked, rode the Great Northern rails, and hitchhiked. They slept wherever they could, and survived on handouts they got along the way. Ragged, hungry, and lonely they began moving into Glasgow in the fall of 1933.

Most were family men trying to earn money to send back home. They gladly did odd jobs for food and were grateful for any work they got. Some banned together in camps for safety. Curious farm boys visited a camp near the project where they said they were treated to baked potatoes and told tales by kindly men.

Hundreds of transients stopped at farms to ask for bread and water. Farmers, with little to share, hung dippers on their pumps and handed out what food they could spare.

The men camped on government land near the dam and looked for work. They slept in small tents or out in the open. They caused few problems and when hope of a job was gone, they moved on.

Other transients came too, life-long bums, vagrants, drug addicts, ex-convicts, alcoholics, and the mentally ill. A local man passing a camp outside Valley City was beaten and robbed by five men.

By November 1933 local relief agencies, medical facilities, and law enforcement were stretched to their limits dealing with the ever growing number of transients. Officials asked the federal government to help build a transient camp at the Glasgow Fairgrounds.

In June 1934 FTS director Edna Hawley met with the district relief supervisor and Glasgow Chamber of Commerce to finalize a camp planned by the Federal Emergency Relief Administration (FERA).

Transients were given food, clothing, and shelter for 75 cents a day, with work in the morning and "education" in the afternoon, all funded by federal programs for *out-of-state transients only.*

Hawley emphasized the camp was designed to salvage men, "most of whom are down and out through no fault of their own."

FTS arranged a 24-hour relief service for transients already in the area. They received two free meals, then were asked to move on. "Asking" was done by law enforcement, local area men, and railroad officials. Residents were told *not* to give money to panhandlers.

Hawley ordered water testing in the transient camps and check-ups for the men who were sick with contagious diseases. She said, "How we meet this problem will depend on whether Glasgow and Montana are put on the map favorably or unfavorably."

Problems continued. In May 1934 a *Glasgow Courier* editorial noted, "Conservative figures estimate the transient population at about 500. More than 200 men are living in a 'jungle' west of town. The depot platform and streets are thick with men who have dropped off freight trains. Panhandlers are numerous. The Relief Station spent $269 the first four days of May to feed these people."

On June 6, the county relief director reported 600 men, almost one-fourth of Glasgow's normal population, had been sheltered and fed in the National Guard Armory during a rainstorm.

The county fairgrounds transient camp, designed for 200 and soon overcrowded, relieved problems in town and fewer men drifted to the boomtowns. Several men earned their food orders by digging water and sewer ditches from city mains out to the camp, and by repairing fences, cutting weeds, and installing grandstand seats.

By fall the number of lone transients decreased from 326 to 230. Fifty "families without means" were being fed and sent home.

Dozens of transient teenage boys and a few girls hitchhiked or rode the rails to Glasgow looking for work. Some moved into the boomtowns. Many ended up in trouble and were sent home.

Several boys were injured jumping on or off trains. A half dozen or more lost their hands and arms. An 18-year-old boy, one of four traveling home to Ohio from a CCC camp, fell under a tanker which severed his leg. Glasgow doctors treated him. He was cared for in Deaconess Hospital until arrangements were made to move him home.

At least seven transients were killed near the Glasgow depot in falls from trains. Others died along the rails between Culbertson and Havre. Some were unable to hang on to cold metal railcars during freezing temperatures. Others misjudged their jumps or were drunk.

Among them was a "neatly dressed" ex-baker from Minneapolis, identified by a fellow traveler. A transient found beside the railroad track was identified by a jeweler who sold him a watch. A Pittsburgh transient with a Navy bad-conduct discharge was found by the track and identified by a "friend" recovering from "apparent intoxication."

A World War I veteran, whose only relative was an elderly aunt in another state, was identified by his discharge papers. The Glasgow American Legion paid for his funeral complete with military honors.

The body of a 24-year-old unemployed musician was found by a railroad special agent. He was buried in an *unknown* grave while the authorities located his father in another state.

A 50-year-old Wisconsin transient who sold baskets in the area, fell from a freight train and died in the Wiota yards. He was identified by his Social Security card. His fingerprints revealed a string of aliases and a prison record for numerous felonies.

Many transients had health problems. A couple from California arrived ill of an *unknown cause*, the man died in the Glasgow hospital. A newcomer from Pennsylvania died in the hospital from sleeping sickness. Others had communicable diseases and terminal illnesses.

Several transients committed suicide. Among them, a 45-year-old man "known for his honesty and worried about his bills," was found in the Milk River. A 50-year-old transient, wearing a new shirt bought at Penney's, with the sales slip in his pocket, died on the railroad track. A man who attempted suicide told nurses his home was "nowhere."

In 1935 a transient was brutally murdered. Deputies at the scene reported finding a burned out car and "a maze of transient men trying to find work." The murder went unsolved.

Transient Crime

Transients stole for food, clothes, cigarettes, alcohol, and a number of other reasons. A Montana Power repairman gave a transient a meal then discovered his belt and climbing spurs were missing. A transient stole a man's pants from the cleaners and tried to sell them.

A transient was caught with two suits and an overcoat from the Lewis-Wedum store, another had 17 pairs of men's socks, and another was caught leaving a store with six pairs of pants under his coat.

Transients stole from each other. A man stole his pal's only pants. An elderly man was beaten in a Williston boxcar and his bed roll and $9 taken. He rode to Glasgow where police took him to the hospital.

A transient who had been given a job at Sinclair Produce stole a crate of tomatoes and sold them in a local bar.

Blankets were especially targeted for theft. Many disappeared from unlocked vehicles and neighborhood clotheslines.

A transient ordered a filling station owner to "Stick 'em up." The owner swung his lunch bucket and yelled "Get away before I kill you." The man ran the other direction.

A woman caught a transient in her chicken coop and chased him out and down the alley with her broom. She would have gladly given him food, but stealing was unacceptable.

Transient criminals sometimes forgot they were in small towns. The owner of Markles Transfer caught a man trying to pass a check signed with an area farmer's name. Mr. Markle knew the farmer, saw his name was misspelled, and the check was on the wrong bank.

Hundreds of transient men and women were arrested for vagrancy, fighting, drunkenness, and disturbing the peace. The law dealt firmly but kindly with them.

Round-up and Fingerprinting

In March 1936 Glasgow police started a transient "house cleaning" that resulted in fifteen arrests. Police magistrate Henry Beverly said, "Some of these fellows are generally in some kind of minor trouble, while others are chronic panhandlers and we believed it was better for everybody concerned to move them out."

Several transients left town when officials announced "We plan to obtain records of all residents who have no visible means of support or who have been questioned or arrested by police."

Seventy-five transients were fingerprinted, photographed, and sent out of town in January 1937. An Identification Campaign in February picked up seventy-five more, and twenty-three in March. Several had prison records.

A number of women with aliases and prison records were arrested on drunk and disorderly, and "other" charges. Most were with an unemployed male. Both of them were ordered out of town.

Gypsy bands, another kind of transient, had been traveling the Hi-Line for years. They still came in the 1930s, entering towns in groups to steal whatever they could, and stopping by farms to pick up animals and produce. Most residents feared them. A few people still believed that *many times after gypsies leave, a child is missing.*

Project Area Crime

Fingerprinting helped identify criminals. The Federal Bureau of Investigation (FBI) prints identified dozens of fugitives at the project. Hundreds of bad men, supposing opportunity and anonymity, went there to do what they were good at. As a result, many of them spent time in local jails and courts, and ended up back in prison.

"Almost every major crime committed since the inception of the project has been traced to some ex-convict." Sam Gilluly, *Glasgow Courier 12/1935*.

A Great Northern special agent arrested a "flashy dresser" wanted for robbery and murder. His suitcase was full of crime details, names and numbers; and letters from women all over the country.

In 1936 the sheriff jailed the eleventh out-of-state fugitive in recent months, including a taxi driver wanted in Minnesota for grand larceny, a man wanted in Canada for murdering two policemen, and a Minnesota convict who did not return to prison after Christmas break.

A 32-year-old construction foreman was found in violation of parole from Folsom Prison. The Corps praised his work, but fired him saying it was "incompatible for him to hold a foreman's position, which was one of trust and responsibility for government property."

Crimes

Bar fights were usually sparked by troublesome drunks, theft, or disagreements. Insults escalated into free-for-alls of men, and some times women, with a bartender trying to move them outside. Several employees were injured in a fight at the Los Angeles Club in 1936. When the owner wielded her "small billy" it was grabbed and used to strike her several times.

Beatings were often rendered by a beater and friends who followed the victim to a dark spot. A doctor was lured to his office late at night and beaten. A woman beat a woman baby-sitting her children.

Disturbing the Peace and drunk and disorderly charges were filed against workers, project people, and tourists alike. Officers were often assaulted by individuals and groups in the process.

Rarely did a disagreement turn deadly. One bystander was shot accidentally during a dispute between two men over a bar. A foreman died after a fight with a worker in the Casino. They were strangers. The worker, who provoked the attack, had a reputation as "trouble."

Drug arrests. In 1935 Glasgow police went after "dope peddlers." Raids netted an addict, posing as a doctor, selling opium derivatives; and a disabled barber and two friends, all addicts, obtaining drugs, with prescriptions. Five men were arrested for drug violations and involvement with beer parlors ad pawn shops.

Forgery. A series of forgeries in northeastern Montana ended with the arrest of an Idaho man believed to be tied to a Midwest mob.

A Wisconsin prison fugitive was arrested while forging a worker's paycheck. Deputies found two government buttons and three Mason & Walsh work buttons he used to obtain free meals in the mess halls.

The most daring forgery of all occurred in December 1934, after the sudden pneumonia death of the Mason & Walsh paymaster. Five men and one woman forged his name on stolen payroll checks and cashed them in the project area for over $4,000. Officers searched aliases and fingerprints until they caught the perpetrator, a parole violator from Alabama, and his four accomplices from North Dakota.

Short change men were hit and runners. Two were caught in Fort Peck and Wheeler. Clerks were trained to beware of them but the short changers were also trained and some got away.

Fraud. A "mail racket man" defrauded mail order houses by ordering items General Delivery, paying for them with a forged check, and picking them up under an alias. A postal investigator caught him and he was charged under his real name.

A "high pressure boy" illegally obtained loans and money from Glasgow businesses. The boomtown businesses had none to loan.

Three men camping near the project were caught selling fur coats valued at $15-$20 for $50-$75. Others were selling "slightly used" typewriters. Others collected donations by impersonating pastors.

Door-to-door con men complicated the lives of honest salesmen, such as the local drycleaner prospecting for new customers.

Murders were few. In 1935 the body of a man, murdered gangland style nine months before, was found in the Missouri River. A baby girl was found murdered near a Glasgow dike. The body of a resident dredge worker, believed murdered, was found in the Milk River.

Teenage girls were warned about friendly strangers. A girl who went for a walk with a man she had just met, was beaten and raped. In spite of his many aliases, her attacker, who had a prison record, was tracked down and rushed to a jail out of town. Officers reported there were "considerable feelings" in the community about him.

At least ten rapes were reported. Not all victims told authorities.

Robbery. A robber was caught about five minutes after robbing a Midway man who had just given him a ride. The *Glasgow Courier* reported, Mr. R. B. exhibited considerable bitterness and addressed profane remarks at the court while being tried."

Two men robbed a group of three, then lost a very fast foot race with them. A worker drinking with a new "friend" was robbed when the friend saw how much money he had.

Robbers broke into Freidle's Midway market and stole $87. They ran when the butcher came out with his meat cleaver. A robber was taking money from a garage cash register when the owner grabbed him by the collar and kicked him into the street.

In 1936 two McCone City men stole 800 pounds of copper wire from the project. They were caught when Valley County Sheriff Ed McPherson stopped by on another matter and one, thinking the sheriff was there about the copper wire, blurted out the details.

Stick-ups. Who were those masked men?

Most stick-ups were attributed to two men in white handkerchief masks described as "one short, one tall, and both nervous."

Originally there were three. During their first robbery in 1935 they entered a Park Grove grocery, which they seemed familiar with, and demanded the cash box. When the owner handed it over they were so nervous that two ran out and left their accomplice inside.

The tall-short duo robbed a Midway meat market of 80 cents. When the butcher asked for a cut, since it was his day's gross, they refused with "Business is business." It was believed the duo also robbed two men of money and watches.

In January 1936 two men, the sheriff believed to be the tall-short duo, were arrested trying to hold up the Roosevelt Hotel in Glasgow. They were fingerprinted and charged with vagrancy.

Two months later, two men, one short and one tall, nervously robbed Markles Oil Company in Glasgow of $20. They wore overalls, winter caps, and white handkerchief masks; and carried a 22-caliber target pistol and a 32 caliber nickel plated revolver.

In 1937 the duo robbed Wheeler's Red Star Oil Station of $100. The owner said that when they threatened him and his son with an automatic pistol, "they were almost as nervous as I was."

Law men believed the tall-short duo pulled a "dozen-odd stickups" before they were caught. Sheriff's officers noted "there wasn't an inch of difference in their height."

Other stick-ups. During the cold winter months there were three robberies. One was at Day's Grocery where two robbers came while the town men were at a fire prevention meeting. They tied Mrs. Day's hands and forced her and a female clerk to lie on the floor while they ransacked the living quarters and stole $300 from the store.

A stick-up man robbed an oil company of $20. He forgot to pull his handkerchief mask over his face and was identified and arrested in a beer parlor with only $11 left of his loot.

Some insurance companies refused to write robbery insurance policies for certain businesses due to unsolved stick-ups and break-ins.

Law officers took a great deal of abuse before drawing their guns. In May 1935 an intoxicated worker was shot in the leg while resisting arrest. A Minnesota worker caused himself a flesh wound when he grabbed a deputy's gun during a free-for-all.

In 1939 a Nebraska man tried to grab a deputy's gun during a bar disturbance. The deputy was shot in the leg. The man was killed when he tried to strangle the deputy who "fired in the line of duty."

Petty theft preferred items were money, radios, watches, clothing, blankets, pocketknives, guns, tools, wheels, tires and inner-tubes, food, candy, and pop. One thief stole 28 sacks of potatoes and a scale.

Domestic abuse calls placed officers between two angry and often intoxicated adults who usually, later on, dropped all charges. Officers reported one couple's house "showed many evidences of disturbance."

Dogs. Many transients and a few irresponsible owners brought their dogs to the project area and later abandoned them. Owners were rarely found and ticketed. Officers rounded up hundreds of unlicensed and "cross dogs" that had to be impounded and destroyed.

Mistaken Identity. A number of people had the same name, for real or use as an alias. Same-name scams varied from trying to collect another man's mail or cash checks, to asking for credit in his name.

Records of honesty are rarely kept, even though on the social scale, honesty at the project area far outweighed dishonesty. A 1935 news story told of a little girl who found a billfold with money inside. Her parents helped her return it to its McCone City owner.

Another story was told of a Fort Peck locomotive engineer who lost his engineer's purse with $310. A worker found it and turned it in to the dispatcher who passed it on to the police who returned it to its grateful owner with the $310 cash still inside.

Part 14

Crime, Alcohol and Gambling

The 18th Amendment to the U.S. Constitution, ratified in 1920, made the manufacture and sale of beverages containing more than 1/2 of 1 percent alcohol by volume, illegal. In 1926 Montana and 23 other states repealed Prohibition in their states, putting the burden of law enforcement on the federal government. Bootleggers and rum runners seized the opportunity to make booze and sell it.

Hard times in the 1930s created a turn-your-head tolerance to illegal alcohol. Some mid- and northeastern Montana farmers were picking up desperately needed cash by transporting or allowing the transport of Canadian alcohol across their property. Vehicles, farm wagons, and airplanes were all being used in the process of getting the product to the central parts of the United States.

A few people were making and selling "home brew."

In 1933 the U.S. Congress passed the Cullen Bill permitting breweries to produce and sell beer with an alcoholic content of 3.2 %, in states without prohibition laws. Bottled and draft beer could be sold in restaurants with meals of 25 cents or more, *if* the meal was eaten there and the proprietor was a citizen. Retailers could sell to the general public. The county board could issue permits to organizations to sell beer if the applicant was of "good moral character."

Beer advertisements could not contain the word "saloon" or give the names or show the pictures of women or children. No beer could be sold to minors under 21 or to Indians.

The state Board of Equalization established three-member License Control boards in each county and they began accepting 3.2 beer license applications. State breweries went into full time operation.

In 1933 beer licenses totaling $5,400 were sold to clubs still to be built along the road to the project and in the anticipated boomtowns.

The 21st Amendment to the U.S. Constitution, which was ratified December 5, 1933, abolished Prohibition. Brewers could now make beer with 3.5 to 4.2 percent alcohol. Taverns could sell 16-ounce glasses for 10 cents, or pints for 35 cents.

A few of the big time bootleggers, already hauling alcohol across Montana, found or built clubs in Glasgow and the boomtowns to sell legal beer at the bar and illegal alcohol out back.

The state goes into the liquor business

The 21st Amendment gave states "absolute control over grain alcohol." The legal sale profits of booze appealed to some politicians. Within two weeks the state opened its first five state-owned liquor stores, supplied with 8,000 quarts of Kentucky bourbon. Billboard ads were prohibited, but the word got around.

Immediately Attorney General Raymond T. Nagle began receiving requests to "get the state out of the liquor business." Most Montanans endorsed the sale of alcohol in drug stores, and accurately predicted opening liquor stores would not stop bootleggers.

In fact, bootleggers began purchasing the state's booze by the legal bottle and reselling it by the illegal glass at a hefty profit.

In February 1934 the state liquor stores advertised new "lower prices." According to *United Press* the Liquor Board planned to put illicit rum venders "on the run." The state's strategy included using its $100,000 appropriation, passed by a special legislative session, to open *more* liquor stores with *more* variety and lower prices, thereby making bootlegging unprofitable.

In addition, the attorney general ordered raids near state owned stores to catch anyone illegally possessing and/or selling intoxicating liquor. The first violator was caught in Glasgow and sent to jail.

Undeterred, the bootleggers kept on selling the state's liquor by the glass in speakeasies, roadhouses, and wherever else they could.

Law officers were ordered to "strike out against the illegal practice of reselling liquor purchased legally at state retail stores."

Beer. Throughout 1934 complaints were made about the behavior of patrons in bars that sold "supposedly non-intoxicating" 3.2 beer. Prohibition of music and dancing was discussed as a possible solution.

In October Wheeler's *Fort Peck Press* reported, "The clerk of the state Beer Board received its 27th beer permit application for 3.2 dispensaries in the Fort Peck dam region."

In January 1935 the Christian Woman's Temperance Union and Council of Church Women asked Valley County officials to regulate beer parlors and dance halls due to objectionable behavior of patrons. Residents of the boomtowns were also filing complaints, and they were including intoxication, disturbances, and DUIs on their list.

The short handed sheriff's department and the Glasgow police struggled to stop back-door and out-of-the-car liquor sales. Three of the "undesirable" beer parlors were permanently closed, ending their alcohol, taxi dancing, and "other practices."

In mid-February owners of the Los Angeles Club and Riverside, located on the Fort Peck highway, were found guilty of possession and sale of liquor. In March the Beer Board was informed both clubs were "at it again." Their licenses were suspended for the next 30 days.

The Montana Board of Equalization stated, "Due to criticism of the conduct of resorts in local towns ... no additional beer permits will be issued within a five-mile radius of the dam unless authorities approve." The existing establishments in fifteen of the boomtowns could remain open, if approved by the sheriff or county attorney.

The Beer Board continued its crackdown, refusing licenses to three bars and reviewing others in Valley and McCone counties. In March Attorney General Nagle stated, "Every open bar in Montana will be closed, the worst shall come first."

Inspectors were ordered to immediately shut down all of the beer establishments illegally selling hard liquor over their bars.

Along with the big timers, small timers, with out-of-town/out-of-state connections were selling alcohol: A lone hauler was arrested at a Glasgow tourist cabin selling gallon lots from a load of alcohol hauled from North Dakota in a car with fake license plates.

A Wheeler taxi driver, from Nevada, was fined $1,500 and bound over to District Court for selling liquor on a government reservation and possessing liquor without excise stamps on the bottles.

The government did not tolerate alcohol law abuse in Fort Peck or at the work sites. An employee was fired and ordered to leave the area after police found his 31 bottles of whiskey.

In April 1935 ten Glasgow establishments were granted state retail and city liquor licenses under a new municipal ordinance, stipulating, "Liquor must be purchased from state liquor stores." Closing was 2 a.m. weekdays, 1 a.m. on Sunday. No minor under 21 allowed in bars.

Getting tougher on violators

In August 1935 the Valley Bar lost its beer license for serving minors and for "objectionable women" of "immoral character" in the guise of "bar maids." The proprietors were arrested and the bar abated a "common nuisance." The complaint asked the owner be restrained from operating another bar, and all furniture and fixtures be sold as chattel.

One owner, a Canadian believed by federal agents to be in the United States illegally, failed to appear in court and forfeited a $500 bond. Officers and credit agencies in Chinook, Malta, Glasgow, and Wheeler were looking for him. The bar was deeded to bondsmen.

A man was arrested at the Idle Hour for possessing illegal whiskey. Three were arrested in a shack near the Wheeler Inn. When officers returned they found one of the men was back in business.

Complaints were also being made about legislators "getting state booze jobs," noting three of the Butte delegation were employed by the Liquor Board. The board sent an auditor, from Butte, statewide to check liquor store books. An Anaconda attorney was appointed to stop the illegal sale of hard liquors.

Petitions again begged, "take the state out of the liquor business."

In December a bartender at the Spot near Lakeview unknowingly sold five straight shots from an out-back bar to the sheriff and four officers. They seized "14 bottles of wine, gin, sloe gin, whiskey, alleged rum and cordials, and one bottle of whiskey colored water."

In March 1936 the Beer Board auditor issued notices that beer parlor owners caught selling or allowing consumption of any illegal whiskey would have their licenses revoked. And in September, "We have been advised that some beer vendors ... have started selling intoxicating liquor ... contrary to our Regulations."

The first charges under the state liquor law regarding possession and sale of liquor without authorization were brought against two Glasgow bar owners at their unlicensed bar.

In September the Board of Equalization sent letters reminding beer vendors, "We will not tolerate a violation ... and will suspend, or revoke, licenses issued where we have evidence of such violation."

At the end of 1936 the Liquor Control Board posted their net profit, a grand total of $1,522,477 for the year.

Saloon Days returned in April 1937. Licensed establishments could sell retail liquor by the drink. Licenses were granted to nine boomtown bars and ten in Glasgow. State liquor store sales during the first six months of 1937 totaled nearly $8,300,000. Stores in Butte, Glasgow, and Wheeler sold the most.

Liquor violation arrests continued into 1938, most of them for non-possession of retail dealer stamps or failure to pay special taxes. But the battle between bootleggers and the state was about over.

In January 1939 the Montana Senate ordered an investigation into the set up of the Liquor Control Board.

Not all bar owners were involved in illegal alcohol and gambling. Their clubs were places to meet, dance, enjoy a drink, and have fun.

Gambling

Illegal gambling was said to be "wide open" in the project area

In September 1934 Montana Attorney General R. T. Nagle ordered all county attorneys, sheriffs, chiefs of police, and mayors, to "close gambling dens forthwith." He further served notice that officers who failed to enforce gambling laws would be prosecuted.

September 28 the *Fort Peck Press* reported a "wide-open gambling setback" when the Los Angeles Club was raided and a "quantity" of equipment seized. Raids continued in 1935. Cards and chips were destroyed. The Wheeler Inn owner and dealer were fined $100 each.

The sheriff was directed to "close and abate" the Los Angeles Club after another raid there. Five men were arrested at half a dozen clubs in Park Grove and outside New Deal. Three club owners were arrested for possessing gambling equipment and an "IOU" machine.

Fall raids in Glasgow turned up five slot machines. They were destroyed with a sledge hammer behind the courthouse. The county kept the $19 contents. In November a slot machine, punchboard, and cigarette machine from the Casino, the largest club in Wheeler, were destroyed and the $10.81 inside given to the County Poor Farm.

A mother pressed charges against the Buckhorn Club after her son lost $540 at Black Jack, and studhorse and penny ante poker.

By 1936 owners of the establishments involved in gambling were becoming wary and weary. The judges were tough, and Sheriff Ed McPherson and his deputies kept on coming back.

In September an area-wide raid was ordered by Valley County Attorney Thomas Dignan and his deputy Otis Hallett. More than a truckload of gambling equipment and liquor were found in a building behind the Los Angeles Club. Three men were arrested at Lakeview Resort. A craps table, slot machine, and $125 cash were seized, and a "21" table shut down. Some $81 from gambling games and slot machines were confiscated from the Casino. Four men were arrested.

Several more owners and bartenders were arrested. They posted $125 bonds totaling $1,100 in fines. The $260.80 from gambling machines was deposited in the County Poor Fund. The machines, valued at $1,000, including an expensive roulette wheel, were burned at the dump. The liquor was turned over to the state Liquor Board.

The owner, a bartender, and four taxi dancers ordered out of town earlier, were arrested at the Bar-X at Valley. Slot machines and more than twenty bottles of liquor were seized. The bar was shut down for allowing minors inside and "indecent behavior by patrons." Its furnishings were sold for court costs. The bartender got 100 days in jail for selling intoxicating liquor. The owner was fined $300.

The entire Fort Peck project area was raided several times, but no other evidence of gambling was found.

In 1937 the Hickey Act legalized certain table games in specified locations. In April 1938 the county attorney stated the Supreme Court decision on the Act, which did not authorize gambling of any kind for money or checks, resulted in a shutdown of Valley County gambling.

Part 15

Montana Highway Patrol–Flying Squadron
MHP received 3,000 applications for 15 openings. Report 1937.

The Valley County sheriff and his few deputies were hard pressed to maintain law and order along with patrolling all the county roads and highways during the phenomenal growth of the project area.

By 1934 the increased traffic, growing population, volume of calls, and the new time-consuming laws for accident reporting, dictated the need for immediate assistance.

Help came in 1935 when the legislature approved formation of the Montana Highway Patrol (MHP). Lou Boedecker, a former Powell County sheriff, was named supervisor. Twenty-four patrol candidates were selected and sent to Helena for thirty days training.

The state was divided into twelve districts, each served by two patrolmen. Purchase was authorized for 19 patrol cars, 18 coupes and one sedan; and five motorcycles, one with a sidecar. A station wagon was authorized for the *Flying Squadron* assigned highway patrol duties during municipal and county functions.

Patrolmen were instructed to strictly enforce traffic laws. Fines and possible prison terms awaited offenders. Most Montanans welcomed uniformed officers on the roads, but a few, who resisted any change in their surroundings, dubbed them a "bunch of Boy Scouts."

The MHP officer assigned to the project area made his first drunk driving arrest in June 1935. A Square Deal carpenter was stopped for having six people stuffed in his two passenger coupe. The patrolman instructed two passengers to get inside the car, two to get in the rumble seat, and two to walk back to Wheeler.

The two-member Flying Squadron got their first major workout during a weekend in June 1935. With the help of sheriff's deputies, they ticketed hundreds of drivers for no driver's or auto licenses, speeding, vehicle light violations, and for carrying freight without a permit. Eleven were arrested for DUI.

The two officers were back for the 4th of July, then returned a week later to assist victims of the Galpin Coulee flood and Wheeler area tornado. Sheriff Al Fassett wrote a letter of commendation to Governor Frank H. Cooney to praise their "exemplary conduct."

In February 1936 the Highway Patrol, along with sheriff's officers, rescued nearly 200 travelers who ignored severe weather warnings and were stranded on the highways in sub-zero temperatures.

The MHP Board adopted new safety rules in 1936 in response to a report that 75-percent of the drivers involved in Montana's 119 injury or death accidents "were in an alcoholic condition."

In July 1936 the patrolmen held a "school" at the project for auto light violators. Drivers were instructed on how to adjust high and low headlight beams, and how to set spotlights to strike only the right side of the road. Repair orders for faulty equipment were written and summons issued if they were not returned.

A 1937 MHP Act empowered patrol officers to ban "mentally or physically deficient drivers" from Montana highways. It also created tests for lights, brakes, and steering devices; and required rear view mirrors and windshield wipers on all vehicles. It added penalties for school zone and other violations.

In July 1937 authorities were thankful to report "no deaths" on the Glasgow-Fort Peck road for the past year.

In November signs for a 30 mph minimum and 45 maximum speed limit on Highway 24 were set in place, further reducing accidents.

Officers of the Highway Patrol and Flying Squadron worked in cooperation with county sheriffs' departments to make roads safer. They contributed significantly to the education of Montana drivers still not accustomed to license and vehicle safety requirements.

From its establishment in 1935 to the end of the Fort Peck project, the Flying Squadron was on hand whenever needed to help during disasters; and to advise, assist or arrest hundreds of travelers on US 2 and other roads leading in and out of the construction area.

Lawmen

The majority of lawmen in the project area, except for Fort Peck town police, had little, if any, enforcement training. Most were area farmers or ranchers who helped keep their communities safe in light of the law and the Golden Rule. Lawbreakers who thought these lawmen would be pushovers, soon had second thoughts.

Glasgow was the first to deal with the crime that came with the Fort Peck project: In 1932 it was a peaceful town of 2,200 with one lone officer, Marshal Walter A. Baynham. He was still summoned by a 1915 alarm system consisting of two red lights, one at each end of town, activated by a telephone operator who received emergency calls.

A curfew for children under 18 was sounded each night at nine (9:30 May-August) with a Fire Hall whistle donated by the Flour Mill.

By 1934 the volume of traffic made it no longer safe for children to rollerskate on main street or in the business district. An increase in crime dictated homes and cars be locked and residents more vigilant.

The problems of rapid growth, plus a new state law that all vehicle accidents be investigated and reported, led the city to organize a police department with six officers. A seventh was added in 1935.

The Valley County Sheriff's Report January through October 1934 reflected the changes: Misdemeanor and vehicle violation arrests 32; grand larceny 5; burglary 3; concealed weapon 1; forgery 1; rapes 2. Calls were up to 331 in November, most of them for traffic accidents, vagrants, and stray dogs.

Regulations would be needed soon to control peddlers, hucksters, and transient retail/wholesale distributors moving into the towns.

A police station/bus depot was built in Glasgow and paid for with funds from a benefit ball with music by the Harness Bull Quartet, and old-time fiddle tunes by Valley County Sheriff Al Fassett.

All sorts of people were coming in great numbers. Policemen and sheriff's deputies found themselves facing more sophisticated and hardened criminals. Jails were full, attempted breaks were common.

In 1935 a robber, being moved to a more secure area, overpowered a jailer and locked him in a windowless cell. The jailer asked a drug dealer, in the only cell with a window, to call out for help.

The dealer went to the window and yelled and hollered "Help!" but people on the street ignored him. A few hours later a police officer happened by and unlocked the jailer's cell.

197

Loss of a respected lawman

Valley County Sheriff Al Fassett was elected in 1932 and re-elected in 1934. In August 1935 county residents were stunned when their "highly esteemed sheriff, and well known fiddler," age 46, died in Mayo Clinic after surgery for a brain tumor. He left a widow and four children. "Hundreds gave final tribute to Al Fassett."

Under-sheriff Charles Reed served as acting sheriff until Warren Thornton was appointed in October. Ed McPherson was elected in 1936 and served as sheriff until his resignation in 1945.

In June 1936 some 47 prisoners were jailed for varying lengths of time. At 75 cents a day each, the food cost totaled $283.50. After only ten paid their way with fines, the Glasgow city fathers passed an ordinance allowing police magistrate Henry Beverley to sentence future lawbreakers to "hard labor" on the streets and roads. If they refused, they were fed more affordable meals of bread and water.

The jailer reported the jail so full in August that "two drunks and an auto thief" had to bunk on the floor. When a complaint was made about "more physical force being used in arrests," the *Glasgow Courier* editor wrote, "It is justified ... in the phenomenon of human nature the sympathy goes to the lawbreaker after he's behind bars."

Glasgow police issued tickets and arrested hundreds of people for driving and auto violations. Most local offenders were fined. Visitors were, usually, given warnings. DUIs received stiff fines.

At the peak of the project, July 1936, there were 434 calls: 80 drivers were arrested, including 10 DUIs within the city limits. The police magistrate levied $789.50 in fines.

Rex. In 1936 an abandoned German shepherd wandered into the Glasgow Police Station. Officers fed him, bought him a license, and named him "Rex." He was their mascot and rounds assistant to Chief Baynham. He once earned a T-bone steak for chasing down and holding two North Dakota teens responsible for several thefts.

During February 1937 the Glasgow Women's Club participated in a jail survey sponsored by the National Federation of Women. They reported the jail, built for 32 inmates, had one bathtub, two lavatories, and worn mattresses. Women's quarters had little privacy. Resources were needed to prevent the spread of contagious diseases, especially TB and venereal diseases.

The women cited the outdated, over-capacity jail and lack of funds as the problem, not the management of the jailer or the sheriff.

Boomtown law and order
Deputies were assigned in Park Grove and New Deal, as needed, for traffic control. Town owners handled most of their own problems.

Wheeler was assigned a deputy in 1935 to control the heavy traffic on Highway 24 through town, and to investigate traffic accidents and violations. He worked from his office in the Valley Hotel while the new police station/jail/bus depot were being built.

Occasionally project people took matters into their own hands. A note in a May 1936 *Fort Peck Press* read: "It is rumored that there are four women that have repeating rifles loaded to the muzzle waiting for the Window Peeping ... to put in a second appearance."

McCone City/County
Mason Knapp was McCone County sheriff 1928-1933, and Henry Beason 1934-1945. Because of the rapid growth and size of McCone City, under-sheriff Orin Miller was stationed there during the project years to keep the peace and control the heavy local and tourist traffic.

McCone City at its peak was seven times the size of Circle, 519 population, and almost as large as the whole county of 4,790.

Courts
District Court in Glasgow
The Honorable Judge John Hurly, former associate justice on the Montana Supreme Court 1919-1922 presided over the 17th Judicial District Court in Glasgow from 1929-1948.

"There's no place for men of your type in this community who come here for the express purpose of 'playing suckers' in what you regarded as a 'hick' community." *Judge John Hurly sentencing a couple of con men who came to the project area in March 1935.*

District Court annual report 1935: 49 defendants, 37 sentenced: larceny 10; assault 3; burglary 6; auto theft 3; embezzlement/fraud 3; forgery 7; rape 6; liquor violations 4; narcotics 1; gambling 4; intoxicated driving 1.

Dismissed case defendants faced other charges. Sentencing: 22 to prison, 2 to juvenile institutions, 5 to local jails, 4 were fined, and 4 put on probation or sentences suspended.

Several cases were disposed without conviction. Nine were dismissed by the prosecuting attorney, two never placed in custody. Of the sentenced, 34 plead guilty, three were convicted by juries.

In the first six months of 1936, 59 cases were set for trial, with 10 criminal and 49 civil cases. Most involved collection and damage actions, and personal injury.

Valley County Attorney Report 1934: Criminal actions 371 with 253 convictions. Third degree assaults 24; disturbing the peace 44; misdemeanors 32; murder 0; petty larceny 44; vagrancy 38. Plus a variety of miscellaneous crimes. Cases received speedy prosecution.

Felony convictions the first six months of 1935 equaled 1934, with a large increase in misdemeanors handled in justice courts. Most offenders entered guilty pleas to avoid expensive trials. Several of the convicted were sent to the state penitentiary in Deer Lodge.

Glasgow Justice Court: A 1936 audit of Justice C.W. Kampfer's books showed: Fees of $4,200 collected August 1934-February 1935, most for justice court fines and costs. Sheriff and court fees were deducted and the balance distributed by the treasurer to local school districts. There was a five-cent overage for the county.

Justice Court in Wheeler

In January 1935 insurance man Frank Breznik presented a petition to the Valley County commissioners asking for a Judicial Township at Wheeler, with him appointed the Justice of the Peace. This was done in September. Breznik held court at the police station/bus depot, ruling on arrests by the deputy sheriff, constable, and Highway Patrol.

The number of traffic and other violations soon warranted a second position. Justice Roy Shane was appointed. A third position was filled by a man who came to town claiming to be a doctor. He served briefly in 1935 before his arrest for allegedly performing illegal operations.

Justices Breznik and Shane tried and fined workers, residents, and visitors alike: $5 for no license plates, large fines for speeding or no driver's license, $5.50 for failure to dim lights, $12.50 for reckless driving, $50 and license revocation for DUI.

Justice Court cases involved vehicle/traffic violations, intoxication, vagrancy, disturbing the peace, gambling, bad checks, and theft. A man was fined $1.50 for stealing his wife's clothes. Some "payday celebrators" were fined $50 for fights in the Wheeler Inn. Offenders were speedily tried, stiffly fined, jailed, and/or told to get out of town.

In an August 1937 "economy move" the county commissioners eliminated five Valley County townships, including Wheeler, thereby eliminating what they called the "kangaroo courts" in Wheeler.

The justices were ordered to close their offices immediately and turn over their books, which they took their time doing.

Court was permanently adjourned.

Part 16

Visitors, Tourists, and Weather
They came from all over the world.

The Fort Peck project had barely begun before its first visitors were on their way. Most of them came out of curiosity, eager to see the largest earth dam in the world under construction. Others came on official business or to see family members at work. Some were drawn by sensationalized accounts of the "wild west towns."

Thousands of vehicles full of tourists turned south off Highway 2 at Glasgow and Nashua and bounced over dirt and gravel roads to the construction sites. From July 12 through September 16, 1934, four-thousand visitors signed a guest registry at a temporary water pumping station near the dam. Thousands of others drove by after hours.

Visitors filled the restaurants, hotels, theaters, and nightclubs. They added significantly to the economy, traffic, night life, and crime.

Tourist booths opened the summer of 1935. Volunteers handed out thousands of maps with information about the project; and gave directions to the visitor access areas of the dam and spillway.

An attempt was made to count the tourists, but, like everything else at the project, tourism was happening twenty-four hours a day, twelve months a year. The several booths were only open in the summer, and of them, only one-fourth to one-third of the vehicles stopped to register. Many visitors arrived before and after hours. Thousands who came September through May were never counted.

The Fort Peck Tourist Information Bureau was operated by the Recreation Association. It opened in May 1935 on Highway 24 at the west entrance to the project. Attendants estimated 80,000 people toured construction sites between June 20 and October 20. July averaged 250 cars a day, fifty-five percent from out of state.

Volunteers counted approximately 50,000 tourists in the summer of 1936, with an unknown number during the rest of the year.

On Labor Day 1937 there were 6,000 visitors, and an estimated total of 75,000 for the year. During the summer of 1938 more than 12,110 vehicles with more than 30,000 visitors stopped to register. Numbers for 1939 were estimated at 50,000 for the year.

Visitors came from every state and many foreign countries. Booth attendants saw "a steady stream of traffic" regardless of the weather.

The Glasgow Chamber of Commerce Tourist Information Bureau opened east of town on the new Fort Peck Highway in 1935. In mid-June the Glasgow Boy Scouts counted 1,800 cars in eleven hours: 1,200 from Valley County, 390 from other Montana counties, and 210 from 30 other states and Canada.

In 1936, as an added attraction, the Glasgow booth displayed a "critter" found near the head of Big Dry Creek. The animal weighed about 350 pounds and resembled an adult sheep. Many believed it was a "petrified sheep." Scientists disagreed. It remained an unknown.

The Nashua Tourist Booth opened in the summer of 1935 as an information center for visitors traveling to the spillway and dam. In spite of the rough road thousands of tourists came by for information.

The Spillway Pavilion was a small building that featured a large model of the completed spillway. It was open most of the year. Visitors were given maps and treated to a great view from the hill.

Tourist Information was available at the Administration Building and most business places, especially at the Green Hut and Vornholt's Drug in Fort Peck. Tour maps and a variety of postcards were sold in boomtown drugstores and other business places.

Aerial tours of the project were offered by several Glasgow and boomtown pilots. One of the flying services ran ads in the September 1934 *Fort Peck Press*, "See Fort Peck from the air: 3 hawks only 75 cents; 2 fine heated cabin planes ... 1/2 mile north of Park Grove."

Most visitors drove their own vehicles, taking self-guided tours on routes marked by large red signs. Others chartered buses or rode with family or friends. A few hired guides at the Fort Peck Tourist Booth.

Observation Points

The first Skyline Road across the dam became "fill" in 1936. A notice of its replacement appeared in the *Glasgow Courier*:

"The new road will be above the face of the dam at every point and will be the permanent means of access from the top of the shafts to the lower portals. From a vantage point near the shaft gatehouse, visitors will be able to get the most comprehensive view of the dam."

The first Fort Peck Tourist Information booth was moved from the west to the east abutment of the dam in May 1937. Stairways were built from the graveled parking lot up to an observation point with guardrails and electric lights.

Visitors were invited to "watch the dredges at work, and the 24-hour movement of men and machines." Pamphlets and maps were available. Several photos of the project were on display. Visitors enjoyed a panoramic view of the dam's two mile main dike section, the boomtowns, Fort Peck townsite, the badlands, and Missouri river.

Sioux Street Circle: On July 27, 1937, a project news item in the *Glasgow Courier* reported that the hill on Sioux Street Circle at the edge of Fort Peck had become a popular observation point.

"Since closure of the dam, all four dredges with their attendant plants are grouped within a small area in the downstream borrow pit ... at night, endless strings of lights connect each unit, giving the valley the appearance of a giant carnival. This won't last long ... when the swinging bridge is completed near Park Grove to allow passage of dredges past the Wiota-Fort Peck railroad, the Fleet won't again be so concentrated. Not since the project started have visitors had the opportunity to see so much activity from one point."

Bus Tours. Hundreds of organizations chartered buses and visited the project: including a 600-member group of the Great Northern Veterans Association; 350 postmasters on their way to the National Convention in San Francisco; a large delegation of Sioux City, Iowa, "fellow Missouri Rivermen"; numerous Canadian and American Legion Posts; and a 60-member North Dakota Good Will Tour.

Twenty Sioux City Stockgrowers visited the dam. They brought their local newspaper editor. He wrote, "It's almost too big for comprehension. Imagine standing on a high bluff some 180 feet above the level of the Missouri, looking down into what looks like a jumbled mass of lumber, steel, shale, mud, cranes, trucks, water, men in an area more than half a mile wide...."

Among the thousands of foreign visitors was the Stavangere, Amt., Norway, tour group who stopped by the dam while visiting Montana and North Dakota Norwegian pioneers.

Visitors came by air. They landed at Glasgow airport and rode the bus to the dam. Among them were the North Dakota Sightseers who landed in Glasgow in their Travelaire biplane and Stinson J-6.

School tours were arranged by the Glasgow, Nashua, and state chambers of commerce. In 1937, Glasgow welcomed 40 Romanian-Canadian students, their teachers, and superintendent.

Official visitors included Col. R.A. Wheeler of the Army Corps of Engineers, Washington, D.C., one of many high ranking American engineers to tour the dam. Corps officers from the Kansas City headquarters came for tours and inspections, many were involved in other Missouri River projects. Four members of the Missouri River Division Office visited in 1936. Several organizations, such as the Nebraska Public Power & Irrigation District, sent representatives.

Dozens of American engineers traveled to the dam to study the various phases of dam and spillway construction.

Foreign engineers included one from Choshinko Hydro Electric and seven from Chosen, Japan; one from the Ogachi Dam of Tokyo; an engineer from a Volga River dam; engineers from the Engineering Institute of Canada; and others from Greece and Australia.

Captain N. Boddington of the British Royal Engineers visited the project in 1934. He created quite a stir when he arrived in his English automobile with its right hand steering and removable top.

In September 1936 about 250 engineers and industrialists from the World Power Conference and Second International Congress on Large Dams, in Washington, D.C., stopped in Fort Peck. They arrived on two special trains and filled seven buses for their trip to the dam.

Others. President FDR's uncle Frederick A. Delano, chief of the National Resources Board, toured the dam in 1935. The "River Preacher," musician Harold Harner, stopped on his fourth trip from Fort Benton to New Orleans. Radio star Jack Benny stopped in 1939.

Thousands of relatives and friends of the project workers toured the work sites and visited the boomtowns.

Promotion, postcards, and poetry

In March 1935 the Glasgow Chamber of Commerce and the Fort Peck Concessionaires distributed a tourist booklet with aerial photos of the project. The Chamber joined state organizations to promote Montana in eastern newspapers. Ads promised "scenic highways ... you can now cross the state two ways on oil ... see the world's largest earth dam under construction at Fort Peck."

The Fort Peck Dam was included in a "Three Great Dams" folder distributed by the Great Northern. In December 1936 a souvenir book *History of the Fort Peck Dam* was written by Corps personnel.

Tourists bought postcards with aerial photos of the project, the thermometer pointing to 60 degrees below zero, a "giant" grasshopper photographed by Cole's Studio, Ernie Pyle's colorful column, and a variety of others that were sold in businesses around the project.

A number of poems and songs were inspired by the hard times, the workers' jobs, and families living in the boomtowns.

Heartfelt poems like L. Hawthorn's "The folks next door are movin' out," were printed in local newspapers.

At least one small volume of poems was published and can be found in some public library archives.

Weather

Hot, dry summer days with wild wind and dust storms. Record low cold winters with deep snow. Northeast Montana had it all during the 1930s. There was no need for anyone to ask, "Will the rain hurt the rhubarb?" There was no rain and there was no rhubarb.

The rain stopped falling in 1929. By 1930 a severe drought had a choke hold on northeastern Montana. In October 1933, as work began on the Fort Peck dam, a hot summer was ushering in a cold winter.

The Corps of Engineers maintained a weather station at Fort Peck, operated by a meteorologist who gathered information via short-wave radio from 200 North American stations. It claimed "97 percent accuracy," and was invaluable to the engineers, especially in the cold winter, while planning construction projects using sensitive materials. Local reports were appreciated by the project people.

1934

January began with snow and freezing temperatures. In the midst of it, officials from the Corps of Engineers headquarters in Kansas City arrived to visit the Fort Peck dam and town sites.

Rain and snow in February caused what weathermen called "the worst road conditions since February 1912." Trucks sank axle deep in gumbo mud that clogged wheels, and stuck on the workers' boots.

June was stifling hot. The driest summer on record was predicted. Workers choked on dust and sweltered in 100 degree heat.

The Assiniboine Indians held their three day Raindance the first week in June at their camp grounds near Frazer on the Fort Peck Indian Reservation. A few days later rain fell over the entire county.

Climatologists noted the weather's "queer antics." On July 13, frost damaged gardens. September 21, several inches of hail preceded a three-day blizzard and "cold snap." Hardware stores sold out of shovels, stovepipes, and dampers.

September 27 a cyclone hit Square Deal, followed by a snowstorm that blocked roads in northern Valley County.

November and December were so fair that weathermen declared the area a "banana belt." The year ended with an old fashioned snowstorm and 27 below zero. A recap of 1934 showed 4.41 inches of precipitation, the lowest in fifty-two years.

1935

"January 12 will be remembered as the day the storm and cold wave struck Montana ... the same date the 1888 storm swept the territories of Montana, the Dakotas, Iowa, and Nebraska taking hundreds of lives." *Fort Peck Press.*

Temperatures dropped to 32 below zero during mid-January. Work at the dam continued, but the spillway shut down at minus 44. Twelve inches of snow fell March 5. Warmer temperatures produced a "mystery fog" that covered the project. April varied from a high of 33 to 82. Rain and Robins were a welcome sign of spring.

July 2 a wild windstorm hit Wheeler during the first evening of its three day 4th of July celebration. Several concession booths were topple, and dust and dirt filled the air. Visitors were injured by flying debris. A number of homes were damaged.

July 7, during the early evening, a sudden cloudburst drenched the project area. Within an hour nearly two inches of rain became a flood surging through the coulees, swallowing one dam and overflowing another before it poured out of the mouth of the normally dry Galpin Coulee on the north side of New Deal.

Victor Archambeault, owner of the Archambeault Addition at New Deal, warned residents and Fort Peck officials at 2 a.m. that a "terrific flood" was bearing down on New Deal, Midway, Park Grove, Valley City, and Parkdale. Men, women, and children, many in their nightclothes, ran through the cold rain into a darkness stabbed by lightning and rumbling with thunder, to reach higher ground.

Emergency crews from Fort Peck rushed to the towns and moved more than 300 frightened, cold, and soaked residents to a barracks for shelter. Several people spent the night at a first-aid station in the Park Grove Drug Store while others spent a long, wet night on the hilltops.

Government officials, Valley County authorities, and the two members of the new Highway Patrol Flying Squadron worked all night assisting boomtown residents and patrolling flooded towns.

Many of the homes in New Deal and along the coulee were filled with water. An estimated 200 homes in Midway and Park Grove had water up to three feet deep inside. Valley City was partially spared when floodwaters spread out before they got there. Parkdale residents ran when backwaters threatened them at dawn.

County officials reported, "This morning the streets are full of stranded cars, driftwood, mud, and other debris washed down."

Nine of the Federal Emergency Relief Administration (FERA) workers set up offices in the Park Grove Drug Store, and school. Their supervisor noted that residents were doing the best job she had ever witnessed "in helping their friends and neighbors."

Fifty more women and children were taken to the Recreation Hall where water, food, and clothing had been brought from Glasgow.

Boomtown owners contributed $200 to buy oil and disinfectants to clean up the towns. Businesses donated funds for sanitation supplies. More than 250 flood survivors lined up for typhoid vaccinations, then went back to work salvaging what they could from their homes.

Chloride of lime was put in outhouses and cesspools, and scattered near flooded homes. Corps engineers removed pump handles and condemned wells for testing. State and county health officials brought in chemicals to control mosquitoes.

The town owners, themselves hit hard, gave two months free lot rent to residents whose homes were damaged or destroyed.

Plans were made for state experts and property owners in New Deal, Midway, Park Grove, and Parkdale to meet and discuss a flood control ditch to protect the towns.

Tornado

The night of July 8 a tornado hit Wheeler, ripping apart tents and small buildings, and destroying frame homes. A 24-year-old woman was killed when her home collapsed. A 36-year-old man was killed while trying to save two women from the wreckage of their home.

Telephone lines were blown down. Dr. C.C. Lull, commander of the Fort Peck American Legion, mobilized legionnaires to help search house to house for the injured and to pick up medical supplies from other townsites after Wheeler stores ran out.

Wheeler news correspondent Rosetta Beachler wrote, "Dr. Lull's office and living rooms were crowded with the injured, bloody, and disheveled suffering from injuries ranging from severe lacerations, bruises and shock, to broken bones. Some, more seriously injured (about 100) were given first aid and taken to the hospitals in Glasgow and Fort Peck. Both J.A. Holland and Charles E. Peterson (two of Glasgow's morticians) brought their ambulances and were busily engaged in bringing the suffering to the doctor's office and taking some from there to the hospitals."

Dr. Lull worked all night, assisted by his mother, two house guests from Kansas, and Ralph Gabriel. Early the next morning two doctors and three nurses arrived from Fort Peck Hospital. The last of the 40 severely injured people were treated at dawn.

The tornado destroyed more than 100 houses in Wheeler and ripped the roofs off others. A Square Deal home was destroyed, and homes in Lakeview and Wilson damaged. The next day, Mason & Walsh sent carpenters to help homeowners rebuild.

More than two-hundred women attended quilting bees in Park Grove and Wheeler to make quilts for families who lost their bedding.

The editor of Wheeler's *Fort Peck Press* reported, "With grim determination to erase the scars of two disastrous storms this little mushroom community ... set out to rehabilitate itself and its 2,000 residents."

Courtesy of Paul McFarland

News of the two storms made national headlines. Several local editors reported "rumors are rampant." The number of lives lost and the danger of a typhoid epidemic were exaggerated. Sensationalized headlines read: "Park Grove rendered unlivable." "Half the houses in Wheeler destroyed." "New Deal wiped from the face of the earth."

The Glasgow Courier editor wrote: "Praise for the mushroom towns who have had more than their share of calamity this week."

He noted that residents made sure their families were safe, then calmly faced their losses, "almost everyone was more concerned for others than themselves.... In Wheeler, neighbors took care of everyone needing help.... Everyone there will always remember the fine spirit of the people who suffered the worst."

The county relief administrator wrote, "Most people took care of themselves ... they have admirable independence and initiative."

More wind storms

July temperatures rose to 102 and more, with only a trace of precipitation. July 25 a wild wind and dust storm followed by rain and hail hit the towns again. An August storm demolished homes in Wheeler and the tent of the visiting Gifford Eryse Players. Two homes were destroyed and one rolled over into a coulee at Wilson.

October brought snow and sub-zero temperatures. A freezing rain sent vehicles skidding off salted roads into ditches. It was the coldest October on record, down to 10 below zero.

November brought more cold weather and the first snow. Work at the project slowed. The four dredges entered winter harbor while other sections of the project shut down for the winter. Hundreds of men were out of work until warmer weather in the spring.

Many boomtown people suffered from a shortage of fuel to warm their homes. They covered their walls and metal coil bedsprings with newspaper, and put hot water bottles in their beds. They poked rags around windows and doors to keep out the wind, and wore their overshoes, coats, and gloves inside the house.

1936

January temperatures dropped to 44 below zero. Ten inches of snow fell. Vehicles stalled. Garages ran out of storage space.

On January 23 the *Nashua Messenger* noted, "Nashua, one of the coldest spots in the United States ... at 48 below ... several cars ... had to be abandoned.... Garage men reported the grease was so stiff the wheels skidded instead of revolving when towed."

February 6, the meteorological center reported, "Fort Peck area was the coldest place in the United States with forty below."

Weathermen blamed Alaska, saying temperatures 300 miles above the Arctic Circle were affecting the weather at Fort Peck.

Sixty Degrees Below Zero

February 15, temperatures plunged to a record breaking minus 60. Almost everything came to a halt. Vehicles would not start. The two operators of the D-8 Angle Dozer snowplows used a blow torch to keep fuel lines from freezing so they could clear snowbound roads.

The Highway Patrol saved 100 to 200 travelers, who, "in spite of precautions, ventured out on the roads and were marooned or injured."

The Patrol praised the ninety-three snow plow drivers who worked long, cold, dark hours trying to clear the roads.

Roads were opened in March when several area men with shovels assisted county plows until the Highway Department plow arrived.

March sub-zero cold held up progress on the project. Men wanted to work, machines did not.

Spring

The Missouri River's spring break-up backed water and ice jams over roads and into the valleys, creating the largest flow since March 1890. The Corps reported 28,200 cubic feet of water per second passed the dam, raising the water level eleven feet. In spite of the debris, the floodwaters were good for the dredges.

April snow and strong winds blocked roads. May had a 24-hour, eleven-inch rain that brought hope for good crops.

Winds blew back in June. Boomtown residents sat in their cars as small buildings and signs went down around them. In Park Grove the Eastern Montana Shows & Carnival light plant and merry-go-round were battered. Two homes in Valley City were destroyed. McCone City residents ran for safety in their dugouts. In Wheeler, rolling dust storms darkened the skies; the first rain drops turned to mud. Temperatures soared to 108, a record high.

June 28 high winds in the area fanned flames that wiped out nearly a dozen stores and businesses in Nashua.

Summer

Windstorms once again raised havoc with Wheeler's 4th Of July Celebration. The huge crowd was pelted with gritty dirt and sand. The Piccadilly Circus Big Top and Ferris Wheel were damaged. The rodeo went on as scheduled but the heat sent many spectators home.

July averaged 98 degrees. The hoped for crops, hay, and even the thistles were dying. The *Glasgow Courier* reported, "Nearly every day sees shipments of livestock passing through Glasgow on the way to markets and some to ranges."

The temperature was at one-hundred in August when the Jefferson churned up silt-covered ice chunks from the Missouri river bottom.

Mother Nature outdid herself putting on a spectacular show of northern lights in October.

At year's end, December 31, 1936, the Weather Bureau recorded: rainfall 8.45 inches (deficiency 6.86 inches); and mean temperatures above normal for the eighth consecutive month.

1937

The first week of January the Fort Peck weather station sent a short wave message to Glasgow saying it was 37 below zero at the project. Cars stalled. Roads were drifted shut. Businesses thawed key holes and heated water pipes with blow torches. On January 21, it was 41 below zero in Glasgow, up from minus 48. Three inches of snow and northwest winds made travel and work miserable.

February 16 the weather station analyst at Fort Peck reminded residents that at 34 degrees above zero it was "84 degrees warmer than a year ago at 50 below."

A Glasgow resident reported seeing a robin, but his neighbor claimed it was only a sparrow in red flannels.

Spring

In March the *Glasgow Courier* reported the "infallible signs of spring," seed catalogs, marbles, blankets on backyard clotheslines, optimists removing storm windows, county folk in town "who haven't been seen for months."

April snow raised hopes that this was the *next year* everyone was waiting for. The Glasgow Women's Club and Fort Peck townsite clubs kicked off their lawn and garden contests. Boomtown families tilled their garden spots and planted seeds.

The second week in May a three day, 34 mph windstorm blew clouds of topsoil through the project, filling work sites, homes, and businesses with dirt. May 28 a windstorm gusting from 48 to 63 mph caused what the weatherman described as "the most severe weather recorded at Fort Peck."

May temperatures ranged from 59 to 93, with only one inch of precipitation, far short of the 12.33 normal.

In the evening of June 4th, a Black Blizzard swept from Glasgow through the project with 63 mph winds darkening the sky with tons of topsoil. The ninety-minute wind overturned small houses in Wheeler. A Lakeview ice-house wall went down, sawdust blew off tons of ice. Power was off at the dam.

A week later a cloudburst dropped four inches of rain in Hinsdale causing major washouts along the Great Northern railroad main line. A 24-hour drizzle became 1.71 inches of moisture. Stockmen had hope they could make it until fall.

A two-inch "soaker" created a record flow in the river, swelling parts of the Missouri drainage basin above the dam. The river rose seven feet, threatening dredge pipelines and sending large pieces of driftwood downstream.

Aerial river surveys were made daily to check flood conditions as the Marias and Teton rivers poured run-off into the Missouri.

Crops looked good until June came "abnormally" warm and dry. August marked 18 months of below normal rainfall. Precipitation was only 9.37 inches out of a normal 22.97.

1938

March predictions were for the best crops in ten years. Then came the worst blizzard in years, with temperatures below zero. Traffic and work at the dam were all stopped by a wild 36 mph wind that drifted snow for forty-nine hours. Roads were closed. The storm raged from the Rockies, across the Dakotas, to Minnesota causing great suffering for humans and animals, but leaving the best moisture in years.

April rain gave farmers and ranchers some hope they could leave the project and return home. There was plenty of water for their stock, and the largest winter wheat harvest since 1927-1928, double 1937.

The third week of June a "near cloudburst" fell over parts of the project area. At 2 a.m. a wall of water from 8 to 10 feet high suddenly poured down Galpin Coulee, over its dam and bridge, and through the towns of New Deal and Midway. It flooded the flats before it ran into the new dredge cuts between Midway and Park Grove. This flood was worse than the one they had in July 1935.

Residents "lightly clad" ran through the cold rain, lightning, and thunder to the hillside. A young couple and their baby sailed across New Deal on the roof of their house. A trailer home floated into Midway, along with barrels, doorsteps, and wood piles. Several sheds and outhouses were washed off their foundations. Debris was caught in the trees and strewn about on the ground.

A dredge crew working in the cuts near Midway pulled people on board until motorboats and the Fort Peck Police arrived to transport them to the barracks in Fort Peck. Several people were sheltered in gas stations on higher ground.

The next morning residents found their homes, cellars, vehicles, and storage areas full of mud and water. Most of their belongings were damaged beyond use.

With the help of each other, the Corps, and county health officials, homeowners and businessmen began salvaging whatever they could; thankful no lives had been lost.

Twin scourges
July 1938 was the mildest in four years. Then August brought a "twin scourge." Hordes of grasshoppers descended on and destroyed or damaged $6 million worth of crops. Wheat rust took the rest.

It rained 4.72 inches in four hours the end of August, the heaviest in fifteen years, causing flooding and damage, especially in Glasgow.

The first snow fell the end of November. The year ended with a dust storm, snow, and sub-zero cold.

1939
January was one of the mildest in years. February turned cold and temperatures dropped to 36 below, interrupting work at the dam.

Nashua floods

By mid-March the Milk River spring run-off was flooding Nashua. Ice jams at the bridge were blasted to let the water pass.

Then word came that the Midway Dam on Porcupine Creek forty miles northeast had broken. A wall of water was heading for Nashua.

On March 23, newspapers reported heavy losses in the town, with many buildings destroyed and others washed off their foundations. The Edgewood Pavilion was moved 1,000 feet and smashed into trees. It later fell into the creek and broke in half.

Dr. Currie and his staff gave typhoid shots to safeguard the health of the town's residents, while officials dealt with sanitation problems. Help came from around the area as residents waited for the water to go down so they could return home and rebuild.

Soon after the floods, a cloudburst and hail hammered Nashua and some 2,500 acres of farm and ranch land in Valley County.

Rainfall in May totaled 2.61 inches. High wind and dust storms interrupted electrical power and phone service, and slowed progress at the dam. In June it rained for 21 days. Crops looked good.

Dust devils targeted the 4th of July celebration in Wheeler. They blew in shortly after the Siebrand Brothers Circus and Carnival had set up. The Ferris Wheel toppled onto the tilt-a-whirl. The midway was torn apart. Business signs, chimneys, and small buildings were blown down in Wheeler and Midway.

Then it rained. The rain was welcome, so the drenched celebrants waited out the big storm, then waded out in the mud to pick up the midway and resume their celebration.

Glasgow was hit with similar weather, but their annual Jubilee and Band Concert, free acts, and dancing went on as scheduled.

Fall weather sent V-shaped formations of ducks and geese flying south for the winter. 1939 ended with a Christmas rain followed by a snowstorm that ended the long dry spell. The dusty, drought- stricken, tough-times years of the 1930s were about over.

1940 would be better and so would the next decade.

When the work's all done.

Play A Tune

Take A Break

Go For A Ride

Go Fishing

Photos courtesy of Stella Smith,
Lois Damstrom, Paul McFarland

Celebrate

Revisiting Project No. 30
Time has changed almost everything.

Dust has long since settled over the Fort Peck Project worksites. Construction workers have moved on, and the care of their dam and spillway has been handed down through the generations. Prairie grass grows over the boomtown sites where shanties and false front stores once stood. A few old buildings, rebuilt or moved away, still remain.

Since 1940 many former project people have returned to reminisce about the *dam days* on the job and in the towns. Their children and grandchildren try to imagine what life was like here in the 1930s.

They drive through Fort Peck to see the updated Administration Building, the Recreation Hall, and the Fort Peck Hotel. They visit the Fort Peck Theatre to take in a show, and hope to see its *ghost.* They move across the street to where the Lutheran Church was a long time landmark, and over to where the old first service station still stands.
There is so much history here!

Remarkable growth and change have taken place since the dam was built, starting with the first of the two power houses in 1941. Engineering technology has changed, they don't build dams like the Fort Peck Dam anymore. The 1930s Corpsmen and workers agree:
They don't build dams like the Fort Peck Dam anymore!

Thousands of tourists come to see the dam and spillway, and visit the Powerhouse Museum. The Fort Peck Interpretive Center, opened in May 2005, is located on the south side river bank near the tunnel outlets. It preserves the history of the dam construction and towns, displays area wildlife, and features pre-historic dinosaurs, including the huge "Peck's Rex." Nearby, paleontologists "research, prepare, mold and cast fossil finds" in the Fort Peck Dinosaur Field Station. A warm water Fish Hatchery was opened a few miles northwest in 2006.

Thousands of visitors come to the Fort Peck area to go boating, birding, camping, fishing, hiking, hunting, and swimming. There is wildlife viewing in the Charles M. Russell Wildlife Refuge, and year-round recreation of all kinds in refined and rustic settings.

Sight-seeing is still popular. From the observation point on the hill at the east end of the dam there is a panoramic view of the lake, dam, river, badlands, and much of the wildlife refuge around them.

It is a beautiful four-mile drive on Highway 24 across the berm of the dam from the west side to the east end. From the two-mile main dam section on the east end, you can see for miles in all directions:

To the south, Fort Peck Lake stretches out to touch a chain of rugged badlands. To the north the Missouri River rushes through the four tunnels under the big dam and exits through the outlets at the powerhouses. As it winds its way through the valley it sends a stream through a channel, on the west side of the river, into the dredge cuts.

Off to the northwest is the former "government town" of Fort Peck. Beyond it, in the cottonwood between a dredge cut and the river, west of Highway 117, is Park Grove, the last of the boomtowns.

Highway 24 runs east up the hill to where the Spillway Building stands guard over the mile-long spillway below, running to the north.

The huge concrete and steel structure and gates are often mistaken for the dam—because the dam in its outward earth-friendly simplicity looks more like an enormous lake-side hill with a highway across.

From the tops of the dam, spillway, and observation point the panoramic view is stunning in its vastness. Seen through the eyes of the 50-cent an hour workers it's an awesome sight.

—30—

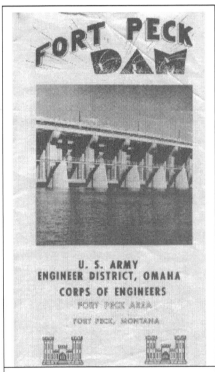

Spillway. Tourist brochure 1961.

Fort Peck Dam

Hydraulic and rolled earth fill
Length: approx 4 mi. (21,026 ft.)
2 mi. main dam, 2 mi. approach
Height: 250.5 feet
Width-top: 50 ft.; Base: 3,500 ft.

Tunnels
Four: steel lined, under the dam
Diameter: 24 ft. by 8 in.
Length: *5,386 *6,011 *6,636
and *7,261 *(1+ mile each)*

Fort Peck Lake
Shoreline: 1,520 miles
Width:16 mi; Length: 134 mi.
Max. Depth: 220 feet

Spillway
Three miles east of the dam
Length: one mile
Overall length: 2.8 miles

Spillway Gates
16 gates 25 ft. high x 40 ft. wide
Weight: 80 tons each

About the Author

Stan, Lois, Lucille
1939
Stella Smith Collection

Klebig Studio

At the end of 1939 my family moved from Wheeler to my great-grandmother's deserted homestead south of the Missouri River in northeastern Montana. There I got first-hand experience as a dryland farmer/rancher living in a little prairie house with ice on the inside of the windows in winter and wild roses around the door in summer.

I was destined to leave at seventeen and a year or so later marry a Midwesterner who shared my love of music. We added six children to our duo and formed a family band playing music for shows and radio.

While my husband Del managed and owned radio stations and our children grew up, I freelanced news and features for several Midwest newspapers, and television and radio stations; earned a BA in English from the University of Wisconsin; and saw my short stories in print.

Once more a duo, Del and I moved to Helena in 1989. He stayed with radio, I spent thirteen years at the *Helena Independent Record.*

All the while, especially after Mom and Dad were gone, this book kept tugging at my heart, struggling to get out of there and into a form I could pass on to my family. When I started researching my project roots I realized this important part of Montana history deserved a book that could be shared with everyone.

I have had many requests for information and it is my prayer that "Fifty Cents" will answer your questions and make you laugh and cry in memory of the hardworking project people who stood up to the Great Depression and in so-doing created the biggest hydraulically filled earth dam in the world.

Lois Lonnquist

Selected Bibliography

This history is based on the research and writings of professional and amateur historians who have diligently preserved our past. Thanks to them and the many librarians in libraries and museums who keep materials organized and available, the many sources, more than I can mention here, were there to guide me through.

Archives Montana Historical Society
Fort Peck Dam Oral History. Cassettes, numbered and dated. Summaries.
Vertical File Collection on Fort Peck, Montana. 1930s.
Northeast Montana weekly newspapers. Microfilm. 1935-1940.
Not in Precious Metals Alone: A manuscript History of Montana, compiled and edited by the Montana Historical Society. 1976.

Books
Baker, Don. *Ghost Towns of the Montana Prairie.* Boulder, CO; Fred Pruett Books, 1997.

Footprints in the Valley: History of Valley County (3 volumes). Valley County History Committee, Glasgow, 1991.

Gilluly, Sam. *The Press Gang, A century of Montana Newspapers 1885-1985.*

Lang, William L., and Rex C. Myers. *Montana: Our Land and People.* Boulder, CO: Pruett, 1979.

Paladin, Vivian. *From Buffalo Bones to Sonic Boom...75th Anniversary Souvenir.* Glasgow, Montana, Jubilee Committee, 1962.

Presser, Marvin. *Wolf Point: A City of Destiny.* Billings, M Press, 1997.

Malone, Michael. Roeder, Richard. *Montana: A History of Two Centuries.* Seattle & London, University of Washington Press. 1976.

Miller, Don and Cohen, Stan. *Military and Trading Posts of Montana.* Missoula, Montana: Pictorial Histories Publishing Company, 1978.

Montgomery, M.R. *Saying Goodbye: A Memoir For Two Fathers.* New York Alfred A. Knopf, 1989.

Murphy, Mary. *Hope in Hard Times, New Deal Photographs of Montana, 1936-1942.* Helena: Montana Historical Society Press, 2003.

Reiman, Roy. Ed. *We Had Everything But Money.* Greendale, WI. Reminisce Books, 1992.

Spritzer, Don. *Roadside History of Montana.* Missoula, Montana: Mountain Press Publishing Company, 1999.

Van Faasen, Jerold. *Making It Happen: A Sixty-year Engineering Odyssey in the Northwest (A Memoir)* Kip Productions, Seattle, WA. 1998

Vichorek, Daniel. *The HI-LINE, profiles of a Montana Land.* Helena. Montana Magazine American & World Geographic Publishing, 1993.

Steinbeck, John. *The Harvest Gypsies, 1936.* Series of articles with Forward Charles Wollenberg. Heyday Books Berkeley, 1988.

Watkins, T.H. *The Great Depression: America in the 1930s.* Boston: Little, Brown and Company, 1993.

Wiley, Frank. *Montana and the Sky.* Montana Aeronautics Commission, 1966.

Wischmann, Polly. *Lists of McCone County.* Author Published, 1981.

World Book Encyclopedia. Field Enterprises Educational Corporation. Chicago, 1974.

WPA Guide to 1930s Montana. Foreword by William Kittredge. University of Arizona, Tucson, London. Compiled and written by the Federal Writers' Project, Work Projects Administration for the State of Montana, 1939.

Golden Anniversary Edition. Glasgow Courier. November 30, 1937

"Our Dam" by Major Clark Kittrell. *Glasgow Courier.* Special Northeastern Montana edition. November 30, 1937.

The Story of the Fort Peck Dam. Corps of Engineers Information staff. 1936.

Fort Peck A Job Well Done: October 1933-August 1977. Reunion Committee 1977.

Fort Peck Construction Workers Directory: Volume I and II, 1937-1987. Fifty years of Service. Fort Peck Dam Workers, 50th Anniversary of Fort Peck Dam. US Army Corps of Engineers, Omaha District Public Affairs Office. 1987.

50th Anniversary Commemorative Issue. District News, Special Edition, Kevin Quinn, Public Affairs Office, Omaha District, Omaha, Nebraska. Summer 1987.

Magazines
Saindon, Bob and Sullivan, Bunky. *Fort Peck Dam: Taming the Missouri and Treating the Depression. Montana, the Magazine of Western History, Montana Historical Society. Helena. Vol. XXVII, Number Three, Summer, 1977.*

Maps
Montana Highway Department. Portions of maps 1932, 1940, 2000.

Diary
Lucy Fisher, Family archives (1932-1937)

Video
Let Us Try: The Construction of the Fort Peck Dam. University of Montana, Bozeman. 1999. Videocassette.

Index

Looking northwest from Highway 24 across the dam.
Fort Peck Interpretive Center beside the Missouri River. The town of
Fort Peck is on the hill off to the left. The powerhouses are off to the right.

Looking southeast from Highway 24 across the dam.
Fort Peck Lake.

Photos by author.

The Way It Was

A Home in the First Boomtown

Bartron Home

Portion of New Deal Main Street

Apartment House in New Deal

McCone City Home

McCone City Dugout Home

Park Grove Homes Among the Trees

Photo 1 courtesy of the Army Corps of Engineers-Fort Peck District
Photo 6 donated to the Fort Peck Interpretive Center by Mary Moylan
Photos 2, 3, 4, 5, 7 donated to Fort Peck Interpretive Center by Heidi Olson